CONTEMPORARY RACISMS
and ETHNICITIES

SOCIOLOGY *and* SOCIAL CHANGE

Series Editor: *Alan* Warde, Lancaster University

COMTEMPORARY RACISMS
and ETHNICITIES
Social *and* cultural transformations

Máirtín **Mac an Ghaill**

Open University Press
Buckingham · Philadelphia

Open University Press
Celtic Court
22 Ballmoor
Buckingham
MK18 1XW

email: enquiries@openup.co.uk
world wide web: http://www.openup.co.uk

and

325 Chestnut Street
Philadelphia, PA 19106, USA

First Published 1999

A catalogue record of this book is available from the British Library

ISBN   0 335 19672 1 (pb)   0 335 19673 X (hb)

Library of Congress Cataloging-in-Publication Data
Mac an Ghaill, Máirtín.
    Contemporary racisms and ethnicities: social and cultural
transformations / Máirtín Mac an Ghaill.
        p.   cm. – (Sociology and social change)
    Includes bibliographical references and index.
    ISBN 0-335-19673-X (hardcover). – ISBN 0-335-19672-1 (pbk.)
    1. Race. 2. Racism. 3. Ethnicity. 4. Minorities. 5. Social
isolation. 6. Marginality. Social. 7. Social policy. I. Title.
II. Series.
HT1521.M215 1999
305.8–dc21
                                                                98-49830
                                                                CIP

Typeset by Graphicraft Limited, Hong Kong
Printed in Great Britain by Biddles Ltd, Guildford and King's Lynn

To Iestyn, Simon and Sharon

For Laurence, Patrick and Ulani

Contents

Series editor's preface

In response to perceived major transformations, social theorists have offered forceful, appealing but contrasting accounts of contemporary Western societies. The speculative and general theses proposed by social theorists must be subjected to evaluation in the light of the best available evidence if they are to serve as guides to understanding and modifying social arrangements. One purpose of sociology, among other social sciences, is to marshal the information necessary to estimate the extent and direction of social change. This series is designed to make such information, and debates about social change, accessible.

The focus of the series is the critical appraisal of general, substantive theories through examination of their applicability to different institutional areas of contemporary societies. Each book introduces key current debates and surveys of existing sociological argument and research about institutional complexes in advanced societies. The integrating theme of the series is the evaluation of the extent of social change, particularly in the past twenty years. Each author offers explicit and extended evaluation of the pace and direction of social change in his or her chosen area.

Máirtín Mac an Ghaill presents an authoritative overview and critique of recent developments in sociological theories of race and ethnicity. As he demonstrates, this is a complex area, increasingly conscious of the complicated relationship between sociological frameworks, methodological strategies and the phenomena subject to examination. The nature of ethnic relations – perceptions, practices, populations and policies – has changed rapidly over the past forty years, often escaping adequate theoretical understanding. In response, the book advances a bold and challenging synthesis which seeks to preserve a materialist core from earlier accounts while incorporating insights from more recent reflection on representation, identity and cultural difference. From the theoretical investigation emerges an evaluation of past policies and an analysis of implications for contemporary political practice. Enriched by his own original research, Máirtín Mac an Ghaill offers fresh, critical yet constructive diagnosis of the origins and development of current conditions and controversies.

Alan Warde

Acknowledgements

A number of people have contributed to the writing of this book. The main influences include working with Avtar Brah and Mary Hickman in editing two collections on the sociology of racism and ethnicity. As is shown in the book, this experience and their own work have helped shape my ideas. Recent research with Chris Haywood on the sociology of sexuality is evident throughout the text. My thanks to Sharon Lambert who has provided much support. Thanks to Mary Hickman and Dave Gillborn for advice. Thanks to Martin Holt, Tony Walters, Jacky Brine, David Gilbert, Peter Jackson, Richard Jenkins and Sharon MacDonald who have read different chapters. For the past few years I have worked on a number of projects examining anti-Irish racism and the experience of the Irish in Britain – more specifically with Irish communities in Birmingham and London. This work has been carried out with Iestyn Williams. He has made the book possible. Thanks for his support in reading through and discussing with me several versions of each chapter. As always, love to Rajinder. Finally, much gratitude to the publishers at Open University Press – particularly Justin Vaughan and Gaynor Clements as well as to John Solomos and the series general editor Alan Warde.

Part I
RE-READING 'OLD TIMES' *as* CHANGING TIMES

Introduction

What is going on?

At one level the questions may seem to be simple. For example: How are we to understand race, ethnicity and racism? How do we construct policies within institutions that challenge racist practices of social exclusion? What are the most effective forms of political mobilization to contest the organized racist violence of extreme right political groups? It may be that in the past it was also thought that the answers were simple. At the start of the new century both the questions and answers seem more complex. In a recent sociological study that I carried out in secondary schools, young, white, working-class students told me that their schools were racist (Mac an Ghaill 1994a). The first time I heard this, I responded by thinking how successful the school's anti-racist policy had been in raising awareness about the position of ethnic minorities. During the following weeks, I realized that I had made the wrong assumption and misunderstood what they were saying. I went back to them and asked them: What do you mean? They replied that the school was racist in favouring African Caribbean and Asian students, while racially excluding white students. At the same time in this school a number of Asian students were violently attacked when they went beyond the safe space of the local inner-city area. This incident was seen by the Asian students as part of an ongoing campaign of 'Paki-bashing' that served to cut them off from the white population, keeping them in their 'racial place'.

Sociology is concerned with answering the question: What is going on? *Contemporary Racisms and Ethnicities* is written in an attempt to answer that question in the context of what often seems to ethnic minorities to be nothing but the same old story of racist abuse alongside new responses to questions of racial difference among the white, Anglo-ethnic majority. A main influence on this book is work that I have carried out with young people living in a multicultural/multiracist city in the West Midlands region of the UK. As some of these young people point out, we have moved beyond the era of post-war colonial migration to that of ethnic minorities born in England, such as Birmingham Irish, Leicester Asians, Liverpool Chinese and London African Caribbeans. This marks a shift from the old certainties of colour as the primary indicator of social exclusion to more complex processes of social inclusions and exclusions that vary across and within regions and institutions. At theoretical, political and policy levels, however, the ongoing story of the post-war immigration of Asians and African Caribbeans as racial outsiders is still being told in an older language of anti-racism. This colonial paradigm is not able to grasp a younger generation's experiences of inter-ethnic social relationships and their engagement with shifting meanings about racial difference at a time of wider rapid social change.

Hamilton (1986: 7) has suggested that: '. . . it is the task of sociology and the other social sciences to "deconstruct" naturalism, and to determine how actions are given their meaning and significance via social action'. Sociology, setting out to make visible the social construction of society, seems to have failed in relation to the concept of race (Guillaumin 1980; Husband 1982). An examination of the concept's history highlights its remarkable continuity and people's deep social investments in notions of racial difference (Miles 1989). The seeming failure of social sciences to challenge 'common-sense' understandings of race converges with recent cultural theorists' scepticism about the progressive political achievements of contemporary Western societies. If social sciences have proved weak as a science of predicting social change, nowhere is this clearer than in relation to current developments across and beyond Europe of racism, nationalism, ethnocentrism and xenophobia.

Contemporary Racisms and Ethnicities is about the relationship of changing understandings of race, ethnicity and racism with wider social and cultural transformations within the British nation-state. The rapid change in the politics of race across a wide range of societies suggests the need to go beyond existing sociological explanations. Questions of migration, nation and ethnic belonging are key elements of rapid social transformations in the late 1990s and the accompanying pervasive feeling of increased anxiety and stress within de-industrialized societies. In short, race and ethnicity are currently of major significance to Western societies in uncertain times. There is, however, little acknowledgement of this in the literature (Solomos and Back 1995). For example, there is little empirical sociological work on how the social transformation of regions and institutions – such as the North–South geographical divide, restructured labour markets, with the decline of manu-facturing and the increase in the service sector, deregulated housing markets, contracted-out health services or redesigned educational agendas – are impact-ing on new forms of racism and new ethnicities. Questions about race, racism and ethnicity are central to explanations of the complex configurations of contemporary social and cultural change. There is, however, a lack of theor-etical development of explanations of such transformations. If much recent debate about postmodernism is about how we are to understand a radically altered social reality, there is a strange silence around issues of racialized social relations and ethnic identity formations (Gilroy 1993). One of the main claims of postmodernists is that we are experiencing a fundamental cultural shift, marked by a sense of discontinuity, fragmentation and uncertainty. Hence, it might be assumed that, in engaging with such questions, ethnic minority communities, many of whom have a long history of social dis-placement, would be an essential reference point to draw upon. In most postmodern accounts, however, these groups are absent, resulting in a failure to address issues of migration, social marginality, cultural belonging and a sense of home (Massey 1994). The impact of these wider changes is particularly difficult to understand with the emergence of unpredictable similarities between anti-racist and racist political discourses across Europe, as well as the highly unexpected current effects, as indicated previously by young, white people, of progressive social policies that were developed in the 1980s. The political success of the French Front National in developing a coherent explanation with wide popular appeal, and in Britain the continuing criminalization of the Irish, and racist attacks – such as the murder of Stephen Lawrence in London and Rosemary Nelson in Northern Ireland – are a reminder of the urgent need to develop alternative contemporary explanations that make sense of people's lives (Hardy, 1999).[1]

Aims of the book: rethinking the black–white dualism in 'coming times'

Contemporary Racisms and Ethnicities is written against a background of the theoretical underdevelopment that surrounds the interplay of racialized social relations and ethnic identity formations with contemporary transformations.[2] The aims of the book are developed in the context of making explicit an extended evaluation of the pace and direction of social and cultural change in this sociological area. First, there is a critical engagement with British sociology of race, ethnicity and racism in 'old times', which provides an overview of the central issues that have defined this area of inquiry during the past fifty years. A specific objective of the book is to bring together early and more recent theoretical and empirical work to provide a critical reflection on the relative adequacy of different sociological frameworks of racism and ethnicity. An advantage of this kind of structure is that it allows us not only to consider the relative adequacy of different theoretical accounts through a series of contrasts, but also encourages a view of these theories as alternative explanations which make different assumptions about ethnic minority and majority communities and associated processes of racialization. In turn this suggests different political and policy interventions at local and global levels.

In the early section of the book there is a critical re-reading of historical and contemporary debates within the sociology of race and ethnic relations. I also draw on comparative material from Europe and the United States (Guillaumin 1995; Balibar and Wallerstein 1991; Goldberg 1993; Wieviorka 1995). A potted history of British race and ethnic relations in the past fifty years reads as follows: early race-relations studies were critiqued by class-based anti-racist analyses, which in turn are now being criticized by a new politics of cultural difference position. The primary focus of race-relations studies was on inter-ethnic relations between minority and majority communities in such institutions as employment, housing and education (Patterson 1963; Banton 1977; see also Barth 1969). They examined minority communities' distinctive cultural attributes, suggesting that social behaviour was to be understood primarily in terms of culture. This culturalist perspective was preoccupied with questions of assimilation or integration of ethnic minorities into British society and the problems facing the 'second' generation, who were seen as being 'caught between two cultures'. Although the culturalist perspective received much theoretical criticism from other sociological approaches, it was nevertheless a significant 'common-sense' explanation of minority communities' experience of British society. It was particularly important in helping to develop multicultural policies. The legacy of this perspective is still to be found in different parts of the country, illustrating the uneven translation of theories into practice.

The race-relations problematic was challenged by Weberian and Marxist analyses on the grounds of its assumed limited theoretical explanation. These argued that a major weakness of the culturalist approach was that by focusing on the 'ethnic attributes' of the black community, the significance of its social class location in advanced capitalist societies was not recognized. The Weberian approach examined the incorporation of different immigrant groups into Britain and the forms of social stratification emanating from status distinctions based primarily on race (Rex and Moore 1967; Rex 1970). For Marxists, the emphasis was on the economic exploitation of immigrant groups with a focus on the interrelationship between class, racism and colonialism (Castles and Kosack 1973; Miles 1982). Weberian and Marxist accounts were of particular political importance in the development of anti-racist theories. They established commonalities of racism among Asians and African Caribbeans and investigated their different institutional positioning within a multiracist Britain. They provided these social groups with a public language to talk about their experience of society in terms of racism.

A main argument of *Contemporary Racisms and Ethnicities* is that recent cultural theorizing needs to recover the history of earlier class-based accounts and in the process re-read 'old times' texts as providing innovative understandings of racial conflict and social change. This enables us, from a contemporary perspective, to engage with the structural continuities of racist and nationalist exclusions, for example in areas of employment, training and social services, alongside the discontinuities of late capitalist society. It also enables us to address key absences in the rather narrow ahistorical accounts generated by current theoretical frameworks, as well as illustrating the complexity of developing conceptually and politically adequate understandings of processes of racialization. Most importantly, analyses of the relationship between racism and class are currently of strategic political importance in challenging a growing pessimism that there is little that can be done, for example, in relation to global forces that are seen to be determining welfare policies at the level of nation-states. This is not to suggest a 'simple' return to class-based explanations. Rather, as is illustrated in this book, new theoretical frameworks and empirical studies of racialized minorities and a de-racialized Anglo-ethnic majority need to re-engage critically with earlier theoretical issues of class analysis, concerning the state, migration and social control. However, they must address contemporary concerns of a restratified working class in relation to the cumulative effects of mass unemployment, the crisis of the welfare state and the restructuring of scarce public resources to an emerging 'underclass', who are experiencing multiple social exclusions. This is part of a broader picture in which global economic restructuring, advanced technological communications and increasing cultural exchange are highlighting a wide range of emerging processes of social exclusion and marginalization that has challenged older models of racism.

A second aim is to explore the emergence of more recent theories in 'new times' that have begun to suggest the need for a more complex understanding of racial difference and ethnic formation. This mapping of a more complex picture has been greatly developed by ethnic minority feminist theorists (Bhavnani 1991; Mama 1992; *Feminist Review* 1995; Hickman and Walter 1995; Brah 1996). The middle section of the book explores a number of high-quality theoretical accounts, offering innovative insights into racial difference and social change in Britain. Of particular influence here has been post-colonial cultural theorists, who have suggested that in constructing human identity we cannot appeal to any fixed or essential characteristics that exist for all time (Spivak 1988a and b; Bhabha 1990a; Gilroy 1993; Said 1993). Furthermore, they argue that we need to move away from theories that suggest that racial and ethnic relations are shaped by a single, overarching factor, that is colour racism.[3] Rather, they maintain that these relations are better understood within the specific contexts in which they are played out. By the late 1990s we have been provided with theoretical frameworks in which the changing nature of minority communities' lives has been much debated. These texts, in reclaiming culture as of central importance to ethnic minority communities, provide a critique of class-based explanations. At the same time, they enable us to analyse systematically and document coherently the production of contemporary ethnic identities (Hall 1992a; Wetherell and Potter 1992). Reading through recent texts on cultural forms of racism and new ethnicities one becomes aware of the current influence of particular ideas around post-structuralism and postmodernism in 'post-colonial' conditions that are discussed in terms of difference, diversity and cultural pluralism. Some post-structuralist theorists have adopted psychoanalytic accounts, highlighting the complex psychic investments that individuals have in dominant racist and nationalist discourses that cannot be explained simply in rationalist terms (Parker *et al.* 1992; Cohen 1992).

In *Contemporary Racisms and Ethnicities* I am particularly concerned to explore a theoretical shift beyond an anti-racist black–white model of racism. The controversial debates during the 1980s around the concepts of institutional racism (the systematic exclusion of black people within institutions) and black identity are illustrative of the decline of the theoretical and political certainties of an earlier period.[4] In questioning the fixed boundaries around colour racism established by earlier race relations and class-based perspectives, it is argued that contemporary conditions are helping to produce multiple forms of racism and new ethnic identifications. A re-reading of these texts in the late 1990s shows them to have been developed largely in reductionist and essentialist terms of 'what white people have done to black people', rather than in terms of the broader category of racialized social relations between a wide range of ethnic groups. A further limitation of earlier work was the undertheorization of subjectivity and ethnic identity formation. Contemporary cultural theory suggests that the changing meanings around racism and ethnicity can be seen to be multidimensional – experienced and negotiated in different ways in specific historical and institutional arenas. There has been a strong tendency in earlier anti-racist work to adopt a monocausal explanation of racial exclusion and inclusion, which disconnected it from other forms of social divisions and cultural processes. Contemporary racialized processes are temporally and spatially specific, and connect in complex ways with other categories of social difference. More specifically, much was written out of the overly simplistic black–white oppositional couplet, including issues of migration, nation-making, religious and cultural identities and generation. Furthermore, in assuming that blacks and whites were homogeneous collect-ivities, there was a tendency to concentrate on inter-racial differences to the exclusion of intra-ethnic differences, both within and between black and white social groups. Hence, racial/ethnic categories can be read as being shaped by, and shaping, the processes of colonization, racism, class hegemony, male domination, heterosexism and other forms of oppression. In short, the book makes the case for seeing changing forms of racialized social relations and ethnic identities as crucial points of intersection of different forms of social differentiation, subjectivity and identity formation (Mac an Ghaill 1994a and b).

Current debates between anti-racists and cultural theorists are providing a limited discussion, with the former emphasizing common experiences of racism and the latter focusing on the differentiated experiences of different ethnic groups and subgroups in ethnic minority communities. In attempting to hold on to the tension between these different accounts of racism and ethnicity, I have found that theory-led qualitative research grounded in indi-viduals' own accounts is productive. It is important in signalling a move beyond the anti-racist colonial paradigm in which fixed racial boundaries were ascribed to a 'first generation' of immigrants and their children. Cultural theorists highlight the limitations of anti-racist accounts that have tended to concentrate on particular sections of selected 'non-white' groups, namely Asians and African Caribbeans. This has resulted in marginalization of the experiences of other 'non-white' minorities, such as the Chinese and Viet-namese, and the under-representation of anti-Semitism, while at the same time underplaying key elements of black and Asian lives, such as religion and culture, that do not fit into an anti-racist liberal secular framework. So, for example, there is a major difficulty for this framework in explaining the position of Muslims in England. In arguing for the need to rethink a black–white dualist model this book critiques the long academic tradition of 'over-racializing' selected groups of 'non-whites', while de-racializing white minorities. The book explains how future studies of ethnic minorities in England, informed by the principle of ethnic inclusiveness, involving the wide range of ethnic minority communities as well as the Anglo-ethnic majority, might help to move beyond the limits of dominant anti-racist accounts in trying to understand the politics around ethnicity, racism and difference. A key question that arises here is whether we can develop a new civic nationalism for the 2000s that challenges the racist and nationalist exclusions currently experienced by ethnic minority groups and addresses the fears of the Anglo-ethnic majority in a rapidly changing de-industrializing society. The book examines this question in the context of a new focus, shifting beyond the 'colonial paradigm' to explore the experiences of established migrant groups and their British/English born children.

A third aim is a critical engagement with the main sociological accounts of the struggle for racial and ethnic equality at a time of rapid social change in which there is criticism from the political left and right of the limits of anti-racism (see Sivanandan 1982; Cambridge and Fuechtwang 1990a). Questions are being raised about the isolation of anti-racism from the wider community and the idea of race being closely associated with the idea of blackness (Dummett 1991; Miles 1993). This is taking place, following the Gulf War and the Rushdie affair, at a time of increased anti-Islamic feelings in Britain and across Europe, named as Islamaphobia[5]. At the same time, there is increased acknowledgement of the range of historically specific racisms in Britain, including, for example, those operating against the Jewish, Irish, Chinese and Greek Cypriot communities (Holmes 1978a; Kushner 1989; Anthias 1992b; Parker 1994; Hickman 1995a). Equally important, within the context of changing 'post-colonial conditions', the developing world is no longer seen as a unitary category with a homogeneous identity, but instead as a range of regions experiencing differential impact on, and responses to, globalization (Hoogvelt 1997). The last section of the book includes a critical review of sociological accounts of the impact on specific institutions of broader socio-economic and political changes, including the dominance of the 'market' in the public sector (Mac an Ghaill 1988; Phizacklea 1990). For example, it is suggested that recent educational developments on forms of racial and ethnic demarcation can be understood in terms of 'the construction of new parental identities, defined increasingly in terms of consumption' (Offe 1985; Williams 1989; Gabriel 1994). Important issues are highlighted here. This exploration serves to illustrate that anti-racism, or in fact anti-racisms, are not unitary, fixed entities but rather historically specific, contextually contingent phenomena that have given rise to a wide range of minority community mobilizations and anti-oppressive responses. At the same time, it emphasizes that public policy initiatives, both at central and local government levels, are not unproblematically translated into practice. Rather, they must pass through pre-existing institutional infrastructures, composed of groups and individuals, within each institution's political culture. Theory-led empirical work enables us critically to investigate what is involved in evaluating different explanations of the way in which ideologies, discourses and representations of race and ethnicity are lived out within different institutions. In other words, the book explores the adequacy of our understanding of the local *production* of racial difference within regional and institutional sites, alongside the *reproduction* of racism at broader national and global levels.

In the dominant policy approach, multiculturalism and anti-racism have often been crudely opposed and misrepresented. In *Contemporary Racisms and Ethnicities* it is argued that we need to take account of the continuities and discontinuities between these paradigms before any useful strategies can be formulated. The new right critique of anti-racism and the internal critiques from a more progressive perspective, such as the Burnage Report's warning about the limits of 'moral anti-racism', are addressed (Palmer 1986; Macdonald *et al.* 1989). There is also an examination of the de-racialization of white people (Hickman and Walter 1995). Equally importantly, I evaluate accounts of the changing forms of mobilization and protest that have developed in ethnic minority communities, including complex cultural and religious identities, as well as the broader anti-racist movements in response to wider socio-economic and political change. This is illustrated through an examination of recent mobilizations by the Irish and Muslim communities, which serve to highlight the limitations of our current understanding of the politics of race and nation in Britain.

Engaging critically with the wide range of literatures explored in the earlier sections of the book points to the need to construct a 'local', English-based account of racism and anti-racism for 'coming times'. The idea of the local is employed throughout the text in several interconnecting ways. This is summarized below and serves to illustrate what the book is about.

- To rethink the dominant anti-racist, black–white dualistic model, which has been overly influenced by American race-relations frameworks, and to develop a response to the emerging vocabulary of the new politics of cultural difference in the context of a 'post-colonial' British nation-state located in the new Europe.
- To move beyond the historical legacy of London-based discourses of anti-racism developed in the 1970s and 1980s and to acknowledge regional variations and accompanying geographies of racism, anti-racism and ethnic-minority mobilization.
- To move beyond the conceptual 'over-racialization' of Asians and African Caribbeans and the correlating 'de-racialization' of white minority ethnic groups. There is a specific concern here with the erasure of the Irish – as the largest labour migrant and ethnic minority group in Britain – from the academic and political map of racism and ethnicity. This is of particular concern with the continuing British military and political occupation of Northern Ireland, and the general uninterest of British sociology in the 'Irish question'.
- To make problematic the status of the ethnic majority, with a particular focus on the crisis in dominant forms of Anglo-ethnicity. This raises the question of whether we can develop a progressive, inclusive understanding of an English sense of nation and cultural belonging.
- To move beyond the homogenization and reification of ethnic minority and majority groups, highlighting *intra*-ethnic as well as *inter*-ethnic differences.
- To explore critically the complex interconnections between different sets of social relations and accompanying divisions. This includes questions of regionalism, religion, generation, gender, sexuality and the urgent need to reinstate social class in examining multi-dimensional social exclusions.

'Old times', 'new times' and 'coming times': making sense of social and cultural change

The changing political conditions of the late 1990s have included challenges to the configuration of the UK involving the development of a new settlement

between Britain and Northern Ireland, the establishment of a Scottish parliament and a Welsh assembly, a new Europe, nation-building in Africa, and
conflicts in east and central Europe and the former Soviet Union. The late
1980s/early 1990s have seen unprecedented change in the politics of race,
nation and racism in Britain, much of Europe and the United States (Gates
1986; Wieviorka 1995). The rise of Euro-racism has been widely reported,
with suggestions that new cultural forms of racism, ethno-nationalisms
and ethnic cleansing have emerged in the context of globalization. We see
the development of quasi-nationalistic assertions of a European 'us' and a
non-European 'them' taking place within highly contested national arenas
in which questions about immigration and what constitutes the nation-
state are major debates. A central element of these changing conditions is
the growing importance of a diverse range of new migrants, 'illegal' immigrants and asylum seekers (Layton-Henry 1990). This has most recently
been highlighted in the media's projection of a moral panic about the arrival
in Britain of east European gypsies from the Czech Republic and Slovakia,
against whom the National Front has protested (Campbell and Connolly
1997).

All historical periods have 'new times', that is social transformations
that mark a break with an older social order. As suggested above, what is at
stake here is understanding the extent and direction of current social and
cultural change. In *Contemporary Racisms and Ethnicities*, by thinking through
conceptions of social change and continuity, I shall explore issues of racism
and ethnicity within a framework that I shall call 'old times', 'new times'
and 'coming times'. There is a danger here of misreading what is intended.
The focus is not on the chronological distinction, suggesting that 'old times'
are displaced by 'new times'. 'Old times' accounts tend to emphasize the continuities of racism in its form and effects. In contrast, 'new times' accounts
highlight the changing meanings of cultural representations of racism as
temporally and spatially specific. A defining feature of the suggested 'new
times' is highlighted in a major debate across European nation-states: namely,
whether there is a shift from an era of classical biological racism to that of
the emergence of 'new', cultural forms of racism (Taguieff 1988; Balibar
1991a; Silverman 1992; Wieviorka 1995).

A main political success of new right dominance in Britain has been to
challenge critical sociological accounts. By the late 1980s the New Right had
taken up and reworked radical sociological critiques of British society. These
were seen by many people as making sense of their lives that were shaped
by the broader national anxieties and political concerns of 'new times'. The
new right promoted itself as constructing a modern Britain, with a radical
agenda that gained the ascendancy, occupying the high moral ground with its
projected atavistic accounts of a consumer-based acquisitive individualism,
the patriarchal family, the strong state and the patriotic British nation. The
response of the mainstream left to the new right's modernizing project has
been to restate 'old times', Enlightenment-based principles, involving vague
conceptions of a social-democratic, welfarist and multiethnic citizenship.
This included the suggested return to notions of community, participatory
democracy and the more recent additions of empowerment and the learning

society. During this period a self-fulfilling prophecy appeared to have captured English society, with its claim that there was no real alternative to the new right's policies. Consequently, by the late 1990s the mainstream left's response can be seen to be uncomfortably accommodating the right's radical version of 'new times'. In contrast to the political convergence between the parliamentary right and left, radical alternative agendas were developed by new social movements, such as feminism and anti-racism, that challenged the Conservative position. It is within this context that *Contemporary Racisms and Ethnicities* is located, exploring the extent and direction of change in relation to racialized social relations and ethnic identity formations in the British nation-state.

An important development in the social sciences over the past twenty years has been the impact of new social movements on re-thinking how we understand social institutions and cultural arenas, such as workplace, family life, education and leisure activities. By the late 1990s, questions of culture, identity and representation have moved centre stage. It is particularly important to move beyond sociological critiques of the new right, which have been a main concern of sociology during the past twenty years. The return of the Labour Party to central government marks the decline of the high point of the New Right project. This shift enables us to explore the different theoretical frameworks made available by new social movements, namely *identity politics* and *the new politics of cultural difference*. In this book, a *materialist* position is taken as underpinning a *politics of identity* and a *differentialist* position as underpinning *the new politics of cultural difference*. Working in this framework highlights the need to connect an understanding of racialized social relations, ethnic-identity formations and a sense of national belonging *with* wider social and cultural transformations.

In this book, the term *materialist* refers to social movements that perceive the organization of ethnic and racialized identities as deriving from fixed bases of social power. Such bases of social power are seen to work logically and predictably, often being illustrated through an individual's occupation of fixed hierarchical positions, such as dominant/empowered (white people) and subordinate/oppressed (black people). This position is clearly illustrated by anti-racism. In contrast, differentialist theorists have emphasized that the living of ethnic and racialized categories and divisions is more contradictory, fragmented, shifting and ambivalent than the dominant public definitions of these categories suggest. Most importantly, a differentialist account of racism suggests that we cannot simply read off social behaviour from a pre-existing black–white oppositional binary structure of 'victims' and 'oppressors'. This has been illustrated for me recently in a report carried out in Birmingham on the economic needs of older Irish men (Williams *et al.* 1997). The older Irish men had access as whites to dominant racist discourses in relation to Asians with whom they live in the inner city. However, the older Irish men were not in a predictable position of white power-holders in relation to Asian doctors and landlords on whom they were dependent. In short, *differentialism* explores such issues as the limits of the way that racial identity categories are portrayed in terms of black and white social groups, how to make sense of the interconnectedness between multiple relations of power, such as gender, sexuality and disability, and the making of subjective identities. Throughout the book I shall highlight the need to engage with both materialist and differentialist approaches in order to generate more comprehensive accounts of racism and ethnicity.

Contemporary Racisms and Ethnicities provides a critical investigation at a time of rapid change of the way in which shifting 'common-sense' institutional definitions of racialized inclusions and exclusions are affirmed and legitimated within social institutions and cultural arenas, where symbolic systems and material practices systematically privilege dominant social groups. The book develops a multi-level analysis that incorporates explanations at the level of the nation-state, institutions and social groups. It is written at a time of a political and cultural interregnum in which the 'old times' politics and accompanying identities are in decline, but we are not sure what to make of 'new times' politics and identities. Hence, the book describes a transitional period, rather than offering a definitive prediction. Within this context, throughout the writing of this book the issue of the obscurity of recent sociological texts is difficult to resolve. The sociology of racism and ethnicity is an unclear field of study in which highly complex theories are being developed that fail to connect with individuals' and social groups' lived experience. Of particular political significance is the claim by the new politics of cultural difference that power is being dispersed, while subordinated groups are experiencing a sense of systematic social exclusion following the centralization of political power over the past twenty years in Britain. Another aspect of the complexity of researching and writing in this area is the question of the elusiveness, fluidity and interconnectedness of new racisms and emerging ethnicities in contemporary societies in which there is an intensified general feeling of uncertainty. In the final chapter I shall explore this further with reference to placing research questions in local institutional contexts.

Currently, a number of texts provide general overviews of the sociology of racism and ethnicity within conditions of late capitalism (Anthias and Yuval-Davis 1993; Miles 1993; Gabriel 1994; Mason 1995; Solomos and Back 1996). *Contemporary Racisms and Ethnicities* is much indebted to these texts. While in no way simplifying the complexities or understating the challenge it presents, this book sets out to make the study of race, ethnicity and racism at a time of rapid change more accessible to a wider readership. Social movements in the 1960s and 1970s provided a new vocabulary of anti-racist politics. More recently, post-colonial writers have suggested a new language around such notions as diaspora (movement of people – cultural dispersal), hybridity (mixing of cultures) and syncretism (pluralistic forms of cultural belonging) (Spivak 1990; Gilroy 1993; Said 1993; Bhabha 1994).[6] Every effort is made in the book to translate what often seems to be abstract theorizing in this area, enabling us to develop a language to engage with issues of racial difference and how we might contribute to the transformative nature of racism within wider frameworks of social justice, civil rights and citizenship. In so doing, I have attempted to present key issues in a number of different ways. This has led to a certain repetition in the text. At the same time this enables each chapter to be read as a separate unit.

Notes

1 Stephen Lawrence was a black, London, 18-year-old student who was murdered in 1993. A public inquiry was set up in 1998 to investigate the events surrounding the murder and, specifically, the response of the Metropolitan police. The Macpherson Report was published in February 1999. Rosemary Nelson was murdered in Northern Ireland in March 1999 (see Hardy, 1999). The Macpherson inquiry makes an interesting contrast with the case of Blair Peach. Peach was killed on 23 April 1979, while demonstrating against a National Front rally in Southall, west London. A campaign was set up to prosecute a member of the Metropolitan police special patrol group, who eye-witnesses reported hit him over the head. No public inquiry took place and no one was charged. A verdict of death by misadventure was recorded. The campaign continues.

2 The book explores the changing processes of racialization of social relations in Britain at a time of rapid change. Banton (1977) used the concept of racialization to refer to the use of the idea of race to structure people's perceptions of different populations. More recently the notion has been used as a key signifier of racial meanings in a range of discourses (Reeves 1983; Miles 1993; Troyna 1993). Small (1994: 32–3) adopts the 'racialization' problematic in order to unravel the relative influence of multiple factors (economics, politics, demography, culture, ideology and myth) in patterns of 'racialized relations'. As Solomos (1993: 1) argues, a main focus here is 'the growth of ideologies which have focused upon race as an important political symbol, the role of anti-racist and black political mobilisation and the impact of social and economic restructuring on racial and national identities in British society'. Changing processes of racialization are operationalized through the impact of changing race imagery in a range of institutional settings as well as processes of deracialization (Husband 1982; Miles 1989; Gillborn 1995). See also pages 68–70 below.

3 See pages 61–4 for fuller discussion.

4 Against this trend the Macpherson Report (1999) has used the concept of institutional racism to describe relations between the London based Metropolitan police and the black community. This provides a good example of the productiveness of holding onto earlier materialist concepts, such as institutional racism, while at the same time engaging with their limitations, that more recent cultural theorists have highlighted. The Macpherson Report also illustrates how anti-racist concepts developed in the 1970s and 1980s, and were unevenly taken up by different institutions in different parts of the country. See pages 61–4 below for fuller discussion.

5 See note 1 in Chapter 3, page 81.

6 See pages 57–60 at the end of Chapter 2 for further exploration.

1 Changing academic *and* political representations *of* race, ethnicity *and* racism

'Old times' as 'new times' – discursive and ideological labouring

'Old times' were once 'new times'. Locating earlier materialist representations of racism, ethnicity and social change within a socio-historical context enables us to see how they resonated with wider social concerns and anxieties of the period. From a contemporary perspective, it is easy to dismiss these explanations by concentrating on their limitations, such as essentialism, functionalism and over-determinism. It is important to note that we are exploring these earlier accounts at a specific moment, when notions of multiple racisms, new ethnicities and diasporic identities are helping to provide innovative sociological frameworks.[1] More recent cultural theorists are addressing the key concerns of culture, identity, subjectivity and difference. A main strength of earlier materialist accounts has been to place on the social map such issues as the social reproduction of racist ideology, the state regulation of racism, institutionalized racial discrimination and cultural exclusion. At present, it is important to hold on to the theoretical and political achievements of this work. This will serve as a useful reminder of the historical amnesia concerning earlier productive frameworks. There is a strong tendency in work on 'new times' to downplay or erase issues such as that of state power, social class divisions, institutional structures and hegemonic cultural capital. In such texts, there is a suggestion that discourses and practices of representation have displaced the need for such terms as ideology and social reproduction. There is often little awareness that racism and ethnicity are the objects of both discursive *and* ideological labour.

At a time of the ascendancy of the cultural, there is a need to return the social to critical theory. Of particular concern is the need to signal the retreat from class analysis in more recent sociological work and to argue for the renewal of social and cultural analysis of class; to map out some of its more intricate and intimate positions as they articulate the shifting boundaries of class, gender, sexuality, ethnicity and generation. However, this is not to suggest the return to a sociological reductionism, which views minorities as unitary social categories, or a structuralist account that reifies racism as a monolithic state practice operating against racialized social collectivities. This chapter is about a re-reading of earlier sociological work, that is, re-engaging with academic and political accounts of minority ethnic communities. This is particularly salient at a time when there is a lack of consensus in sociology about how we conceptualize our concern with commonalities of experience and specific national and regional experiences of globalization (see Mason 1995). As Smith (1993: 50) maintains: 'Notwithstanding romantic ideas about the boundedness of space, the fixity of place and the reality of "race", the world is on the move. The impetus for this mobility comes from a series of economic and political restructurings accompanying the rise and fall of colonialism, the maturation of industrial capitalism and the advent of the postmodern world.'

Cultural studies has been very successful in establishing the strategic significance of media representation of racial difference in Britain (Van Dijk 1991; Fitzgerald 1992). This has been most graphically illustrated with reference to the coverage of the Rushdie affair. However, cultural studies has tended to underplay the production and circulation of cultural representations of racial difference, failing to locate them within historically specific institutional contexts in which they are lived out. A dominant understanding of representation is found in reflection theory, which suggests that representations simply reflect a pre-existing reality that exists independently of its representation in discourses. A second understanding argues that the way things are represented has a constitutive role in actively constructing the object, giving 'questions of culture and ideology, and the scenarios of representation – subjectivity, identity, politics – a formative, not merely an expressive, place in the constitution of social and political life' (Hall 1992b: 254). This book is working with the latter meaning, highlighting the multiple interpretations of key concepts in discussions of racism and ethnicity. However, out of the many possible meanings in particular situations, specific meanings are privileged or preferred as a result of the way the representation is constructed and the context in which it is experienced (Barthes 1977; Henriques *et al.* 1984). There is another important aspect to the question of representation. Spivak (1988a and b) describes two ways of understanding the act of cultural representation: representation as interpretation and representation as 'speaking for' others. In Chapter 5, this is further explored with reference to a re-reading of multiculturalist and anti-racist modes of representation of racial difference.

This chapter begins with an argument about the importance of a historical perspective, highlighting that there is a long history to how ethnic minorities have been at the centre of social change in Britain. This is followed by an outline of the early culturalist-based race-relations approach against which a class-based materialist approach was developed. The chapter explores, from historical and contemporary perspectives, the relationship between class and racism in late capitalism. Most importantly, a historical perspective enables us to trace the structural continuities alongside the discontinuities with reference to racism at a time when there is much talk of social and cultural change.

Remembering and forgetting the past: history as present – present as history[2]

Novelists and playwrights, such as James Baldwin, Brian Moore, J. M. Synge and W. B. Yeats, appear to be better placed than social scientists to record the central importance of cultural memory for how we live our lives. They are particularly good at capturing the way cultural memory mediates the complex interweaving of individual biography and wider social practices. The suggested re-reading of 'old times' makes explicit the act of remembering. Bhabha (1986: xxiii) maintains that:

> Remembering is never a quiet act of introspection or retrospection. It is a painful re-membering, a putting together of the dismembered past to make sense of the trauma of the present. . . . It is such a memory of the history of race and racism, colonialism and the question of cultural identity, that Fanon reveals with greater profundity and poetry than any other writer.

Within a British context, the Irish are frequently portrayed as being regressively obsessed with living in the past; that is, 'the Irish can't forget'. Said (1993: 266) in *Culture and Imperialism* places this remembering in context, noting that:

> The high age of imperialism is said to have begun in the 1870s but in English-speaking realms it began well over 700 years before as Angus Calder's gripping book *Revolutionary Empire* demonstrates so well. Ireland was ceded by the pope to Henry II of England in the 1150s. He himself came to Ireland in 1171. From that time on an amazingly persistent cultural attitude existed towards Ireland as a place whose inhabitants were a barbarian and degenerate race.

In response to the British, the Irish claim that the 'British can't remember'. It may be that this couplet of cultural remembering and forgetting, as central processes of the racialization of time and place have wider resonance for contemporary social relations between Britain and its former colonies (James 1938; Renan 1990). Sociology theorists, with their tendency to search out general patterns, need to pay special attention to holding on to the significance of the historically and geographically specific. As Keith warns (1993: 17–18), 'generalisations . . . by suppressing memory . . . become the vehicles through which time is lost and places forgotten'. One of the reasons why the Irish and other former colonized groups may retain their collective memories is not reducible to some pathological obsession with the power of the oppressor. What is underreported in race-relations literature and tends to be absent from the British popular imagination is that much of Britain's history has taken place 'outside' of Britain. There is a sense in which 'racialized others' know more about the indigenous British than the latter know about themselves. This interrelationship needs to be located in a broader framework of dominant–subordinate social relations, in which there is an understanding that racialized minorities, who have been positioned at the margins, know much about the ethnic majority positioned at the centre because they have to – in order to work out how to survive in what often seems to be a hostile social environment. For example, all English people may not be racially hostile to the Irish but for the Irish there is no way of knowing who is and who is not. Hence, safe public spaces for Irish people are limited by potential situations of racial conflict of which English people are unaware.

Re-reading 'old times' is a highly contested area of inquiry. Academic books have catalogued selected histories of post-war representations of race and ethnic relations. These academic representations include key figures, dates and places that help us to interpret the particular meanings of these times (Benedict 1943; Little 1947; Glass 1960; Patterson 1963; Banton 1967; Rex 1970). *Contemporary Racisms and Ethnicities* is concerned with stories of social and cultural belongingness; that is, the question of who is included and who is excluded, with reference to ethnicity, racialization and citizenship. The stories embedded in the shifting semantics of race are, of course, historically specific in the production of racialized political subjects. We can trace the shift from a narrative of immigration from New Commonwealth countries and Pakistan (NCWP countries) (1950s/1960s), through one of institutional discrimination against black ethnic minorities and their 'finding a voice' (1970s/1980s), to a narrative of the search for a lost white British national identity in the context of an ambivalent Anglo-ethnic response to 'Fortress Europe' (1980s/2000s).

Contemporary Racisms and Ethnicities adopts a socio-historical analysis of British sociology of race, ethnicity and racism, with a specific focus on its own inclusions and exclusions. This enables us to rethink the contemporary dominant anti-racist model of a racial dualism of black and white, tracing the contextual specificity of multiple racisms and new ethnicities by desegregating specific origins, causes and effects of racialization in particular periods. Earlier theories need to be contextually located, in order to explore what they were developed in relation to and against. At the same time, it is necessary to develop a clearer framework to explore the complex geographies of racism involved in a regionally based politics of location. In turn, this allows us to identify the continuities alongside the discontinuities in challenging what seems to be the inevitable logic of racism as a natural biological or cultural force. Currently, this is of particular significance when cultural theorists tend to overemphasize change, difference and diversity in Western nation-states. This is also important when there is a sense that no one theory can give the whole picture of an increasingly complex global arena that is experiencing rapid transformations. As Solomos (1993: 230) has argued with reference to the interrelationship between shifting meanings around racism and ethnicity and wider processes of social change: 'Race and ethnicity are experienced and negotiated in quite complex ways within contemporary British society, and it is difficult to generalise that there is a common perspective which characterises British society as a whole.'

A historical account suggests that there is potential for the transformation of shifting forms of racialization, national belonging and cultural difference. There emerges a clearer understanding that different material conditions and accompanying symbolic signs produce different effects in local spaces. This enables us to place the contemporary micro-political realities of racism, xenophobia, ethnocentrism and nationalism in the bigger picture and on a longer time-scale. As Rizvi (1993: 3) has argued in relation to the complexity of racism in contemporary society: 'Its exploration requires historical sensitivity as well as political commitment. To research racism is to investigate how various practices of representation are racially formed, and how it is possible to engage in different practices of representation.' Such an approach challenges the determinist notion of history without agency and rescues submerged voices. A historical account of the sociology of racism also serves to link current community political mobilizations to their histories of protest in colonial and 'post-colonial' conditions. In so doing, we move beyond images of a unitary history, for example of Asian and African-Caribbean communities, and begin to record the underreported forms of resistance to racialization that are not reducible to academic accounts of anti-racist movements (Gilroy 1987, 1993). This also helps us to go beyond the exclusive focus of materialist accounts of blacks and whites, to explore the continuing political significance of anti-racism with reference to other 'non-white' minority groups and white minority ethnic groups. These forgotten histories of protest highlight the different cultural forms of state incorporation of minority communities that are linked to their period of entry into Britain. They enable us to begin to ask critical questions about the relationship between minority communities and anti-racist movements. They also open up questions concerning the disconnection of anti-racism from other social movements, including trade unionism, Northern Ireland struggles, ecology, feminism and 'queer politics', as well as links with Europe and Euro-racism. Furthermore, this historical background enables us to understand contemporary forms of contestation by recent migrants, 'illegal' immigrants, refugees and asylum seekers from increasingly diverse places (Sivanandan 1989; Gabriel 1994).

Racialized minorities as a lens to wider social transformations: Anglo-ethnic internal discontents

Contemporary issues around racialization and cultural difference can be seen to be *constitutive of* as well as being *constituted by* wider socio-economic, political and cultural changes. Notions of decentred forms of cultural racism and new ethnicities are being developed within a wider arena of 'the cultural logic of late capitalism', which in turn they are helping to shape (Jameson 1991). Earlier migrations and associated forms of racialization can also be read as a barometer of social and cultural transformations taking place in Britain and other European societies at specific periods (Holmes 1978b; Mosse 1985). This dialectical relationship is particularly visible at times of real or imagined crisis in the nation-state. The history of British race relations is littered with changing racialized images in which national 'internal political discontents' were displaced on to earlier migrant workers and currently on to established minorities and more recent migrants. At a time of crisis in dominant public forms of national arrangements, ethnic minority communities are coerced into carrying the Anglo-ethnic majority's sense of moral disorder. This involves complex processes of social exclusion and psychic expulsion of abjected groups who are represented as a threat to the maintenance of social and symbolic borders. At the same moment, the construction of a 'pure us' and 'polluting them' may be read as illustrating the centrality of the latter to the former (Kristeva 1982).

The interplay between social change and shifting racialized discourses has a long history. It can be seen in the nineteenth century, during what Kumar (1978) has called 'The Great Transformation'. The rapid changes brought about by British industrialization and urbanization, as a leading capitalist society, were intimately linked to its imperialist project, as part of wider structural transformations in the world economy that fuelled demand for migrant labour. Irish migrant workers and emigrants represented strategic economic and cultural elements of this project. Economically, Ireland as the emigrant nursery to the world economy provided a reserve army of cheap and flexible labour for British capitalism (Kearney 1990; Mac Laughlin 1994). Engels (1969: 116), in *The Condition of the Working Class in England*, records the part the Irish played in England's industries. He argues that: 'The rapid extension of English industry could not have taken place if England had not possessed in the numerous and impoverished population of Ireland a reserve army at its command.' Culturally, specific subject positions were produced for the Irish as 'colonial others', in the context of a 'shared life' between immigrants and the 'host' society at the imperial centre (Jackson 1963; Holmes 1988; Dummett and Nicol 1990). This was an important moment for the British, in the re-production of their collective self-identity as a 'superior race', who actively disidentified with the Irish as an 'inferior and degenerate race' (see Miles 1982: 121–50). Curtis (1968) describes the pervasiveness of popular images of the Irish that circulated in Victorian England. There was a wide range of markers of difference that juxtaposed the dirtiness, drunkenness, laziness and violence of the alien Irish with the purity, industriousness and civiliza-tion of the English. As Hickman (1995a: 49) argues, at this time dichotomies of race and nationality were frequently conflated in popular journals and newspaper editorials. Lebow (1976: 40), in his study of the impact of racial stereotyping on colonial policy, illustrates this with a quotation from *Frazer's Magazine*, a middle-class journal, in 1847:

> The English people are naturally industrious – they prefer a life of honest labour to one of idleness. They are a persevering as well as an energetic race, who for the most part comprehend their own interests perfectly and sedulously pursue them. Now of all the Celtic tribes, famous everywhere for their indolence and fickleness as the Celts everywhere are, the Irish are admitted to be the most idle and most fickle. They will not work if they can exist without it.

A second example is the post-war immigration of people from the New Commonwealth countries and Pakistan (NCWP). This occurred at a time of great socio-economic and political change in Britain. In other words, a 'new times' was in the process of being built. This reconstruction included the development of the social democratic settlement that was underpinned by an expanding industrial economy and the establishment of the welfare state. Economically, the NCWP immigrants were a replacement labour force, filling key labour market roles. Culturally, this was a critical moment, in a historical period in which the empire came 'home', as the British were in the process of decolonizing. At this moment the contemporary notion of a British 'race-relations problem' became associated with the presence of 'coloured immigrants', who were positioned as a key signifier of the new social order. This association was pervasive, becoming fixed across the political spectrum, in academic and political representations, on policy makers' agendas, in the media and in the popular imagination.

By the late 1970s the British Labour government's 'winter of discontent' signalled the collapse of the post-war social democratic settlement as a modernizing force. In a declining industrial society, new discourses emerged, with the state reworking racialized representations of the black community, who at this time were experiencing increased racial hostility, including the organized violence of the National Front. A number of commentators have spoken of the growing crisis of hegemony in Britain during the 1960s leading to the formation of a new authoritarian consensus through the 1970s (Nairn 1977; Hall *et al.* 1978; Centre for Contemporary Cultural Studies 1982; Anderson 1983; Gilroy 1987). Gamble (1988: 11) describes the background to the global crisis of this period and its impact on the local organic crisis of British capitalism.

The crisis in the regime of accumulation and the shifts in the political organisation of the world system which took place in the 1970s were the fundamental changes which made a new politics possible and necessary. But the content of this new politics was often provided by local concerns, specific to institutions and circumstances of particular countries. Nevertheless here too certain common themes can be seen. The institutions and policies of social democracy came under attack almost everywhere. The challenges were made through ideological debate as well as by new political programmes and movements. Many of these challenges began before the appearance of the global crisis of accumulation and hegemony. But they became much stronger once the political and economic foundations of the post-war order had been undermined.

For Hall *et al.* (1978), at an ideological level, race came to signify the social crisis; providing the 'arena in which complex fears, tensions and anxieties ... (could) be most conveniently and explicitly projected and ... "worked through"' (Hall *et al.* 1978: 333). They insisted that this was not a crisis of race but rather that race provided the lens through which the crisis was perceived and mediated; the crisis was largely thematized through race. Racism was no longer the preserve of the extreme minority but became naturalized, that is part of the 'normal' everyday experience of the population. With a move towards national popularism, racism provided a mobilizing force. The creation of a moral panic about race, particularly made visible in the social construction of the 'black mugger', provided the basis for a shift to the implementation of a form of popular authoritarianism.

By the 1980s, with the New Right in the ascendancy, a new political landscape was constructed with a shift to de-racialized discourses (Centre for

Contemporary Cultural Studies 1982; Gilroy 1987). Questions of culture, nation and belonging as central elements of the new modernization project came to displace openly racist talk. More recently, Keith (1993: 232), commenting on this period, has provided an original analysis of the interrelationship between the criminalization of black youth as the logical outcome of the racialization of British society that resonated with the economic restructuring of the 1980s. He argues: 'that it lends a legitimacy to the measures of social control this restructuring requires and also that the very reproduction of racial divisions in society is in part a function of this process'. Signalling the need for more sophisticated theoretical frameworks, in order to understand what is going on in Britain, he maintains that: 'The outcome is no less invidious, the reality no less morally obscene, but the processes at work belie easy categorisation.'

The limits of the culturalist race-relations problematic: a materialist critique

During the 1970s and 1980s a major concern of the materialist position was the nature of racially structured British society. There were a number of critical sociological approaches to this question. Before discussing these, it is necessary to contextualize the materialist position. This enables us to explore the dominant culturalist perspective of the race-relations problematic, towards which critical sociological perspectives were highly disparaging. The materialist critique of culturalism is currently being superseded by differentialist accounts that involve a reclaiming of culture, locating it at the centre of contemporary analysis. From a perspective of the late 1990s, it is argued that in critiquing the limits of culturalism materialists erased the centrality of culture to questions of racial difference. This serves as a useful reminder of the partiality of all theories, including recent developments, which are always constructed within specific political contexts.

A re-reading of earlier literature on British race relations reveals a long history of the discarded social images of minorities. As pointed out above, African Caribbeans and Asians were the major focus of British sociology of race relations in the 1970s and 1980s. The dominant ethnic approach focusing on minority communities' distinctive cultural attributes suggested that social behaviour was to be understood primarily in terms of culture (Ballard and Driver 1977; Banks and Lynch 1986). Ballard and Driver (1977: 543) were influential representatives of this approach, and appropriately entitled their paper 'The Ethnic Approach'. They argued that:

> When West Indians first came to Britain as migrant workers in the 1950s, it seemed to many that they were black Englishmen and Englishwomen. Their own group interests and identities were often suppressed by the needs of the moment. Now both they, and especially their children, are developing and demonstrating more open hallmarks of their ethnic affiliation, of their experience of being West Indians in Britain . . . Asians in contrast have a much less openly aggressive impact upon the British scene. Yet the issues have been more numerous in their case . . . While

we cannot disregard the inescapable fact of colour, many social tensions associated with race relations are really centred around cultural differences. . . . Economic disadvantages and ethnic diversity are two sides of the same coin. . . . The negative concept of racial disadvantage fails to understand the positive vitality of ethnic minority institutions. To act as if minorities did not create a corporate existence of their own is unrealistic and absurd. A central political issue at all levels in our society is how much acceptance is to be given to the separate development of ethnic communities.

This culturalist perspective suggested that as a result of ethnic minorities' being prevented from assimilating into British society, they, especially the 'second generation', were emphasizing their common culture and celebrating their ethnic belonging. This was demonstrated in the symbolic significance of Rastafarianism for young African Caribbeans and in the readoption of the wearing of turbans and saris for young Asians (Ballard 1979). Adopting a discourse of deficit, the main social images constructed by this culturalist position portrayed minority communities as a 'problem' (John 1981). Ethnicity was assumed to act as a 'handicap' to their assimilation or integration into British society. So, for example, the difference in the educational performance of Asian and African-Caribbean young people was frequently explained in terms of the assumed pathological structure of the African-Caribbean family and kinship organization. In contrast, the assumed cultural unity of the Asian extended family network was seen as providing the necessary support for the younger generation (Khan 1979; Lawrence 1982). This reductionist problematic contrasted the assumed underachievement of young African Caribbeans with the assumed linguistic difficulties of young Asians, who were seen to be 'caught between two cultures' (Community Relations Commission 1976). Some theorists working with this approach also acknowledged the positive elements of ethnicity; thus Driver (1980) suggested that the improvement in the academic performance of African-Caribbean females resulted from the strengths of their ethnic structure, such as the strong matriarchal African-Caribbean family organization. However, it was the negative aspect of ethnic differences that was the major concern of race-relations discourse.

Within a culturalist perspective the term ethnicity was employed as a politically neutral category while serving as a racially coded euphemism for the black community with the British-born 'second generation', contradictorily assigned the same immigration status as their parents (Anthias and Yuval-Davis 1993). These academic representations are an example of the central role of bureaucrats in the welfare professions involved in the process of converting political questions into technical and administrative problems (Gramsci 1970). In contrast to the black community, the cultural attributes of the Irish, the largest ethnic group in Britain, were of little concern. So, for example, English teachers were not interested in learning about Roman Catholic religious practices, Gaelic football, or *ceilithe*, nor, more significantly, did they assume that such knowledge was necessary in order to understand the educational performance of students of Irish origin. Working within the black–white dualistic model, it was assumed that the Irish as white Europeans had assimilated into British culture (Mac an Ghaill 1988; Hickman 1995a). At the same time, as with white migrants and their children, the 'ethnicity' of the Anglo-ethnic majority population was unproblematically taken for granted. In short, the main ethnic group was erased from the culturalist perspective which operated with ethnicity as its central concept.

Although the culturalist perspective received much theoretical criticism from other sociological approaches, it nevertheless was a significant 'common-sense' ideological explanation of minority communities' experience of British society. Most importantly, the assumptions of this culturalist perspective were shared by race-relations theorists, policy-makers and welfare professionals, including teachers and social workers, and the more repressive agents of social control, such as immigration officials, the police and the courts. The significance of the ethnic approach can be seen in relation to the implementation of a range of multicultural initiatives within public sector institutions. Historically, the shift from the official national policy of assimilation to integration in the mid-1960s involved public-sector employees becoming informed about the cultural background of black people (Mac an Ghaill 1988; Ball and Solomos 1990; Gillborn 1990). Presently, the historical legacy of the culturalist position is often underplayed. A concern with selected black people's distinctive cultural attributes, most particularly African-Caribbean and Asian cultures, remains a central focus of institutional practices in civil society. This is illustrated, for example, by the state's collection of data on ethnicity for equal-opportunities purposes.

During the 1980s a number of criticisms of the culturalist position were developed. Bourne with Sivanandan (1980: 345–6), in their examination of race relations in Britain, attacked the ethnic school with its emphasis on cultural relations for detracting from the black community's real struggle against racism. They maintained that:

> Culturalism in practice leads to a cul-de-sac nationalism, defeatism, inward-looking, in-breeding incapable of changing the power relations in society . . . cultural pluralism, the framework, and multiculturalism, the solution, deal with neither (institutional) racism, nor class questions. Reactive ethnicity or cultural resistance can only be a resistance to racialism in British society. Racialism is not about power but about cultural superiority. Racism is not about cultural superiority but about power; and the resistance to racism must in the final analysis be political resistance, expressed perhaps in cultural forms.

Bourne and Sivanandan made a distinction between the experience of colour prejudice and the institutionalization of prejudice in the power structures of society, that is, a distinction between racialism and racism. They claimed that the ethnic approach was exclusively concerned with the former. Sivanandan (1983: 5), returning to this theme in a talk given to the Greater London Council Ethnic Minorities Unit, argued that 'ethnicity blunts black struggle' by creating cultural and generational divisions in the black community. From a materialist position, a major weakness of the culturalist perspective was that by focusing on the 'ethnic attributes' of the black community, it failed to recognize the fundamental significance of social class location in advanced capitalist societies. As Mercer and Prescott (1982: 102) argued: 'The most significant feature of the minority experience is not their ethnicity but their place in the class structure. Their relative powerlessness ensures that they will remain in a subordinate position politically and culturally. Again in these circumstances a meaningful cultural pluralism is impossible.'

Revisiting materialist accounts of racism: 'old times' as changing times

One of the most important debates in theoretical and empirical work on racism explores the interconnection between racism and class (see Anthias and Yuval-Davis 1993: 61). Earlier class-based materialist analyses provided cutting-edge explanations about racism and social change. These accounts offered a range of explanations as to why socially constructed race categories continued to have such popular resilience in the 1970s and 1980s. They established commonalities of experience of racism, investigating the different institutional social positioning, particularly of Asians and African Caribbeans, living in multiracist Britain (Cohen and Bains 1988; Anthias 1990). In so doing, they highlighted the *different realities* of living in a racially structured society, in which there was little day-to-day contact between white and black communities. Black people's contacts with whites tended to be limited to interaction with employers and state representatives in civil society who had disciplinary and regulatory power over them, such as immigration and welfare officials and teachers. The research documented to varying degrees the pervasiveness of white racism in relation to, among other things, British immigration legislation, housing, schooling and labour markets, welfare in-stitutions, policing practices and media representation. These studies charted histories of racial inclusions/exclusions and the associated range of changing processes and institutional techniques that were deployed in the economy, the state and civil society, alongside the construction of a range of collective responses of resistance. At the same time, these studies were strategically of political significance in providing key information that informed policy changes on racial discrimination, particularly at the level of the local state, that was translated into multicultural and anti-racist institutional practices. From the perspective of the political uncertainty at the end of the twentieth century, materialist accounts may be read as being developed in an era of relative optimism in which it was believed that social science research could contribute to shaping social change, leading to greater racial equality.

The materialist theoretical position was important in establishing the structural impact of dominant social class relations and divisions on the black community. The most stimulating work during the 1970s and early 1980s on class analysis of racially structured societies in the context of social change, at the level of both the national and world economy, was developed by left Weberian (Rex and Moore 1967; Rex 1970, 1973; Rex and Tomlinson 1979), and Marxist and neo-Marxist theorists (Castles and Kosack 1973; Nikolinokos 1975; Sivanandan 1976, 1978; Hall *et al.* 1978; Hall 1980; Phizacklea and Miles 1980; Centre for Contemporary Cultural Studies 1982; Miles 1982).

Hall (1980: 2–6) suggested that work carried out during this period on racially structured societies could be divided into two broad tendencies: the economic and the sociological. Hall includes the work of Rex in the sociological approach. These materialist frameworks argued for the need to go beyond conventional models of social pathology and subjective discrimination, to examine the structural subordination of the black community. The economic was so called because economic relations and structures were seen, in the final analysis, as having a determining effect on the nature of the social formation. The sociological tendency was characterized by the analysis of race within a framework capable of being defined by a number of social or cultural considerations depending on the specific context, the economy being only one of these considerations.

Rex's work was of central significance in developing a class analysis within what came to be called British race relations. Rex (1973: 157), critical of the classic Marxist definition of class as determined by the relationship to the means of production, suggested that: 'Class position in a modern society cannot be solely and simply defined in terms of men's [sic] relations to the means of production or simply in terms of the workplace. It refers to a whole complex of rights, which though they may be in the long run derivative from a man's [sic] industrial position, has implications in many other social spheres as well.' In the Weberian tradition he saw classes as existing in each of the primary market situations of employment, housing and education. Rex and Moore's (1967) work remains a classic non-reductionist sociological study of the operation of institutional racist mechanisms working against the black community and maintaining members of that community in the different 'allocative systems' at the lowest positions. Rex, in his later work with Tomlinson (1979), developed theoretically this analysis of blacks as forming an underclass, which suggested systematic disadvantage compared with the white working class that they experienced across all of the allocative systems.

More positively, the concept also suggested that in not identifying with white, working-class political and cultural institutions and community life, blacks had formed their own organizations that must be understood in relation to a 'wider political conflict, arising from the restructuring of a formerly imperial society' (Rex and Tomlinson 1979: 275). Having established this concept as of central theoretical significance, Rex and Tomlinson (1979: 275–6) then presented a summary of their conclusions, emphasizing the distinct class position of blacks and the role of racism in maintaining social divisions between the white and black working class. In examining the implications of their study, they rejected the optimistic analysis that could be made by a superficial reading of their survey data, that the decreasing differential treatment of blacks could be overcome, with the implementation of more liberal policies and increased powers to the Commission for Racial Equality. Having examined the life chances of blacks in each of the primary market situations, they concluded that there was in fact increasing polarization between black and white populations. Rex and Tomlinson (1979: 294) claimed that in the future the black community, and in particular the young, would continue to develop self-help political strategies, linked to a developing world revolutionary perspective that they found in operation in Handsworth, in the Midlands city of Birmingham. There were a number of criticisms of Rex's theoretical formulation of the relationship between race and class (Gilroy 1980; Hall 1980). For Hall, a weakness of the sociological tendency, including Rex's work, was that Weberian analysis ultimately produced a set of descriptive plural explanations which lacked an adequate theorization and avoided 'the necessity to specify the articulating mechanisms and the modes of dominance between these different types' (Hall 1980: 16) of production processes. From the perspective of the late 1990s, materialists would suggest a similar argument with reference to the differentialist position that Hall has been central in developing in Britain.

The economic approach to the question of racially structured societies focused on a political economic analysis; as Nikolinakos (1975) pointed out, the study of racism is a study of political economy. A major starting point for Marxist analyses of the political economy of race was Peach's (1968) study of West Indian migration to Britain, with its central thesis that black immigration was primarily determined by post-Second World War labour shortages and that immigrants acted as a 'replacement population' in non-growth sectors of industry where whites were unwilling to work. Castles and Kosack (1973) provided support for this view of the role of immigrant labour in advanced capitalist economies with their work on the occupational location of migrant labour in Germany. They argued that cheap immigrant labour was of particular benefit to capital for a number of reasons. These included the low cost of black labour and its social reproduction, and its contribution to the survival of labour-intensive industries and to increasing the capital intensity of production, through, for example, the overrepresentation of black workers on shift work. In this sense black labour was seen as a super-exploited stratum of the working class (Phizacklea and Miles 1980).

An inadequacy of much of the literature stemming from the economic approach was the tendency to reduce social relations and divisions to a function of the needs and requirements of the economy. This led to an instrumentalist view of the state as working directly and unproblematically in the interests of capital. Also, since all European immigrants were frequently lumped together, as for example in the work of Castles and Kosack, the differences between immigrants in Britain and those in Europe and immigrants' specific mode of incorporation into post-war British society was inadequately analysed. Sivanandan (1976), addressing himself to the role of the British state as a central mechanism in the distribution of labour in the production process, could be seen as attempting to qualify this weakness in suggesting that since 1971, with the erosion of their legal status, immigrants in Britain increasingly came to occupy the same disadvantaged position as those in Europe. However, the problem of reductionism and the viewing of immigrants and the state as operating functionally and unproblematically in the interests of capital remained.

Sivanandan and Miles are two major theorists in the sociology of racism who have produced wide-ranging accounts of the continuing importance of general political economic (materialist) analyses of racism in advanced capitalist societies (Sivanandan 1989, 1990a; Miles 1982, 1989, 1993). Sivanandan's account of the history of black resistance in Britain is discussed in Chapter 5. Miles is recognized by a wide range of theorists as one of the most influential Marxist theorists on class and racism (Wetherell and Potter 1992; Anthias and Yuval-Davis 1993; Gabriel 1994; Hickman 1995a; Solomos and Back 1996). His critics tend to move too quickly to accuse him of 'simple' class reductionism. Rather, he can be seen to have produced one of the more sophisticated non-functionalist Marxist accounts. His own academic biography reads as a modernization of conceptual frameworks, addressing the dynamic relationship between class and racism. For Miles (1989: 9–10):

> ... the influence of racism and exclusionary practices is always a component part of a wider structure of class disadvantage and exclusion; the real challenge is to contextualize the impact of racism and related exclusionary practices, partly to highlight the specificity of that impact and partly to demonstrate the simultaneous continuities in the class positions and experiences of (in the case of Britain) people of Asian and Caribbean origin and people of indigenous origins. In other words, in the light of the extensive evidence of the existence and impact of racism and related exclusionary practices, the task that remains is to unravel the different forms and levels of determination, the articulations between racism, sexism, nationalism and the exclusionary practices which are derived from these ideologies, in the context of the reproduction of the capitalist mode of production.

During the 1980s, Miles was a key theorist in the shift from the race-relations problematic (a phoney and misleading field of study) to the sociology of racism; a shift from race to racialization (Miles 1982). His work at the time was important in doing the hard work of arguing for theoretical and methodological clarity and rigour in what became an overinflated concept of racism among theorists and political activists. A number of commentators have identified limitations of his claim that racism is primarily a form of ideology (Gilroy 1987; Anthias and Yuval-Davis 1993). However, with the ascendancy of cultural analysis, Miles' work on ideology is an essential reminder that racism is the object of ideological and discursive labouring. Drawing attention to the power of 'negative' formulations of ideology, he critically explores processes of legitimation, rationalization and justification (Wetherell and Potter 1992). For example, his writing is exemplary in examining the ideological work of the state in the regulatory process of racialization, albeit that 'the distinctions he draws between economic, political and ideological processes are not as clear-cut as he suggests' (Wetherell and Potter 1992: 33). In Miles's work, we see excellent interrogative work in his search for the ideological distortions of racism and how it is played out in people's lives. Differentialists, employing a different epistemological approach, have shifted from a concern with establishing the factual status of truth claims as to whether race *really exists* to one of understanding *how truth claims attain their status as facts* and the effects of these constructions. However, what is often missing from differentialists' work is Miles's consistent and exhaustive analysis of the construction of racial categories. This is partly explained by the way in which differentialist accounts of racism often abstract practices from institutional contexts. In contrast, Miles' work is historically sensitive and empirically grounded, exploring the complexity of economic, political and ideological relationships in shaping our understanding of racial conflict and social change in conditions of late capitalism (Phizacklea and Miles 1979, 1980). In his work on the migration of labour, he highlighted the narrow focus of the question of migration within the sociology of racism. For Miles (1980: 5), the object of analysis should be not an exclusive concern with colour racism but the wider context of the vast spatial movements required by the development of capitalism as a national and international phenomenon. In this way, he provides a conceptual framework that goes beyond the black–white dualistic model that systematically distorts our understanding and analysis of the lives of migrants (and minority ethnic groups) in Britain. Finally, unlike much of the earlier and, indeed, contemporary work in the sociology of racism, Miles has not been overly dependent on American race-relations models. Rather, he has drawn on European analyses of racism and nationalism and has made the changing politics of Europe – with reference to work on the nation, the state and immigration – a central object of his analysis (Miles 1993, 1994a and b).

Although Marxist theorists in the 1970s and early 1980s acknowledged that in order to understand the class position of blacks it was necessary to understand the ideological and institutional mechanisms that produced the social division of labour, they failed to carry out such analysis. Hence, in practice an economic reductionist approach remained, with racist and nationalist ideologies portrayed simplistically as mere expressions of ruling-class interests. An important exception to this was the work of Hall *et al.* (1978). Following Hall *et al.*, in attempting to fill this gap, in earlier work (Mac an Ghaill 1988) I viewed the relationship between the economy and institutional sites in civil society, such as education and training, not as a functional relationship but as a contradictory and disjointed one, focusing on historical and spatial discontinuities. My particular concern was to explore the limits of this relationship and the means by which the contradictions were resolved to the disadvantage of overdisciplined working-class Asian and African-Caribbean young people, by examining their position in relation to the education system and future destinies in local labour markets.

A number of Marxists and neo-Marxists, drawing on work such as that of Althusser (1971), Poulantzes (1975) and Gramsci (1971), attempted to go beyond a class reductionist position and the accompanying instrumentalist view of the state (Gabriel and Ben Tovim 1978; Hall 1980). The most dynamic contribution came from the Centre for Contemporary Cultural Studies (CCCS) at the University of Birmingham. Along with Stuart Hall, other members and associates of the CCCS, most notably Cohen, Gabriel, Gilroy and Solomos, have provided some of the key texts over the past twenty years that have been, and continue to be, major influences in contemporary debates about race and racism in Britain. Hall's (1980) essay 'Race, Articulation and Societies structured in Dominance' was of major significance in arguing for the relative autonomy of racism from other socio-economic and political relations in capitalist societies. Hall's theoretical intervention into the debate on race and class was later developed by other members of the CCCS. Of particular importance was the publication of *The Empire Strikes Back* (Centre for Contemporary Cultural Studies 1982), which was developed conceptually against both the race-relations problematic and Marxist writers such as Miles. In this work the Centre set out to investigate the changing politics of race, class and nation in the 1970s and early 1980s. It was important in generating new non-reductionist ways of conceptualizing the relationship of race and class within Britain, going beyond Hall's (1980) original conception that remained in a Marxist framework. It successfully established a new theoretical point of departure, locating the growth of repressive state structures and new racisms within the dynamics of the global crisis of capitalism and the specificities of the deep-seated structural crisis of British society. A starting point of the book was that the working class in Britain did not constitute a continuous historical subject. There was a central concern to investigate the notion of race as an inherently contestable social and political category.

For Gilroy, one of the key contributors to *The Empire Strikes Back*, an element of primary importance to the specificity of the black struggle was the centrality of cultural forms of resistance. Here, race was not reduced to a question of ethnicity or custom but rather racist and anti-racist ideology and black resistance were seen as elements of class conflict. Gilroy (1982: 302) maintained that:

> Though for the social analyst 'race' and class are necessarily abstractions at different levels, black consciousness of race and class cannot be empirically separated. The class character of black struggles is not a result of the fact that blacks are predominantly proletarian, though that is true. It is established in the fact that their struggles for civil rights, freedom from state harassment, or as waged workers, are instances of the processes by which the working class is constituted politically, organised in politics.

This was a very important point that had remained underexplored in the race–class debate; not only were race and class analytically distinct but connected sets of relations, they were also mutually constitutive of one another – in Hall's terms, British class formation was predicated on race structuration. Hickman (1995a) has provided an interesting historical examination of this articulation with reference to the migration of the Irish to Britain in the nineteenth century. Her work suggests that further investigation in this area has the potential to produce a re-reading of this period.

Contemporary Racisms and Ethnicities is working within a specific framework that is exploring the differing positions of materialist and differentialist theorists. However, there is always a danger in an ideal-type approach with such a construction of categories, as they are not always found in pure form; nor is it possible simplistically to allocate sociological theorists to one or other category. Social reality is more complex, with theorists straddling the categories and adopting shifting discourses as their work develops. In labelling academics there is a risk of reifying what are often loose classification systems and implying that they may not change from one position to another. This warning is particularly salient at a time of rapid social and cultural transformation, when theorists may be more likely to shift positions. Hence, the categories materialist and differentialist are used as a heuristic device and may be read as unstable theoretical positions with transitional fusions and unexpected alliances emerging. For example, Anthias and Yuval-Davis (1993) and Solomos and Back (1996) in their theoretical overviews of sociology of racism in the 1970s and 1980s identify a number of these convergences, particularly with reference to similarities between former CCCS members and their old theoretical adversary, Rex. The extensive work of Hall and Gilroy over two decades has led the way in contemporary analyses, shifting from materialist frameworks to a differentialist position. Re-reading *The Empire Strikes Back,* it can be seen to be a harbinger of the shift from a materialist to a differentialist position. Gilroy's later work, for example *There Ain't No Black in the Union Jack* and *The Black Atlantic,* can be seen to develop this shift further towards an engagement with post-structuralist and postmodern influences. There is much disagreement as to where to locate Hall and Gilroy's complex, nuanced bodies of work. At different points in this book I identify different theoretical emphases that are to be found in their writings.

Perhaps a more consistent position is held by Phil Cohen, a former member of the CCCS, who has developed highly original theoretical and conceptual frameworks that hold on to the productive tensions between materialist, differentialist and psychoanalytic positions. Furthermore, unlike much recent culturally based theoretical work in this area, the richness of his analysis is grounded in empirical investigations of specific institutional sites within a 'post-colonial' Britain characterized by time–space compression. Currently, Cohen is director of the Centre for New Ethnicities Research, at the University of East London. The work at the Centre has inherited the dynamism associated with the CCCS in the 1970s/1980s in developing innovative theoretical frameworks for the twenty-first century, which marks a break with earlier race relations and anti-racist positions that tend to be grounded exclusively in the experiences of post-war New Commonwealth and Pakistan immigrants and their children. Cohen's unit is producing a new generation of theory that is conceptually and politically capable of critically investigating the continuing importance of the interplay between multiple forms of racism, shifting ethnic identities and changing class formations. Alongside this there is an engagement with the psychodynamics of the production of ethnic minority and majority communities. In other words, he brings together social structures and inner dramas in illustrating the shifting contours of young people's cultural and political identities within conditions of late modernity.

Anthias and Yuval-Davis (1993: 65), in their critical re-reading of sociological work in the 1970s and 1980s, identify a range of materialist positions that link race to class: 'Rex's underclass thesis, migrant labour theories, racism as an ideology that is relatively autonomous of class, Gilroy's view that class formation is linked to race, and the dual labour market approaches'. They point to the difficulty of reviewing this work, as these writers may draw on one or more of these formulations (see Anthias 1990). In *Contemporary Racisms and Ethnicities*, the materialist position includes a wide range of perspectives, including Sivanandan, Miles, Gabriel and the early work of Hall and associates at the CCCS. Some of the most contentious debates were between these theorists; however, from a differentialist position, their accounts share the limitations of a materialist perspective. Although some of the texts point to a relative autonomy in the distribution of social power, a main organizing principle of a materialist analysis remains, namely that the nature of social being can be logically read off from institutional structures. For materialists, subjectivity that is undertheorized is assumed to be coherent and rationally fixed. One consequence of this is that state institutions are conceptualized as reflecting the possible identities that can be taken up and lived out. A further limitation of a materialist position is that it is unable to realize the significant challenges of new social movements, which are to create theoretical frameworks that can accommodate a range of inequalities, such as those around ethnicity, class, gender, sexuality and disability. In short, a materialist position produces difficulties in articulating an inclusive account of multiple forms of social power.

A main argument of this chapter is that contemporary cultural theorizing needs to recover the history of earlier materialist accounts and in the process re-read 'old times' texts as providing innovative understandings of racial conflict and social change. This enables us to engage with the structural continuities – alongside the discontinuities – of late modernity. It also enables us to address key absences and closures in current theorizing, as well as illustrating the complexity of developing conceptually and politically adequate accounts of racialization for future times. Materialist representations of the relationship between racism and class are currently of strategic political importance in challenging the postmodern excess of moral relativism and indeterminacy, while reminding us what many differentialists have forgotten. New theoretical frameworks and empirical studies of racialized minorities need to re-engage critically with earlier theoretical issues of class analysis, with their focus on the political economy of racism, the centrality of the process of racialization in structuring and maintaining capitalist relations in the colonial period, the ideological work of the state in the regulatory process of the control of immigration, the labour process of migration, hegemonic influences in civil society and their differentiating effects on minority ethnic groups' access to public sector resources.

Decentring of class: decoupling of class and racism?

The decoupling of social class and racism needs to be located in the wider sociological arena of the decentring of social class. The claim that the significance of social class is declining both as a collectivity and as a primary political actor has long been the subject of comment (Nisbet 1959). During the past decade, social class has been increasingly marginalized in sociology. A major critique from culturally based postmodernists claims that recent changes constitute a fundamental shift that traditional class analysis is inadequate to address (Smart 1990; Lash and Urry 1994; Joyce 1995). As Harvey (1993: 93–4), writing of the political situation in America, has noted: 'The very idea of any kind of working class politics was likewise on the defensive, if not downright discredited in certain "radical" circles, even though capitalist class interests and the captive Republican Party had been waging a no-holds-barred and across-the-board class war against the least privileged sectors of the population for the previous two decades.' Similarly, Ainley (1993: 1), writing in a British context, claims that there is no longer much agreement among social scientists on the meaning of the social classifications that used to be the key terms of their craft. He is particularly concerned about the analysis of society in terms of social class that has been largely abandoned in favour of description by measures of social status. Ironically, the decentring of social class analysis has occurred at the same time as an increasingly globalized capitalism has produced unprecedented levels of poverty and wealth in de-industrializing societies at regional, national and international levels (Bottomore and Brym 1989; Hamnett *et al.* 1989; Sivanandan 1990b; Hout *et al.* 1993; Westergaard 1994). As Hoogvelt (1997: xi) points out: 'Today there are over 1.2 billion people in the world living in absolute poverty and misery, and their number is growing, increasingly enveloping those who previously formed part of the rich, First World, and of the semi-developed second world. Furthermore, the gap between the richest and poorest quinquile of the world's population is twice as big today as it was 30 years ago.'

There is a history involved in the theoretical decoupling of racism and social class, with the shift from the problematic of capitalism to one in which issues of modernity and postmodernity have become key analytic frameworks. The implications of this theoretical shift remain underexplored for the study of racialized social relations and ethnic identity formations. Solomos and Back (1996: 16–17) have pointed out that the racism–class couplet reached its high point in the 1980s, although it continues to influence research agendas and teaching. As they argue, however, a number of recent developments have meant that the neo-Marxist critiques of the 1980s were not able to cope with the complexities of theorizing racism in the 1990s. They suggest that: 'The first of these is the crisis within Marxism itself. In this context some have called for a radical revision of class analysis (Castells 1983; Gilroy 1987; Anthias 1992a) in order to incorporate political movements which mobilize around forms of identity other than class. Others have suggested a need to move away from Marxism as a framework of analysis and have taken on board some concerns of post-structuralism and postmodernism (Gates 1986; Goldberg 1990, 1993).' Such writers suggest that, within 'post-colonial' conditions, dif-ferentialist accounts are more productive in exploring contemporary concerns with multiple racisms, new ethnicities and cultural difference.

Postmodernists have developed conceptual frameworks in which such notions as globalization, consumption, post-industrialism and complex iden-tity formations are currently providing cutting-edge analysis. Beck (1992), in his influential work *Risk Society*, sets out a general theory of social change. His main thesis is that Western societies are experiencing 'a surge of indi-viduation' (Beck 1992: 87) in which postmodern change is bringing an end to class and other social forms of industrial society. He makes an exception of Britain, however, of which he says: 'Class membership is very apparent in everyday life and remains the object of consciousness and identification. It is evident in speech . . . in the sharp class divisions in residential areas . . . in types of education, in clothing and in everything that can be included under the concept of lifestyle' (Beck 1992: 102). At the beginning of the twenty-first century, social class origins in Britain remain a key predictor of future location in the labour market, place of residence, education opportunities, and possession of high-status cultural capital (Mac an Ghaill 1994a; Wright 1997). In a class-divided society, work remains 'the most significant determinant of the life-fates of the majority of individuals and families in advanced industrial societies' (Crompton 1993: 120). It is in this context of late capitalism that the development of contemporary forms of racism and new ethnicities is being lived out (Sivanandan 1989, 1990b). The differentialist emphasis on the proliferation of identities and the dispersal of power may serve to underplay materially structured asymmetrical relations of power that constitute hegemonic, class-based, racialized divisions (Sivanandan 1990a). We need to bring together changing forms of racialization and ethnic belonging with the more general debates on the extent and direction of social and cultural change in late modernity.

Reconceptualizing decentred cultural forms of class in late capitalism

In arguing for the need to revisit class analysis, it is important to re-emphasize that the reconceptualization of the class–racism couplet must be critically located within current structural and cultural changes (Miles 1989, 1993; Sivanandan 1989, 1990b). For example, Harvey (1989: 59), commenting on the new phase that capitalism has entered, maintains that: 'The tension that has always prevailed within capitalism between monopoly and competition, between centralization and decentralization of economic power, is being worked out in fundamentally new ways . . . capitalism is becoming more tightly organized through dispersal, geographical mobility, and flexible responses in labour markets, labour processes, and consumer markets, all accompanied by hefty doses of institutional, product and technological innovation.' Most importantly, in the late 1990s we see the increased visibility of the British state's intervention in the recomposition of a 'post-colonial' working class in a de-industrializing society as part of a wider restructuring of the global economy. A crucial element of this recomposition is the current crisis in the welfare state, and central government's response in terms of the management of collective consumption, as a new cultural landscape is constructed within deregulated markets of education, housing, health and social care. Cohen (1990: ix), writing on the reshaping of working-class identities, in relation to the demands of 'post-industrial' capitalism notes that: 'The ideology of the enterprise culture has been institutionalised into particular pedagogic and disciplinary forms, and a new generation of working-class children find themselves being schooled, or trained, for their subordinate roles in the political economy of Thatcherism.' This approach appears to be continuing with the Labour government. For Harvey (1989: 359), the challenge of the new political project involves the 'renewal of historical-geographical materialism [that] can indeed promote adherence to a new version of the Enlightenment project . . . a project of becoming rather than being in the search for unity within difference' (see also Todorov 1986). As Balibar (1991b) suggests, racism as a total social phenomenon needs to be located in the wider social framework. In thinking through how contemporary forms of racialization are linked to wider changing conditions, European theorists have developed a number of innovative frameworks. For example, Balibar and Wallerstein (1991), Silverman (1992) and Wieviorka (1995) have addressed the impact of the decline of social-class forces within the post-war globalized economy, the crisis of the nation-state, the weakening of the welfare state and accompanying forms of social dislocation. They examine how these forms open up new spaces for racism and anti-racism.

In arguing for the reconnection of racism to class analysis, *Contemporary Racisms and Ethnicities* is not suggesting that we return to earlier theories of socialization, cultural difference and collective resistance that tended to emphasize an oversocialized, bipolarization of class differences, in which racism was reductively read as an epiphenomenal effect of deeper class causes. Rather, we need to incorporate a more dynamic, decentred class position, which sees state institutions as *reproducing* wider class divisions, but also locally *producing* a range of class-based identities. These identities involve complex social and psychic investments that multidimensional social subjects come to occupy and live out. Another way of presenting this argument is to suggest that we need sociologically to re-engage with central theoretical problems – such as the structure/agency, macro/micro, society/individual and social order/ social change divisions within the context of global capitalist conditions – while at the same time addressing the limitations of these binaries (Jameson 1993; Lash and Urry 1994; Harvey 1996). For example, in an earlier study exploring working-class ethnic minority students' urban experiences, I identified the limits of class-based theories in understanding the local production of working-class identities with reference to the interplay between changing social destinies and subjectivities. Social reproduction theories were inadequate in providing an account of the relationship between social structure and agency in relation to such 'non-economic' factors as family life, education and popular consumption (Mac an Ghaill 1994a).

The site of production traditionally has been assigned the dominant space in which class formation and reproduction take place, with sites of consumption, such as housing and education, taking a secondary place (Rex and Moore 1967; Mac an Ghaill 1988; Smith 1989). A renewed theoretical interest in class analysis needs to engage with a key argument of recent cultural theory, that class-based communities have been displaced by consumerized lifestyles in a new world of 'rock videos, theme parks and shopping malls' (Lyon 1994: 50). Gabriel (1994: 98–126) provides such an account in his exploration of the interplay between class struggles, consumption and the environmentalist movement, with reference to black employees working for McDonald's. He suggests the need to re-examine the constitution of classes and that one way to move beyond the limited debates around fixed locations is to make a distinction between class location and class formation. He notes that black and ethnic minority employees in this service sector do not neatly follow class lines, and points to the uncertainty around such questions as to whether consumption struggles are more effective than orthodox forms of collective action. While the political climate is more favourably disposed to consumption demands than to trade unionists, he concludes that there is little evidence to suggest that consumption demands are challenging the wide range of forms of racism in operation.

At the same time in revisiting social class analysis, we need to employ a more systematic sociological approach to spatial and temporal issues, which will provide new ways of exploring racialized exclusions and ethnic belonging. This is very well illustrated by Cohen (1998: 5), who, in his work in the East End of London, critiques earlier explanations of working-class racism that employed disembodied notions of ideological racialized divisions.

> Yet as we were to discover there was another, less obvious island story waiting to be told, one which did not quite fit these terms of reference. It was a story of white working class ethnicity whose racialization could not be explained in either purely local or global terms – it was neither a legacy of inbreeding or of imperialism. The histories and geographies which many of our white informants unfolded for us evoked another space and time compressed by technologies of power which were not so much centred on concentrations or dispersals of capital and labour as such but on the articulations of bodies, cities and texts.

The concluding chapter picks up Cohen's themes in critically exploring working-class and middle-class Anglo-ethnicities for a younger generation living in a multiracist and multicultural city.

Notes

1 See Chapter 2 for further exploration of these terms.
2 See Hobsbawm (1992) and Gabriel (1994).

Part **II**

'NEW TIMES': *from* IDENTITY POLITICS (MATERIALISM) *to the* NEW POLITICS *of* CULTURAL DIFFERENCE (DIFFERENTIALISM)

2 Racialized subjects: culture, identity *and* difference

Sociology of racism and ethnicity: the cultural turn and social change

Part II of the book is concerned with exploring the suggested shift from 'old times' to 'new times'. The purpose of Chapter 2 is to outline the general philosophical issues about identity and subjectivity that have emerged since the 1980s and that have important consequences for understanding ethnicity and racism. Chapter 3 explores these issues from a more specifically sociological perspective with reference to the question of rethinking the black–white dualistic model of racism.

This chapter highlights the search for a new vocabulary to capture the complexity of academic and political accounts of racialized and ethnic identities in 'post-colonial' Britain. There is an exploration of the emergence of a fragmentary literature in 'new times' that has begun to suggest a more complex conceptualization of racial difference. This exploration serves to make problematic changing forms of the racialization of social relations, highlighting the active cultural production of racial and ethnic identities within local (national and regional) spaces. Differentialist texts argue that there is a need to move away from theories that suggest that racial difference is shaped by a single overarching factor. In reclaiming culture, they provide a critique of materialist accounts, such as the anti-racist black–white dualistic model. At the same time they enable us to analyse the social and discursive production of contemporary racial and ethnic differences.

The concept of culture has become a central theme in a wide range of current debates about social change in social and human sciences. In what is referred to as the 'cultural turn', there has been a shift away from the study of structure alongside an increased critical interest in language and how it is used to produce meaning in social life. It is in this context of theoretical advances, particularly in postmodernism and post-structuralism, that post-colonial writers have argued for the need to return culture to the centre of the debate on how we are to understand contemporary changing meanings of cultural forms of racism and new ethnicities. For example, Donald and Rattansi (1992) have brought together a collection of articles that provides a critical rethinking of the interplay between culture, race and politics. The focus is on the making and remaking of culture and ethnic identity formations. Said (1993) highlights the heterogeneous nature of these processes of cultural production by arguing for the need to perceive the politics of culture within 'overlapping territories' and 'intertwined histories'. Other post-colonial writers have suggested the emergence of new identities marked by what they call diaspora, hybridity and syncretism (Spivak 1988a and b; Bhabha 1990a; Gilroy 1993).[1]

A major weakness of earlier materialist-based sociological work on racism has been the inadequate conceptualization of racialized and ethnic identity formations. More recently, theorists drawing on post-structuralism, psycho-analysis and semiology have provided new ways of thinking about subjective identities (Henriques *et al.* 1984; Wetherell and Potter 1992). They have critiqued dominant theoretical and 'common-sense' explanations of racial-ized differences, with their taken-for-granted definitions of majority (white) and minority (black) ethnic group identities, which are implicitly assumed to be ahistorical, unitary, universal and unchanging categories. For example, in *Changing the Subject* Henriques *et al.* (1984: 3) provide an account of this more complex picture. They describe how they use ' "subjectivity" to refer to individuality and self-awareness – the condition of being a subject – but understand in this usage that subjects are dynamic and multiple, always positioned in relation to discourses and practices and produced by these – the condition of being subject' (see also Bhabha 1986; Sarup 1996; and Zaretsky 1996).

Identity politics (materialism) and the new politics of cultural difference (differentialism)

Chapter 1 explored the interplay between racism and social class in earlier materialist representations. This interplay was seen as one of the most pro-ductive elements of British sociological explanations of racial oppression. By the 1980s these earlier academic and political representations were criticized for class reductionism and economic determinism. It was claimed that such representations were conceptually inadequate in explaining the complex social and psychological processes involved in the development of changing forms of racialized and ethnic identity formations. Placing the capital–labour relationship at the centre of theory was seen as closing off more open approaches. New social movements, including feminisms, black struggles, national liberation movements, gay and lesbian rights, and anti-nuclear and ecology movements, challenged the privileging of class relations, through which other social categories were mediated (Mercer 1990; Weeks 1990). The question of identity has emerged as one of the key dynamic concepts in the context of rethinking change in late modernity. It is suggested that socio-cultural change is marked by the disintegration of older social collectivities – such as social class – and increased fluidity of social relationships, with an accompanying interest in identity and subjectivity (Bradley 1996). More spe-cifically, there has been a focus on the pluralization of identities involving processes of fragmentation and dislocation (Laclau 1990; Giddens 1991; Hall 1992a; Mercer 1992a). As with many terms used in social and cultural studies, identity is not easily defined. For Weeks (1990: 88): 'Identity is about belonging, about what you have in common with some people and what different-iates you from others. At its most basic it gives you a sense of personal location, the stable core to your individuality. But it is also about social relationships, your complex involvement with others.' The concept of identity is a highly resonant term that is used in a wide variety of ways in different contexts. Sociologically, its high conceptual value emerges from its contribution to new frameworks, which open up innovative ways of exploring the relationship between individuals and society. Most importantly, as Mercer (1990: 43) argues with reference to social change: 'Identity only becomes an issue when it is in crisis, when something assumed to be fixed, coherent and stable is displaced by the experience of doubt and uncertainty.' This doubt and uncertainty is experienced at individual, social and psychic levels, circumscribed by the local–global nexus of cultural transformations. In the context of Britain in the late 1990s, race and ethnicity have come to speak a wider sense of social dislocation in a 'post-colonial' de-industrializing society. An underexplored set of questions emerges from an English/British ethnic majority identity position, concerning a collective national past and future. Who are 'we'? Who were 'we'? Who have 'we' become? Who can 'we' become? Social and cultural theorists have concentrated too much on the exclusions of those positioned as subordinate, such as ethnic minorities. Presently, there is a need to begin to develop frameworks that explore the changing collective self-representations of dominant forms of Anglo-ethnicity and the accompanying material and symbolic systems and practices that produce this ethnicity that is not named as such. For example, in teaching situations there is often unease among English liberal professionals about discussing their own ethnic majority status, while at the same time they hold highly developed explanations of the position of ethnic minorities in contemporary Britain. Similarly, English liberals are uneasy about their own national identity. Hence, while celebrating other nationalities, they feel embarrassment or wish to dissociate from the British/English nationalism.

A clear understanding of the meaning of what has come to be called identity politics is currently hindered by a confusion over terms that different social and cultural analyses employ. Much of this work has taken place in the United States, where new social movement theory has suggested that such a confusion may be overcome by understanding anti-oppressive positions in terms of collective identity formations (Seidman 1993; Epstein 1994). As Gamson (1995: 391) points out: 'The shared oppression, these movements have forcefully claimed, is the denial of the freedoms and the opportunities to actualise the self. In this *ethnic/essentialist* politic, clear categories of collective identity are necessary for resistance and political gain.' With reference to understanding racism, anti-racism and culture in a British context, there is a need to be sensitive to the socio-historical development of new social movements. For example, contemporary accounts of anti-oppressive positions, such as an anti-racist stance, tend to fuse different moments in social and cultural theory. It is important to hold on to an analytical distinction between an earlier moment that came to be identified as *identity politics* and a later moment, that of the *new politics of cultural difference*. This is not to suggest a linear development from one to the other. On the contrary, the distinction between these moments emphasizes a highly contested and complex tension between what are often inappropriately labelled essentialist and anti-essentialist accounts. As pointed out in the introduction (p. 12), in this book, a *materialist* position is taken as underpinning a *politics of identity* and a *differentialist* position as underpinning *the new politics of cultural difference*. My preferred terms are materialism and differentialism. Where appropriate, identity politics and the new politics of difference are used. A fuller understanding of these terms will emerge as you make your way through this chapter, in which the debate between these positions is illustrated through the differentialist critique of a materialist-based anti-racism.

Materialist accounts of racialized identity formation

An important development over the past twenty years in opening up theoretical spaces has been the impact of new social movements on retheorizing social and cultural arenas. They have reconceptualized the structural and phenomenological aspects of institutional sites, including the workplace, education and domestic life (Seidman 1993). In general, these social movements have retained the theoretical and conceptual foundations of earlier social scientific theories such as structural Marxism. This legacy is most obvious in class-based academic accounts of racism, such as those of Rex and Tomlinson (1979), Sivanandan (1982) and Miles (1993). Of central importance is how new social movements examine the mutually informing relationship between the prescribed/proscribed social and cultural status of specific collectivities and the corresponding social relationships and practices that they generate in different institutions and broader social groups. For example, innovative anti-racist work has stressed the importance of examining how particular areas of institutional life – such as the production and circulation of knowledges, access to cultural resources, the occupation of geographical space, and the interaction between dominant and subordinated racialized groups – have contributed to the reproduction of racialized inequalities within and beyond institutional arenas (Brah and Deem 1986; Cohen and Bains 1988; Mac an Ghaill 1988; Gillborn 1990). In this way, new social movements tend to concentrate on the processes that reproduce racial inequalities and the corresponding effects of identity on social equality. For example, it is through the processes of reproduction of racial inequalities that identity formations take place. As a result, particular social injustices impart the essential nature or identity of 'whites' and 'blacks'. These fixed boundaries that were in the ascendancy in the 1970s and 1980s were established and policed by political and academic discourses.

A central concern to understanding the formation of racialized identities has been the role of the particular social structures in the reproduction of social inequality. For example, the use of anti-racism as an overarching conceptual framework to explain racialized relations continues to be influential, albeit often unacknowledged, in understanding identity formations in institutional spaces. Racism, as a complex and multi-level distribution of automatic power for whites, located in interpersonal relations and institutional structures, is seen as a key dynamic in structuring unequal relations between blacks and whites. Social positions between black and white people are hierarchically ordered, with whites' unequal access to disproportionate amounts of power resulting in the structural oppression of blacks over whites. Of primary importance in this work are the ways that different collectivities – blacks and whites; males and females; heterosexuals and gays/lesbians – exist in unequally structured oppositions. In these oppositions, the defining features of identity tend to be intrinsically located within the position occupied.

This chapter explores the shift from *identity politics (materialism)* to the *new politics of cultural difference (differentialism)* in explaining the formation of contemporary ethnic and racialized identities. More specifically, I focus on the interrelated elements of the complexity of interconnecting multiple forms of social power, including class, gender, sexuality and ethnicity; temporal and spatial dimensions of racialized identities; the absence of subjectivity and the need to go beyond an overly rationalist account that erases social psychological and psychoanalytical dimensions.

Differentialist accounts of identity formation: the implosion of social categories and the distribution of social power

As discussed in Chapter 1, earlier materialist representations of race sought to challenge the validity of biological explanations of racial differences. The focus was on highlighting the *structural causes* of racist oppression. During the past decade, in examining the changing nature of race and racism, researchers have drawn on a range of differentialist theories that have been less concerned with the ontological question of whether race *really* exists and have shifted their focus to examine the *effects* of such truth claims. It is argued that issues of race and racism should be located within regimes of truth. As Foucault (1980: 131) suggests: 'Each society has its regime of truth, its general politics of truth: that is, the types of discourses which it accepts and makes function as true; the mechanisms and instances which enable one to distinguish true and false statements, the means by which each is sanctioned; the techniques and procedures accorded value in the acquisition of truth; the status of those who are charged with saying what counts as true.' Here race is conceptualized as a decentred (destabilized) complex of social meanings that are constantly in the process of being transformed by political struggle (Omi and Winant 1986; Gilroy 1987). In turn, racism is understood as a pre-eminently socio-historical concept. Rizvi (1993: 13) explains that: 'This is so because a discourse "inherited" from the past is often reconstituted and rearticulated if it is to be used to make sense of the world in its new context. Racial categories and meaning are given concrete form by the specific social relations which they express and the historical context in which they are embedded. But such rearticulation is never uniform or complete.'

Locating their analysis in recent debates about modernity and post-modernity, differentialist theorists explore the implications of a constantly changing nexus of representations, discourses and power relations for new forms of politics in Western societies. Rattansi and Westwood (1994: 4) provide a clear illustration of this approach, in what they call a 'postmodern frame':

> The postmodern frame draws upon a wide range of authors. Bauman, Giddens, Foucault, Derrida and Laclau and Mouffe all figure in a framework which emphasises the significance of a set of key themes: the 'postmodern' condition as a reflection on the nature and limits of Western modernity; an analysis of modernity which focuses upon its typical dualities, for example the chronic disembedding and reinvention of traditions and collective identities; the marginalization of Western modernity's Others in the constructions of Western identities; the impact of new forms of globalization; the decentring and de-essentialization of both subjects and the 'social'; an appreciation of temporality and spatiality as constitutive of identities and the 'social'; a consideration of the relation between the 'psychic' and the 'social'; and an engagement with questions of sexuality and sexual difference.

Drawing on differentialist frameworks, post-colonial theorists are making a major contribution to our understanding of the construction of the 'other' in colonial and post-colonial discourses. Said's (1978) work on Orientalism has been a major critical influence (Spivak 1988b; Bhabha 1990a; Young 1990). Referring to the long-established tradition in Anglo-European scholarship of constructing the Orient as exotic and other, Said (1978: xiii) quotes Marx: 'They cannot represent themselves, they must be represented.' Orientalism can be understood as 'a mode of discourse with supporting institutions, vocabulary, scholarship, imagery, doctrines, even colonial bureaucracies and colonial styles' (Said 1978: 2). The discourse assumes and projects a sense of fundamental difference between a Western, occidental 'us' and an Eastern, Asiatic, oriental 'them'. Throughout his scholarly work Said provides a rounded picture that is historically sensitive, holding on to the discursive and the ideological and thus arguing for a complex view of power as necessary in understanding the production of racist knowledge. Orientalism has emerged as a significant theme in recent media discussion of the Middle East, including the Gulf War and Islam and in the analysis of contemporary travel and tourism writing. Gabriel (1994: 131), in discussing Said's construction of 'otherness as lesser' through cultural institutions, explains how it continues to permeate the 'post-colonial' world, 'from tourism to charitable events like Band Aid and Comic Relief, through multinational advertising to the Gulf War. It pervades our educational system from school curriculum to higher education courses on "business administration" and "planning" for students from "developing" countries.'

Stuart Hall has been one of the major contributors in developing a differentialist account of identity formation from within a British context, exploring the implosion of older stable social categories, such as class and black identity. He (1991a: 47–50) suggests a number of elements of identity, which he sees being opened up particularly in psychoanalysis and feminism.

The first is that identities are always incomplete, that is, always actively in the process of being formed. Second, identity means a process of identification, marked by *splitting*, between that which one is and that which is the other; and *ambivalence*, that is, 'the attempt to expel the other to the other side of the universe is always compounded by relationships of love and desire' (Hall 1991a: 48). In turn, the impact of this process of defining oneself in terms of otherness acts back on the self. Third, identity is always in part a narrative, involving selective representations that contribute to one's sense of oneself. Fourth, the plural processes involved in the production of identity described above, indicate that 'signification depends upon endless repositioning of its differential terms'. Hence, 'meaning in any specific instance depends on the contingent and arbitrary stop' (Hall 1991a: 51).

The notions of discourse and discursive practices are of central importance in differentialist approaches to the deconstruction of 'progressive' racial categories, such as the term black. Discourse refers to specialized and common-sense regulated systems of meaning through which we make sense of the world. These systems of meaning are constructed in and through particular practices, which make available social identities or subject positions, and which simultaneously entail relations of power. For example, we identify ourselves as black or white, or as an ethnic minority or majority, and could not do so if categorizing discourses of race and ethnicity did not exist. In this limited sense, we can be said to be 'produced' by discourses and discursive practices. Differentialist theoretical accounts have been important in moving beyond social reproduction models that assume that individuals are unitary racialized subjects occupying predictable power positions. It is argued that we need to understand how ethnic and racialized minorities and majorities 'are not unitary subjects uniquely positioned, but are produced as a nexus of subjectivities in relations of power which are constantly shifting, rendering them at one moment powerful and at another powerless' (Henriques *et al.* 1984: 225). This more complex framework, with its suggestion that we are positioned in various discourses and that there are a range of subject positions that we may occupy within different contradictory discourses, is useful. It helps us in understanding the contextual specificity in the cultural production and reproduction of ethnic formations, which shape social relations between and within minority–majority communities in Britain.

Wetherell and Potter (1992: 75), in their study of how Pakeha (white New Zealand settlers) make sense of their own history and actions towards the Maori minority, provide an innovative account of discourse analysis of racism. In discussing the construction of subjectivities, they argue against limiting psychological models in which: 'The individual comes to be seen as a somewhat detached and self-contained entity, and the social becomes defined as an *external* landscape, a structure of groups and group divisions outside the individual, which need to be incorporated into subjectivity in some way.' Rather, they suggest that the psychological field is constituted through the social domain of discourse. They maintain that this approach helps to explore connections between power and subjectivity that are opened up in new ways. For example, seeing ' "subjectivication" as a double process where people become subjected and regulated through the kinds of identities assumed in discourse' (Wetherell and Potter: 79). In conceptualizing discourse as a social practice, their focus becomes the everyday world of conversations and texts. In order to emphasize their concern with the implementation of discourses in actual settings, they use the concept of interpretative repertoires. They explain:

> By interpretative repertoires we mean broadly discernible clusters of terms, descriptions and figures of speech often assembled around metaphors or vivid images. In more structuralist language we can talk of these things as systems of signification and as the building blocks used for manufacturing versions of actions, self and social structures in talk. They are some of the resources for making evaluations, constructing factual versions and performing particular actions.
>
> (Wetherell and Potter: 90)

One of the main theoretical contentions of a differentialist position is to argue for the de-reification of simple models of coercive state and institutional power that assumes it is uniformly held by a single dominant group. Social power is not just repressive but also has a productive capacity. For Wetherell and Potter (1992: 80) the contrast between materialist and differentialist perspectives concerns whether one prefers versions of history that try to specify who did what to whom and why, or versions that are more concerned with how the 'what', 'whom' and 'why' are constituted. They maintain:

> It is a matter, too, of locating power with specific agents, structures and social classes or dispersed power throughout social formations. It also involves whether one defines powerful discourse through its authors (so that powerful words are simply the words of the powerful), or whether the power of discourse becomes evaluated through the kinds of authors or subjects that it creates.

From a differentialist perspective, power does not reflect a deeper reality, but rather, the categories of the social collectivities *are* aspects of social power. The disruption of social categories is a strategic practice in a differentialist politics (Smith 1994). This approach produces a specific understanding of the distribution of power. For example, Foucault (1988) suggests that subjectivity is contextually located through institutional exercises of power. It is through the discursive and material formations of social boundaries with their exclusionary effects that social power becomes articulated. However, these boundaries are never completely fixed, as their fluid nature re-creates and re-produces unpredictable inversions of social power.

Materialist analyses have attempted to go beyond a hierarchy-of-oppressions approach, emphasizing the complex interconnectedness between different social categories. However, as Brah (1992: 128) suggests: 'The search for grand theories specifying the interconnections between racism, gender and class has been less than productive.' Materialist frameworks offer little sensitivity to the way in which, in particular institutional spaces, ethnic and racialized identities exist at the intersection of a range of social relations and come to 'speak' these often in unpredictable ways. There is little sense that power relations of subordination and resistance are actively produced as well as reproduced. In contrast, the novelist James Baldwin has captured this complexity, writing that: 'We . . . are all androgynous . . . born of a woman impregnated by . . . a man . . . each of us, helplessly and forever, contains the other-male in female, female in male, white in black, black in white' (see Leeming 1994: 378). In a similar way there is a need for sociologists to map out some of the more intricate and intimate social relations in local spaces, as they articulate the relational logic of shifting boundaries of different social divisions. Exploring the simultaneous relationship between analytic concepts such as ethnicity, gender, sexuality, generation and class is a significant facet of differentialist strategies. This suggests that in order to understand racialized and ethnic identities, researchers need to examine the simultaneous articulations of a dispersed, localized and shifting nexus of social power. In short, we need to understand how ethnic identities are simultaneously classed, gendered and sexualized. In social relations, people occupy certain positions simultaneously. A working-class identity is at the same time a sexual identity and an ethnic identity. We need to think about not the ways social categories accumulate but the ways they inflect. When we talk about the notion of power, we have to think about it relationally, thinking about powerful in relation to whom. In this way, we do not look at power as an either/or division but as being much more relational. We can say power is shaped relationally: one group is both powerful and powerless. For example, particular social relations of race simultaneously 'speak' gender and sexuality: to be a 'Paki' is also to be a 'poof', is to be a 'non-proper boy' (Mac an Ghaill 1994b). Furthermore, the simultaneous speaking of race/ethnicity and sexuality can also be mapped out as class-based, as certain styles of gay identities resonate with forms of middle-class Englishness (Mac an Ghaill 1996a). This is still a largely undertheorized area, while at the same time there is little empirical work available to illustrate how these interrelationships are lived out within local cultural arenas. It is important to note that the relationship of racialized and ethnic identity formations with wider social relations remains unresolved, as is highlighted in postmodern-based accounts of racism that abstract practices from institutional contexts (Seidman 1993).

There are theoretical advantages in adopting Foucault's de-reification of simple models of coercive state and institutional power, which serve to open up the dualistic approach of anti-racism, with its assumption that power is uniformly held by a single dominant white group. However, Foucault's complex body of work, including different emphases in earlier and later work that are often conflated, raises a number of unresolved questions, including what constitutes power relations. A key absence in Foucault's work is an adequate account of the origins of discourses or how they change; power appears to be defined in such broad terms as to be indeterminate. In short, within this framework, we are not clear how institutional structures operate to maintain power relations. As Hall (1988: 53) argues: 'The problem with Foucault . . . is a conception of difference without a conception of articulation, that is a conception of power without a conception of hegemony.' The concept of hegemonic racialized ethnicities – for example, ascendant forms of Anglo-ethnicity – that are constructed in relation to and against subordinated ethnicities is useful in exploring the construction of contemporary social relations. Adopting the original Gramscian (1971) insight that was used in the context of class, we can examine the asymmetrical nature of racialized social relations, arguing that dominance is never secure but must always be won. Furthermore, this is not achieved simply by coercion but by the winning and shaping of consent for the dominant racialized 'common-sense' view, which involves the building of strategic alliances. New Right discourses in the 1980s on Britishness, the nation and cultural belongingness illustrate how particular political ideologies need to resonate with and rework wider concerns and anxieties in order to gain and maintain an ascendant position (Mac an Ghaill 1994a).

In placing power at the centre of an analysis, it is important to comprehend fully the complexity of its dynamic in institutional sites. Materialist theorists tend to emphasize the continuity of racist structuring of institutions, marked by social marginalization and exclusion. In contrast, differentialists, arguing that there is no universal characterization of racism, focus on the contextual specificities of different historical forms of racialization operating in local spaces. In most accounts of racism and ethnicity there is a failure to attempt to hold on to the tension between the two positions. There is a continuing conceptual and political problem involved in moving beyond materialist-based monocausal explanations that employ 'simple' models of power. At the same time, there is a tendency for differentialist accounts to be rather abstract; often disconnecting from personal accounts and institutional locations. In looking at dominant racial and nationalist discourses in relation to the institutional construction and regulation of minority and majority ethnic groups, I would emphasize the need to locate these discourses in their specific spatial and temporal contexts. That is, we need to acknowledge the significance of social institutions, alongside cultural industries, in which shifting, contradictory practices operate. As Gabriel (1994: 180) argues: 'This is not to say that institutions are solely responsible for all forms of cultural expression, but to acknowledge that most, if not all, of the material aspects of our lives: where we live and how we live, for example, cannot be fully understood without reference to institutional sites.' Working in this framework, a continuing tension emerges in placing the contextual specificity of local practices within the broader arena of state, economy and civil society. This broader arena contains institutional patterns of a racially structured social order and associated dominant racialized divisions and inter-ethnic social arrangements. It is important to emphasize that differentialist accounts need to be placed in this broader arena of global relations of dominance and subordination in late capitalism, which circumscribes the ways in which both minority and majority ethnic groups manufacture their local identities in the nation-state. For example, in a British national context, the bigger picture of racialized social relations has been currently made visible in relation to the regulation of new migrants, refugees and asylum seekers, the passing of the Asylum and Immigration Bill, the debate about the issuing of passports to people from Hong Kong, and the de-racialization of state policy. Drawing on materialist and differentialist accounts, to analyse the racialized nature of power relations in different social spaces highlights certain unresolved theoretical difficulties, particularly regarding an understanding of structures of asymmetrical racialized power relations operating in 'post-colonial' conditions, alongside more fragmentary multiple racisms, new ethnicities and the dispersal of social power.

Constructing difference and recognition–deconstructing sameness and misrecognition

The question of identity has been of major political significance for post-war new social movements in Britain. In focusing on the 'taking up' of identities, there has been a particular concern with how social and symbolic systems classify people and mark social collectivities (Mercer 1990; Weeks 1990; Back 1996). More recently, the questions of 'difference' and 'otherness' have become organizing concepts across a number of disciplines. Earlier work in linguistics, anthropology and psychoanalysis has provided different versions of the centrality of difference with reference to the social, cultural and psychic dimensions of contemporary living. Philosophically, differentialist theorists have employed a notion of difference to challenge the Enlightenment claims of universality, rationality and a unified subject. The work has been important in opening up the field of enquiry and highlighting emerging/shifting social identities at a time of rapid change. More specifically, it is suggested that the claiming of difference makes possible the forging of new identities. Although much of this work remains at an overly abstract level, nevertheless a notion of racial/ethnic difference has become pervasive across academic and popular representations. During an anti-racist phase of race equality, race specific subject positions, such as black and white identities, were produced and inhabited. Presently, at a time of uncertainty the concept difference is invoked, in an era marked by complex, multiple, cross-cutting forms of social exclusion. This argument is often supported by reference to the continuing educational underachievement of white working-class boys, which is compared with the academic success of particular groups of male and female ethnic minority students. This is further explored in Chapter 5, in terms of a suggested shift from policy discourses of 'simple' racial inequality to discourses of 'complex' social exclusions.

In moving away from earlier sociological models of socialization differentialist theorists have stressed the need to reformulate a conception of identity formation as highly relational. Hence, questions are opened up about the relationship between the self and others and the shared terrain of public space at both global and local levels, at a time of increased awareness of the politics of positionality. As Woodward (1997: 1) makes clear:

> Often identity is most clearly defined by difference, that is by what it is not. Identities may be marked by polarization, for example in the most extreme forms of national or ethnic conflict, and by the marking of inclusion or exclusion – insiders and outsiders, 'us' and 'them'. Identities are frequently constructed in terms of oppositions such as man/woman, black/white, straight/gay, healthy/unhealthy, normal/deviant.

The past thirty years of the Northern Ireland 'Troubles' highlight the power of national, ethnic and religious identities to shape social interaction, with opposing social collectivities making claims to different national identities. However, academic and media representations of Northern Ireland politics and, more recently, the representations of the conflict between Serbs and Croats in the former Yugoslavia illustrate the potential limitations of 'deploying the notion of difference within liberal plural political discourses in which both sides are projected as equally to blame, while this difference has been historically forged within relations of domination and opposition' (Woodward 1997: 3).

This is part of a larger problem, namely, the popularity of the term difference has resulted in its becoming overly inflated, with little conceptual clarity of what it means and how it might contribute to the transformative nature of the politics of racism, while engaging with broader issues of social justice, civil rights and citizenship. In particular, in many current texts in which difference is portrayed as positive, there is a failure to provide a more rounded picture of difference as being marked both symbolically through representational systems *and* materially and socially through processes of inclusion or exclusion of social groups. Brah (1992: 140–4) provides a way forward. She suggests the need to engage with four categories of difference: experience, social relations, subjectivity and identity. In the context of conceptualizing black and white feminisms as non-essentialist, historically contingent discursive practices, she argues that the key issue is not difference *per se*. Rather, a number of questions are raised about who defines difference, how different categories of women are represented within discourses of difference and whether difference differentiates laterally or hierarchically.

In contrast to the conceptual and political visibility of 'difference', the idea of 'sameness' remains underexplored, subsumed under the concept of identity. Questions of sameness, identification and belonging are currently of particular salience and demand urgent critical engagement. This requires the development of conceptual frameworks that will enable us to achieve a more comprehensive understanding of the cultural zone within and through which dominant and minority social groups live out and negotiate their differences *and* similarities with others and between themselves. There are a range of areas that may prove particularly productive in such an investigation. First, Gilroy (1997: 304) provides a number of historical examples, in which he explores the complex relations of sameness and difference within Fascist and extreme nationalist movements in the twentieth century. He explores the significance of symbolic systems, encapsulated in the black shirts for the Fascists in the 1930s and the 'ox-wagon trek of 1938' for Afrikaner nationalism in South Africa, emphasizing that: 'signs of sameness have often degenerated readily into emblems of supposedly essential or immutable differences'. Currently, at a time of crisis in dominant forms of Anglo-ethnicity in 'postcolonial' conditions, Gilroy's work provides a useful framework in which to examine the processes of British/English cultural belonging as the ethnic majority rebuild a collective national identity. Second, conceptions of racial difference, based exclusively on colour racism, serve to position the Irish in Britain as racially the same as the white English. For the Irish, however, the cumulative experience of historical and contemporary forms of anti-Irish racism, the British occupation of Northern Ireland and their own national and ethnic sense of belonging to Ireland means that they actively disidentify with the British. As Connolly *et al.* (1995: 1) suggest: 'Ambivalence and binary thinking are always part of the colonizers' relation to colonial Others and are locked into British ways of thinking about Ireland and the Irish. But the Irish have been both racialized and included, constructed as threatening and yet part of the British "family" because they are white.' Developing broader frameworks of racial difference and sameness that are inclusive of ethnic minority groups in Britain, such as the Irish, may help us to reconnect the issue of colour (whiteness) to wider questions of class, migrant labour, nation and cultural belonging (Hickman and Walter 1995). Third, new ethnic identities marked by hybridity and syncretism are being manufactured among diasporic groups within the changing morphology of urban sites (see below). These ethnicities highlight a complex interweaving of sameness and identification as well as of difference and disidentification, among socially non-mobile ethnic minority and majority working-class young people.

Subjectivity and the production of racialized subjects: narrating the self and doing culture

One of the most surprising aspects of earlier literature in race relations and anti-racism problematics has been the undertheorization of subjectivity. In contrast to a materialist position, with its primary focus on the fixed relations between social collectivities, a differentialist position involves a deconstruction of binaries that are seen to constitute identity. An implication of this is to argue that subjectivity is dynamically constituted. At a social level, this perspective suggests that having a singular, coherent and rational subjectivity is inadequate because the interplay between different institutional regimes of power continually re-produces a variety of subjectivities. It is argued that rather than social collectivities authoring self-identity through their intrinsic authentic claims, social collectivities are dependent on the establishment of other social groups. One way to conceptualize responses to the complex interrelationship of changing processes of racialization and wider social and cultural transformations is to view them as a set of narratives of self-production that are dispersed through a multiplicity of power relations. Hence, individuals are not the passive recipients or objects of structural processes. They are not such '*tablae rasae*, to be injected or even constructed with the ideology of the day' but are constructively engaged in the securing of identities (Rowbotham 1989: 18). The limitations of theorizing subjectivities in relation to state and institutional racist practices is that the question of agency may appear as a simple one-dimensional product of minority communities' cultural contexts. This is of particular significance in relation to the reductionist overarching explanation evident in materialist accounts such as anti-racism, in which the signifier of colour leads to a narrative of social closure and predetermined outcomes. By theoretically shifting from a focus on product to process, both minority and majority ethnic groups can be seen as examples of *doing culture*.

One way of conceptualizing ethnic identity formations that is spatially and temporally sensitive to a complex politics of location, is to carry out empirical work in institutions to establish what is going on (Mirza 1992; Mac an Ghaill 1994a; Gillborn 1995). This is further illustrated in the concluding chapter.

One of the shifts from a materialist to a differentialist position in examining the formation of racialized and ethnic identities has been the focus on the constitutive dynamics of subjectivity. In a number of seminal papers, Stuart Hall has developed conceptual frameworks that capture the complexity of black identity formation and shifting subjectivities. He (1992a: 275–7) has distinguished between three different conceptions of identity: that of the Enlightenment subject, the sociological subject and the postmodern subject. The first two underpin materialist accounts, whereas the last informs a differentialist approach. Hall suggests that: 'The Enlightenment subject was based on a conception of the human person as a fully centred, unified individual, endowed with the capacities of reason, consciousness and action, whose centre consisted of an inner core which first emerged when the subject was born, and unfolded with it. . . . The essential centre of the self was a person's identity' (Hall 1992a: 275). The sociological subject developed in the context of a changing and increasingly complex modern world. Sociologists began to understand that the inner core of the subject was not autonomous and self-sufficient but formed in relation to the culture and symbols of wider social arenas. Here identity serves to bridge the gap between the personal 'inside' and public 'outside' worlds. As Hall notes: 'The fact that we project "ourselves" into these cultural identities, at the same time internalizing their meanings and values, making them "part of us", helps to align our subjective feelings with the objective places we occupy in the social and cultural world' (Hall 1992a: 276). Hence, the focus is on the production of a fixed, essential, stable and unified identity. The third conception is that of the postmodern subject, which is located within the fundamental transformations taking place in late modernity. In contrast to the other two models, the postmodern subject is historically defined without a biological or cultural essence. Hall maintains that: 'If we feel we have a unified identity from birth to death, it is only because we construct a comforting story or "narrative of the self" about ourselves. The fully unified, completed, secure and coherent identity is a fantasy. Instead as the systems of meaning and cultural representation multiply, we are confronted by a bewildering, fleeting multiplicity of possible identities, any of which we could identify with – at least temporarily' (Hall 1992a: 277). This is an interesting conceptualization of contemporary identity formations, as it challenges both earlier models of the subject and the materialist conception of the black collective subject developed in identity politics accounts.

Hall, working in a differentialist framework with a particular emphasis on the emergence of new ethnic identities and the decentring of the black subject, has highlighted that at a social level, the idea of having a singular 'identity' is problematic because social situations produce various subjective positions that may be occupied. As suggested above, in its philosophical sense, identity as a form of identification of essential being is inappropriate. What constitutes identity is a range of subject positions that cannot be contained in a singular category. For example, such subject positions can be seen as being constituted by a range of narratives that speak identities (Redman and Mac an Ghaill 1996). These narratives regulate normative subjective positions. As an individual can be located in a range of social relations at one time, the formation of ethnic identities through a range of discursive positions is a highly complex, ambivalent and unfinished process. In this way, 'black' and 'white' subjectivities are conceptualized as processes of *becoming*, characterized by fluidity, oppositions and alliances between particular narrative positions.

Materialist critics of Hall's differentialist position question the assumption that notions of new ethnicities and decentred subjectivities will necessarily produce progressive outcomes. For example, Gabriel (1994: 176) argues that: 'Certainly the focus on the politics of representation, at the expense of the relations of representation, would seem premature given the restricted access of would-be immigrants, migrants and refugees to Europe; the rights of black European residents, the escalation of racial attacks on different minority groups of migrants, immigrants, refugees and Jews.' Lloyd (1994: 236) provides a fresh critique of Hall's differentialist accounts, locating her analysis within the combined elements of increased European racism and alongside the question of the need to fully grapple 'with the implications of the broader constituency made available to organizations like the National Front through their new-found discourse claiming respectability'. Rather pessimistically, she maintains that until this is further developed, it will be both difficult to change the terms of the debate and dangerous to do so without taking up a strong position against the New Right.

In response to these criticisms, it may be argued that Hall's work attempts to hold on to the productive tension between materialist and differentialist positions with reference to a changing black cultural politics. This is taking place in the broader context of the contemporary implosion of 'progressive' social categories, illustrated by the high-profile political debate around the term black. As explored in Chapter 1, Hall and his associates at the Centre for Contemporary Cultural Studies in Birmingham were key contributors in the early 1980s to placing the black community's common experiences of racism on the sociological map (Hall 1980; Centre for Contemporary Cultural Studies 1982). Their work was of central importance in promoting the construction of 'the essential black subject' as an organizing category of a new politics of resistance. This collective identity transcended ethnic, religious and cultural differences in the black community and provided a key mobilizing space for a generation of anti-racists. Hall (1992b) has led the way in tracing the shift away from the materialist certainties associated with this earlier 'moment' in black cultural politics, which he claims is giving way to a politics centred around these cultural differences. Identifying what he calls the end of the innocent notion of the essential black subject, he maintains that: 'What is at issue here is the recognition of the extraordinary diversity of subjective positions, social experiences and cultural identities which compose the category "black"; that is, the recognition that "black" is essentially a politically and culturally constructed category, which cannot be grounded in a set of fixed transcultural or transcendental racial categories and which therefore has no guarantees in nature' (Hall 1992b: 254). Aware that there is a danger of misreading the 'new' phase, he refers to a second 'moment' in black cultural politics involving a change from a struggle over the relations of representation to the politics of representation itself. In drawing attention to this 'shift', he explicitly states that he is not suggesting that a differentialist position is displacing a materialist position. Rather, as he maintains: 'The original critique of the predominant relations of race and representation and the politics that have developed around it have not and cannot possibly disappear while the conditions that give rise to it – cultural racism in the Dewsbury form – not only persists but positively flourishes under Thatcherism' (Hall 1992b: 253). Hall's work continues to be central to developing an understanding of an increasingly complex politics of location, moving beyond the either (black identity)/or (ethnic identity) oppositional stances that are often taken up by materialist and differentialist theorists.

Techniques of the self and performance: how ethnic subject positions are inhabited

As argued above, Foucault's earlier work on the production of identity as an effect of discourse has been influential in rethinking contemporary ethnic and national identity formations. However, at times this approach reads like a displacement of political economic determinism by discursive determinism, with its accompanying emphasis on the regulation and disciplining of the subject. In his later work, Foucault has suggested exploring identity as a technology of the self, where subjectivity is a socio-historical formation of dispersed institutional arenas of power (see Foucault (1988) and Rainbow (1984)). This work develops the notion of agency, enabling us to explore more sensitively the specific historical dynamics of the production of complex and diverse racialized/ethnic subjectivities. One of the main concepts adopted by recent theorists is the notion of the techniques of the self, that is modern forms of managing/producing the self. Foucault speaks of four types of technique 'that he says agents practise on themselves to make themselves into the persons they want to be' (in Martin *et al.* 1988: 18). They are: technologies of production, which permit us to produce, transform or manipulate things; technologies of power, which determine the conduct of individuals; technologies of sign systems, which permit us to use symbols of signification; 'technologies of the self, which permit individuals to effect by their own means a number of operations on their own bodies and souls, thoughts, conduct, and way of being so as to transform themselves in order to attain a certain state of happiness, purity, wisdom, perfection or immortality' (Martin *et al.* 1988: 18). As Nixon (1997: 323) maintains, in his work on masculinity, of particular significance here is that: 'Foucault's comments on "practices of the self" open up the possibility of conceptualising the articulation of concrete individuals to particular representations as performance based upon the citing and reiteration of discursive norms; a performance in which the formal positions of subjectivity are inhabited through specific practices or techniques.' An exploration of these techniques begins to address the absence of a conceptualization of the body in earlier literature on racism and ethnicity.

The move from a materialist to a differentialist position can be seen as signalling a shift from a concern with *labouring with* the racialized body, for example in work on black slavery, labour migrants and the overrepresentation of minority ethnic communities in low-skilled employment, to that of *labouring on* the body, for example in the work on the complex investments of a younger generation of white, working-class men inhabiting black youth styles. One way of moving forward here is to link questions of the body to an exploration of the function of binaries within the formation of ethnic, racialized and national identities. For example, this process might involve deconstructing how Anglo-ethnicity gains an ascendant position in relation to ethnic minority groups through these binaries. In doing this, ethnic identity formation can be read as performative. From a differentialist position performative suggests that ethnic, racialized and national identities are a continual establishment and articulation of binaries. The linking of techniques of the self and performance opens up an exploration of the concrete ways in which context mediates how racialized subjects deal with the lived realities of specific institutional locations. In response, materialists have criticized differentialists for assuming that identities are available to everyone, with the opportunity to take up, reposition themselves and become powerful. In the area of sexual politics, Butler (1993), working from a differentialist position, has challenged this interpretation. She argues that the very conditions of identity formation are the interrelated cultural matrices of institutional and psychic gendered/sexual practices. As lived-out and state-regulated cultural representations, these practices in themselves become ontological evidence of an essential identity; even though, according to Butler, such evidence is illusory.

Psychodynamic dimensions: identifying–disidentifying/investing–disinvesting

Differentialist accounts of subjectivity have been complemented by a differentialist reading of psychoanalysis. A major limitation of much theoretical and empirical work on social relations between ethnic majority and minority communities in materialist representations has been a failure to incorporate critical social psychological and psychoanalytic perspectives (see Henriques *et al.* 1984; Cohen 1987; Bhabha 1990a; Greenslade 1992; and Mama 1995). Racism cannot be reductively conceptualized in terms of a simple binary social system, composed of a juxtaposed Anglo-ethnic majority (superiority) and ethnic minority groups (inferiority). Relations between these social collectivities involve a psychic structure, including such elements as desire, attraction, repression, transference and projection in relation to a racialized/sexualized other (Pajackowska and Young 1992). This echoes one of the main themes of Isaac Julien's film *Young Soul Rebels* (1991). In the film's exploration of the construction of black masculinity, Julien focuses on issues such as white men's ambivalences, transgressions and envy towards black men. In other words, there is a need to bring together social structures and inner dramas. Rutherford (1990: 22), drawing on the work of Derrida, describes the inner logic of the psychic relations of domination. He writes:

Binarism operates in the same way as splitting and projection: the centre expels its anxieties, contradictions and irrationalities onto the subordinate term, filling it with the antithesis of its own identity; the Other, in its very alienness, simply mirrors and represents what is deeply familiar to the centre, but projected outside of itself. It is in these processes and representations of marginality that violence, antagonisms and aversions that are at the core of the dominant discourses and identities become manifest – racism, homophobia, misogyny and class contempt are the products of this frontier.

There is much work to be done in this area in order to understand the ambivalent structure of feeling and desire produced in different cultural spaces (Fanon 1970; Gilman 1985; Baldwin, in Troupe 1989). In an English context, in a study I carried out with young Irish gay men who had recently moved to England, they discussed a range of split responses that were manifested in terms of the interplay between racial and sexual fear and desire and the associated contradictory elements of repulsion, fascination and misrecognition (Mac an Ghaill 1996a). Implicit in their accounts as economic and sexual migrants is the suggestion that ethnicity, sexuality and class can be seen as crucial points of intersection of different forms of power, desire and identity formation. Furthermore, as the young Irish men point out, at a time of crisis in dominant public forms of Anglo-ethnicity and heterosexual arrangements, they, as a racial and sexual minority, are forced to carry the burden of the ethnic and sexual majority's sense of moral disorder (Weeks 1990; Mercer 1994). The young Irish men contextualized the specificities of their highly contradictory immigrant masculine identity, emphasizing how dominant English responses combine internal doubt and external anxiety that is projected on to them (see Rose 1994; Dunphy 1997).

There has been a tendency in materialist explanations to view white British people's holding on to a fixed national identity as atavistic, negative and exclusionary. In contrast, constructions of a black collective subject living in a racist society are granted positive political mobilization potential. Differentialist accounts have opened up these debates, illustrating the complexity involved in claims to ethnic absolutist positions, at a time of convergence between racist and anti-racist discourses (Gilroy 1987; Silverman 1992). This was illustrated by the young Irish gay men in terms of the policing of sexual boundaries among themselves through appeals to external threats to a subjective sense of their national identity. They discussed the implications of Irish gay migrants being able 'to switch' between ethnic and sexual minority/majority social positions. In so doing, they served to highlight, from the different perspectives of majority/minority cultural positions, the political investments in the maintenance of fixed collective identity boundaries in specific contexts. Homophobia was spoken through nationalism which was taken up as a cultural resource to make claims for an authentic Irishness through which homophobic practices operated. From an Irish heterosexual position, to be gay as an Irish man in England was to become like 'them', to become English. Such a strategy was highly effective in policing (hetero)sexual boundaries.

We need to locate racial/ethnic and sexual politics within the current socio-economic decline of a de-industrializing British economy with an accompanying sense of dislocation, bringing together the occupation of subject positions at individual, social and psychic levels with wider social relations. An unexamined cultural element of Britain's decline is the crisis in Anglo-ethnicity and its social and psychic interconnections with the construction of dominant English/British formations of class, gender and sexual identities. As Johnson (1992: 273) has stated: 'The growing consciousness of gender and nationality, race or ethnicity necessarily challenges earlier evaluations of past episodes. [These identities] undermine the moral framing of class-based accounts; they point up their masculinity or Anglo-ethnicity. This produces painful feelings and difficult dilemmas, as attachments to old heroes . . . are qualified.' In other words, we need to shift the focus of academic inquiry to include the ethnic majority alongside ethnic minorities; an inquiry that is historically as well as regionally sensitive to living in a 'post-colonial' society, in which different class and gender groupings of the ethnic majority are displaying and projecting much anxiety concerning their/our future as a nation and their/our collective position in it. Anxieties about national identity and the felt need to police the boundaries of the nation expressed through racialized practices and the erasure of desire for the racialized other suggest that, in part, the Anglo-ethnic majority's investments in nationalism and national belonging stem from dynamics whose origins lie in the unconscious (Fanon 1970; Mercer 1992a and b). Cultural and sociological readings of psychoanalytic theory offer important insights into the ethnic majority's investments in the subject positions made available in national, ethnic and racial discourses.

Diaspora, hybridity and syncretism: a new kind of cultural condition

Post-colonial writers have made an important contribution to our understanding of emerging forms of identity, subjectivity and forms of belonging at a time of rapid social and cultural change in Britain (Bhabha 1990a; Gilroy 1993; Spivak 1988a and b). Most importantly, they have suggested that in constructing human identity, we cannot appeal to any fixed or essential characteristics that exist for all time. Furthermore, they have been at the forefront of arguing that we need to rethink theories that suggest that racial and ethnic relations are shaped by a single overarching factor, that is colour racism. Rather, they maintain that these relations are better understood in the specific contexts in which they are played out. Terms such as hybridity, diaspora and syncretism, which are associated with the new politics of cultural difference (differentialism), have become key conceptual tools in understanding the cultural conditions of late modernity in Britain. For example, Avtar Brah (1996: 16), in her book *Cartographies of Diaspora: Contesting Identities*, illustrates the shift from earlier meanings of diaspora, which referred to the movement of Jewish people, to contemporary meanings and the use of the term in new cultural theory. She makes her own original contribution, holding on to the tension between materialist and differentialist accounts, by suggesting that we think of the concept of diaspora as an interpretative frame for analysing 'economic, political and cultural modalities of historically specific forms of migrancy.' She continues that the term diaspora provides fruitful ways of exploring the relationship of these migrations across fields of social relations, subjectivity and identity. In recent empirical work on the experience of the Irish in Britain I have found the concept of Irish diaspora most productive in trying to make sense of the lives of an 'old' ethnic group in new times, without appealing to an essentialist notion of Irishness, which would underplay important differences among them. Working in this framework a number of questions emerged. How do a group of older immigrants, who have spent most of their adult, working lives in Britain, continue to refer to Ireland as 'home'? In what ways does this exclude or not exclude their having a sense of Britain as their 'home', particularly with reference to their children's lives. What effects have there been on a group of people who have lived *in*, but not necessarily felt *of*, British society? What are the implications of these complex modes of belonging for the next generation, who are developing new forms of national and regional identification within multicultural urban areas? It may be added that the experience of the Irish in Britain is of specific sociological interest, as the Irish are both included and at the same time excluded from belonging to the (British) nation.

Changing forms of black culture have been a primary focus for postcolonial writers. For Gilroy (1987: 155–6): 'Black expressive cultures affirm while they protest. The assimilation of blacks is not a process of acculturation but of cultural syncretism. . . . Accordingly, their self definition and cultural expressions draw upon a plurality of black histories and politics. In the context of modern Britain this has produced a diaspora dimension to black life.' A number of researchers have explored this in studies with young people, illustrating a wide range of new pluralistic forms of collective belonging that broaden the public sphere of multicultural society (Hewitt 1986; Jones 1988; Mercer 1992a; Mac an Ghaill 1994b; Back 1996). They describe how young people are involved in constructing new syncretic versions of transculturally based identities. This involves emotional investments and cultural attachments around popular cultural forms, such as music and sport, that act as significant resources in their creative explorations of the shifting contours of cultural and political identities among and between ethnic majority and minority young people. This work is particularly important in showing subjectivity/identity not as a product, not as something possessed, but rather as a complex and multifaceted process – the focus shifts from a materialist emphasis on *being* ethnic to a differentialist emphasis on *becoming* ethnic.

For Bhabha (1994: 2), 'The social articulation of difference, from the minority perspective, is a complex, ongoing negotiation that seeks to authorise cultural hybridities that emerge in moments of historical transformation.' He sees cultural translation and hybrid identities of metropolitan immigrants and minorities as disrupting older binaries of power relations between dominant colonizers and dominated colonized. Hybridity is represented as a new location of resistance to essentialist identities and associated political demands.

In his work on 'narrating the nation', Bhabha (1990b) employs the concept of hybridity to challenge the assumption that the concept of the national interest is a meaningful analytical category. He develops an alternative position in the context of constantly changing boundaries of national imagined communities, in which he asks: 'What kind of cultural space is the nation with its transgressive boundaries and its "interruptive" interiority?' (Bhabha 1990a: 5). Gilroy (1993: 4) provides an answer to this question in his book *The Black Atlantic*. In what he calls the intermediate space of 'transcultural mixing' which spans the boundaries of nation-states, we can see the emergence of a new kind of cultural condition. He writes:

> I have settled for the image of ships in motion across the spaces between Europe, America and the Caribbean as a central organising principle for this enterprise and as my starting point. The image of the ship – a living micro-cultural, micro-political system in motion – is especially important for historical and theoretical reasons. . . . Ships immediately focus our attention on the middle passage, on the various projects for redemptive return to an African homeland, on the circulation of ideas and activists as well as the movement of key cultural and political artefacts: tracts, books, gramophone records, and choirs.

As is explored in the next chapter, the popularity of the term new racism has raised critical questions about its distinctiveness as a new *cultural* form of racism. Young (1995) raises similar questions about the use of the term hybridity which, as he points out, has a longer history than is presently acknowledged. However, generally, the more recent popularity of the terms diaspora, hybridity and syncretism means that there has been less critical engagement with them. This is because writers such as Gilroy and Bhabha, as post-colonial writers, are providing important conceptual frameworks that resonate with the changing conditions of late modernity, which is opening up the question of the constitutive dynamics of subjectivity while at the same time offering an alternative to the limitations of the cultural essentialism of identity politics (materialism). Furthermore, diasporic communities may seem to be a central signifier for the wider society's sense of dislocation. Solomos and Back (1996: 145) have produced an early critique of this work, raising important questions about the assumed progressive outcomes of syncretic cultures of diaspora communities. They cite the work of Bhatt (1994), who has challenged the assumption that contemporary forms of fundamentalism and neo-traditionalism in minority communities are emerging through a return to pre-modern religious influences. Rather, he maintains that what he calls 'reactionary ethnic formations' are the result of hybridity and cultural syncretism. This is a particularly difficult area, conceptually and politically, for anti-racist analysis, both in terms of its secular-based ideology and its exclusive focus on colour racism, which has underplayed the significance of cultural and religious influences in the formation of contemporary ethnic communities. In critically discussing cultural hybridity, Solomos and Back also provide an interesting exploration of the use of the key symbol of Nazi iconography – the swastika – as an example of a syncretic cultural form. They maintain that:

The point that we are making through this example is that we cannot neatly divide the debate on ethnicity and identity into 'repressive essentialism' on one side and 'liberating hybridity' on the other. Racist and extreme nationalist movements are not necessarily preoccupied with asserting a narrow and xenophobic co-incidence between race and nation: historically speaking they have also embraced transnationalism.

(Solomos and Back 1996: 150)

Terms such as hybridity, diaspora and syncretism that highlight a shifting racial semantics in Britain are key concepts for 'new times'. With reference to diasporic identities, which Connolly *et al.* (1995: 2) see as holding a promise for the future which breaks with the imagined binaries of the past, these concepts imply that identities have to be struggled over and constructed rather than assumed. Connolly *et al.* add that the struggle focuses on a range of difficult questions around issues such as: 'essentialism, the claim for rights to certain national identities and the tensions internally within diasporic communities about what it means to belong where, and indeed to belong to several places' (Connolly *et al.* 1995: 2). These questions are explored further at different points in the book.

Note

1 This work is examined further in the final section of this chapter. See also Brah (1996).

3 Rethinking racisms *and* ethnicities: rethinking *the* black–white dualism

Rethinking racisms and ethnicities: producing new political subjects

The representation of racial difference has a long history as one of the most contested arenas in the social and human sciences. This chapter examines the continuing complexity that marks current academic attempts to represent issues of racialized social relations and ethnic identity formations. There is a concern with changing forms of racialization. More specifically, there is an exploration of the theoretical shift beyond the black–white model of racism – the colour paradigm – towards one in which cultural and religious identities are foregrounded. In questioning the fixed boundaries around colour racism that were established by political and academic discourses in the 1970s and 1980s, there is the suggestion that conditions of late modernity are helping to produce multiple forms of racism and new political subjects that are not reducible to 'victims' and 'oppressors'.

Black and white social collectivities: colour racism and institutional racism

At present, it is fashionable to focus on the limits of earlier sociological representations of racism developed in materialist-based, anti-racist frameworks. Differentialist critiques of terms such as black identity and institutional racism have provided important contributions to our understanding of the interrelationship between changing forms of racism and wider cultural transformations. However, at one level recent criticisms appear to involve a certain historical amnesia concerning the specific moment and the attendant concerns of these political interventions. Terms such as black identity and institutionalized racism need to be read in the context of what was in place at the time of their origin, in attempting to name and explain the increasing systematic social subordination of racialized black groups. Current critiques of what are too easily dismissed as essentialist categories often overstate their case and fail to acknowledge that materialist accounts were developed in particular historical circumstances for specific strategic purposes. During the 1970s political activists and academic researchers reported the high levels of racial violence against Asians and African Caribbeans, which was underwritten by racialized state practices, including the passing of the 1971 Immigration Act (Sivanandan 1982; Solomos 1993). Sivanandan stressed how the fight against racism strengthened the class struggle while developing the growth of unity between the Asian and African-Caribbean struggles in defending their communities. The *Race Today* collective (1979: 52) captured the political mood of the time. It reported: 'The election campaign of '79 will be remembered for the extra-parliamentary intervention of the black communities of Britain who have . . . taken to the streets to oppose the presence of the N.F. (National Front) in their areas. The demonstrations called by the joint I.W.A.s (Indian Workers Associations) and S.Y.M. (Southall Youth Movement) occupied the streets leading to the town. They were driven there by police equipped with riot shields.'

This was the specific historical juncture in which the 'New Commonwealth' immigration and settlement of British subjects became the dominant paradigm in academic, political and popular representations, with colour racism projected as the key index of 'real' racism. Materialist accounts were of central significance in establishing the power differentials around the signifier of colour. A major aspect of a materialist position is the assumption that broader social structures organize and sustain the relations between social collectivities such as whites and blacks, middle class and working class, males and females, and heterosexuals and gays/lesbians. For example, from an anti-racist stance, the notion of racism, as a complex and multi-level distribution of automatic power for whites located in interpersonal relations and institutional structures, is seen as an overarching dynamic in structuring unequal relations between whites and blacks. This 'structured' reading of social relations allows an anti-oppressive position to predict and intervene in individual behaviour and social processes. Power from a materialist position is conceptualized as a negative repressive force. In this way, social identities are reproduced through the systematic restriction and control of social collectivities. Methodologically, attempts to understand the impact of institutional processes on different social collectivities, or more specifically the racialized collectivities of whites and blacks, has resulted in the development of epistemologies of power that centralize and prioritize members of those collectivities. This membership epistemologically reveals the 'true' nature of social relations. It is therefore an individual's authentic claims to membership in structured hierarchical oppositions that define and create the conditions of oppression. From a materialist position, black and white social collectivities are effectively spoken through the concepts of black identity and institutional racism.

As Back (1996: 142) points out: 'Black identity has its historical roots in the "negritude" movement developed in Africa and the United States in the 1920s/1930s and in the Afro-American civil rights and Black Power movements in the 1960s.' There is discussion at different points in *Contemporary Racisms and Ethnicities* about the decentring or destabilizing of the term black with the emergence of new ethnicities. The term institutional racism was developed during the 1960s in the United States, in the context of the Black Power movement's struggles. Carmichael and Hamilton (1968: 3), in their book entitled *Black Power*, defined racism as 'the predication of decisions and practices on considerations of race for the purpose of subordinating a racial group and maintaining control over that group'. They distinguished between two related forms of racism, that of overt and individualized racism, and covert and institutionalized racism. While individualized racism resided in the explicit actions of individuals, institutional racism referred to the practices and the non-practices that helped to maintain black people in a disadvantaged position. The latter was ideologically underpinned by 'the active and pervasive operation of anti-black attitudes and practices. A sense of superior group position prevails: whites are "better" than blacks; therefore blacks should be subordinated to whites' (Carmichael and Hamilton 1968: 5).

It is important to place the 'take-up' of the concept of institutional racism in Britain within its socio-historical context. By the late 1970s it was adopted by anti-racists and developed against what was seen as multiculturalists' overly psychologically based explanations of racial discrimination that focused on individual prejudice. The notion of institutional racism was influential in Britain and taken up by academics, public-sector professionals and policy makers (Dummett 1973; Miles and Phizacklea 1984). Its use was particularly strong among liberal state professionals, such as teachers and social workers, who had direct experience of the social location of Asians and African Caribbeans in the local sites of workplace, housing and schooling. The Commission for Racial Equality (CRE) (1985: 2–3) noted that: 'For too long racism has been thought of in individual psychological terms reducible to the actions of prejudiced individuals. The concept of institutional racism draws attention to the structural workings of institutions which exclude black people regardless of individuals' intentions.' As Gillborn (1990: 9–10) points out: The CRE's understanding of institutional racism resonated with the legal definition of 'indirect discrimination', which made it unlawful to apply conditions that 'disproportionately affect particular racial groups' (CRE 1985: 3). A number of criticisms from a materialist perspective have emerged concerning the term institutional racism (Mason 1992; Williams 1985). Miles (1989) produced one of the most rigorous critiques of the term as part of a wider concern with the conceptual inflation of racism. Most importantly, as Williams (1985: 335) argued: there is no 'one to one relationship between the idea and the effect, the ideology and the material practice. . . . I do not accept definitions of racism and institutional racism which conflate ideologies and practices, but agree that ideologies influence the development of institutions, can be systematic within them, and have material effects on the organisation of the institution.'

From a re-reading of materialist texts in the 1990s, much of the work around institutional racism can be seen to have been conceptualized largely in reductionist and essentialist terms of 'what white people have done to black people', rather than the broader category of racialized relations between a wide range of ethnic groups, who experience different forms of racialization in specific contexts. A further limitation was the undertheorization of subjectivity and ethnic identity formation. At the same time, there was a strong tendency in much of this work to adopt a monocausal explanation of racial exclusion and inclusion, which disconnected it from its articulation with other forms of social divisions and cultural processes. More specifically, much was written out of this overly simplistic black–white oppositional couplet, including issues of migration, class location, national belonging, gender dynamics, religious and cultural identities and generational social positioning. Furthermore, in assuming that blacks and whites were homogeneous collectivities, there was a tendency to concentrate on inter-racial differences to the exclusion of intra-ethnic differences, both within and between black and white social collectivities.

The controversial debates around the concepts of institutional racism and black identity are illustrative of the decline of the certainties of earlier materialist representations. More specifically, a differentialist understanding of institutional racism challenges the view of racism as a monolithic force that can be read off from the assumed responses of individuals, informed by a black–white dualism. Rather, within particular institutional sites there are a range of contextually based racist ideologies and discourses that may place subjects in subordinate positions. These racialized processes are temporally and spatially specific, and articulate in complex ways with other categories of social difference. In attempting to hold on to the tension between materialist and differentialist representations of racism, I have found that theory-led qualitative research grounded in minority and majority ethnic subjects' own accounts is productive in moving beyond a position that dismisses earlier frameworks as having no explanatory value on the basis of their reductive and essentialist stance (Mac an Ghaill 1994a). Such work carried out in 'postcolonial' conditions in changing urban spaces serves to signal a shift from materialist explanations – the colonial paradigm – in which fixed racial boundaries were ascribed to an early generation of immigrants and their children. The more recent focus is the experiences of established migrant groups and their British/English-born children living in diasporic communities.

The Americanization of British race relations

British interest in US race relations is part of a broader historical interest in US political and cultural systems that continues in the 1990s with frequent media references to the Anglo-American 'special relationship'. As Kettle (1996: 23) points out concerning US elections, 'the similarities between America and Britain are too easily accentuated and the differences too readily ignored'. Equally significant is the continuing centrality of the United States in contemporary theoretical accounts. As Billig (1995: 143) argues, in postmodern texts the United States 'is believed to be the place where the future can be observed most clearly. Jean Baudrillard, for example, sees Disneyland as the microcosm of the whole West, exemplifying perfectly the orders of hyperreal simulation, which represent the near future of the world (Baudrillard 1983, 1988)'.

In highlighting the Americanization of British race relations and the need to rethink the black–white dichotomy, it is necessary to stress that the

American model has helped to make sense of what was going on in Britain with the increased state and popular racial violence against Asians and African Caribbeans, outlined above. Edgar (1981: 218) describes the racial politics in the United States in the 1960s/1970s, in which he places the Black movement as a central inspiration and strategic influence on a wide range of new social movements. He writes that: 'Without Black Brotherhood, there would have been no sisterhood: without Black Power and Black Pride there would have been no Gay Power and Gay Pride. The movement against the abuses of powers of the State . . . derived much of its strength and purpose from the exposure of the FBI's surveillance and harassment of the Black Panthers and the Black Muslims . . . only the Environmental movement did not have the Black Movement as a central organisational fact or as a defining metaphor and inspiration.' In Britain, among new social movements, particularly in public-sector institutional sites such as social services and education, second-wave feminism might claim this pivotal cultural position (Rowbotham 1997). However, most male theorists in sociology, and more specifically in work on racial difference, have systematically erased feminist contributions, including the important debates generated by black and ethnic minority feminists within Britain (Carby 1982; Parmar 1982; Bourne 1983; Amos and Parmar 1984; Walter 1984; Bryan *et al.* 1985; Phoenix 1987; Brah 1991, 1992, 1996; Mirza 1992, 1997; Bhavnani and Phoenix 1994; Hickman 1995a and b; Mama 1995). More recently, most male theorists, working in a differentialist framework, have continued to underplay the significance of British feminist academic and political contributions. Interestingly, in contrast, American black feminist accounts, such as those of Toni Morrison and bell hooks, are often cited.

In suggesting the need to rethink the black–white dichotomy, it is not intended to deny the strategically important contribution of the American black movement at this particular historical moment, which resonated with black people across a wide range of societies. Furthermore, whereas the rise of Fascism and, more specifically, Nazi anti-Semitism was highly generative of earlier theories of racism, the American black political struggles of the 1960s alongside the Vietnamese resistance to American imperialism were of pivotal significance for the post-1960s British generation in their political coming of age. The main argument here is that British theorists, in adopting the American model often failed to adapt it to the 'peculiarities of British nation-state' with its specific class formation and reproduction, as part of the wider historical legacy of European colonialism and imperialism. It is worth noting that other models of political mobilization were not taken up by the British left. For example, 1969 was a key moment in relations between Ireland and the British state, marking a critical stage in Irish resistance to Britain's political and cultural occupation of Ireland. A wide range of elements constituted this resistance, which included the civil rights movement concerning political representation, campaigns around issues of discrimination in employment and housing as well as the military struggle (Beresford 1987). The war in Northern Ireland was, and continues to be, represented in European countries as a neo-colonial struggle between the British state and Irish nationalists. In contrast, the British left continued a long tradition of portraying the Northern Ireland struggles as not being of central political and conceptual importance to an understanding of the politics of race and nation. The legacy of this is still evident at the beginning of the twenty-first century, with Northern Ireland remaining Britain's testing laboratory for repressive legislation, surveillance technology and riot control equipment (Hardy 1997: 4). Recent changes in Northern Ireland with the Good Friday Agreement, opening the way for a new political settlement between Northern Ireland and Britain, may in the future increase the academic and political interest of the British left.

More recently, Phillips (1998: 6), writing of the 50-year anniversary of the arrival of the *MV Windrush Empire*, which brought West Indian immigrants to Britain, points to the limitations of importing African Americans to explain what it is like to be black in Britain. He notes: 'few people make the distinction between us and African-Americans, who look like us but are in virtually every way different. Our experience of slavery was industrial, theirs domestic. They have always been Americans, we colonials. We live next to whites and share schools and neighbourhoods; they live in segregated cities where whole areas never see a white face unless it's peering out of a police car.' The limitations involved in the cross-cultural American–British comparison may be illustrated by examining what is referred to as the 'ethnic mix' in each society. As Hall (1992a: 307) has pointed out in his discussion of the dramatic 'ethnic mix' of the United States population: 'In 1980, one in every five Americans came from an African-American, Asian American or American-Indian background. In 1990, the figure was one in four. In many major cities, whites are now a minority. . . . By 1995 one-third of American public school students are expected to be "non-white".' In contrast, Peach (1996: 17) has written of the relatively small 'ethnic mix' (understood in terms of 'non-white' people) in Britain. He writes that: 'The 1991 census · counted an ethnic minority population of just over three million out of a British population of 55 million – 5.5 per cent. South Asians make up nearly half of this total. Indians numbered 84,000, Pakistanis 477,000, Bangladeshis 163,000. The Chinese numbered 157,000. The Caribbean population numbered 500,000. The Africans 212,000.' Furthermore, as Mason (1995: 35) points out in examining the 1991 census, the ethnic minority population that is largely concentrated in England is overwhelmingly resident in the most urbanized and densely populated areas with 44.8 per cent of the minority ethnic population living in London and 14 per cent in the West Midlands. West Yorkshire, Greater Manchester and areas of the East Midlands are other regions that have a high minority ethnic group residence (see Owen 1992).

More importantly, in making such cross-cultural comparisons, there is a need to examine the different migrations both between and within the societies, in terms of their historical and spatial specificity and in relation to the question of how different migrations are located within wider socio-economic, political and cultural dynamics. This in turn leads to questions concerning different forms of collective incorporation, negotiation and re-sistance with reference to the interplay of racism and other social relations in late capitalist societies (Hickman 1995a). As Hall (1980: 339) suggests, there is a need to know: 'how different racial and ethnic groups were inserted historically, and the relations that have tended to erode and transform, or preserve these distinctions through time – not simply as residues of previous modes, but as active structuring principles of the present society'. Racial categories alone are not a sufficient explanation of the complex configurations of racialized minorities. Rather, there is a need to investigate changing social geographies, shifting occupational structures, internally differentiated economic, political and cultural identifications, complex consumption patterns and new social movements, in the context of the social and cultural spaces opened up in the conditions of late modernity (Wieviorka 1991).

A more productive use of American sources can be found in Small's (1994) work on the similarities between African-American and British-based African Caribbeans. This is a sophisticated comparative approach, highlighting the historical processes involved in the European racialization of Africans. However, at the present time the reductionist black–white binary of colour racism is more limited as a general theory of racism in the context of a highly diverse pattern of British racialized groups. Recently, British postmodern and post-structuralist theorists on racial difference, while emphasizing the need for contextually based cultural analyses of local situations continue to overconcentrate on American texts. More specifically, they tend to focus selectively on specific generational sectors of African-American experiences, while remaining silent about other racialized groups. For example, in Britain few people are aware of the impact of contemporary forms of racialization on Asian Americans or American Indians. There is a tendency for British social and cultural theorists to draw on high–profile American media representations, such as the beating of the black motorist, Rodney King, by four white Los Angeles policemen; and Judge Thomas and the O. J. Simpson trial. They then generalize from these incidents, suggesting that they serve to illustrate how race relations are developing in Britain.

The above has explored the limitations in a contemporary British context of the American-influenced dualistic model of race relations in terms of a black–white dichotomy. It may be added that the dynamic edge that the model gave to an earlier generation may also be of decreasing value in contemporary America. Castles and Miller (1993: 1) describe the 1992 Los Angeles riots that were first portrayed as a return to the black–white 1960s race riots. However, they suggest an alternative reading of what was referred to in the media as the nation's first multiethnic riot:

> Few of the businesses destroyed by arson and looting were white owned: about half belonged to Koreans, and around a third to Latinos – mainly Mexican Americans and Cubans. Most of the looters were black, but there were a sizable share of whites. Moreover more than a third of those killed were Latinos, and so were about one-third of the 13,000 people arrested in the week of the mayhem. About 1,200 of those arrested were illegal immigrants, who were turned over to the Immigration and Naturalisation Service for deportation. The white against black violence of the Rodney King (a black motorist beaten up by the police) case may have precipitated the disturbances, but other ethnic and social divisions played a major part.

There is increasing evidence of a shift from a 'biracial' to a 'multiracial' society, as is suggested in the changing ethnic composition of the United States, with the rise in the young Hispanic population outstripping that of young blacks (Kettle 1998: 18). However, in arguing for a broader explanatory framework, which takes account of changing ethnic and racial dynamics, there is a danger of this detracting from the ongoing reality of the systematic racism experienced by blacks in America. Most recently, this has been illustrated in the town of Jasper, Texas, with the brutal torture and murder of James Byrd by three white neighbours. The murder has drawn attention to the reorganization of American white supremacist groups, such as the Ku-Klux-Klan and the Aryan Brotherhood.

Shifting processes of racialization

Historically, one of the major ways in which the concept of race and social change has been problematized in the social and human sciences is through the use of the term racialization. Its usefulness is indicated by the fact that it has been adopted by theorists from a wide range of perspectives, including those from a race-relations problematic, as well as materialist and differentialist positions (Banton 1977; Reeves 1983; Miles 1989; Smith 1989; Solomos 1993; Small 1994; Holdaway 1996). Theorists have deployed the concept in different ways in order to address the limits of conventional accounts of race and racism. From a materialist perspective, theorists have challenged the notion of distinct races as biologically given and pointed to the need to explore the conditions under which specific processes of racialization result in differential outcomes. This work has been particularly successful in examining the cumulative institutional effects of ascribing reified meanings to minorities, particularly Asians and African Caribbeans. As Green and Carter (1988: 23) have argued, processes of racialization in post-war Britain were 'structurally determined, politically organized and ideologically inflected . . . within the relations of domination and subordination'. Miles (1982) provided an early account of this with reference to post-war labour migration to Britain. More recently, Keith (1993: 239) has cogently captured a differentialist understanding of race and racialization, while not losing sight of relations of domination and subordination. Arguing that race is not an essential characteristic, he suggests that:

> The pervasive practices of racism, however and the evolution of racial formations over time and space . . . guarantee some correspondence in the harsh reality of the day-to-day world between the ideological fictions of racial divisions between people and the empirical circumscription of specific groups in society. The generation of racial divisions in society is most easily grasped by use of the notion of racialization, which stresses both the reality of the group formation process as well as the social construction of differences between the racial collective identities so formed. The process of racialization is also of particular significance because it is one of the principal means through which subordination is produced and reproduced in an unjust society.

There has been a tendency in earlier sociological accounts to conceptualize racialization as uniform both across and within different societies.
Most importantly, as Solomos (1993: 244) argues: 'The paradox of attempts
to construct a uniform conception of racism is that they seem to lose the
ability to explain the dynamics of change and conflict. In so doing they fail
to analyse the processes which lead to the racialization of social relations in
particular societies.' More recently, differentialist accounts have emphasized
the need to develop a more complex understanding of racialization. However,
there have been few attempts to explore the logic of the differentialist position
by moving beyond the continuing exclusive focus on blacks as the object of
inquiry.

Consequently, a main issue that has tended to be underplayed in the
literature on racialization is the collective subject position of whites, which
operates in a hegemonic logic in which 'whiteness' is absent to the 'racial
majority', who assume that racialization is 'something to do with blacks'.
Whiteness as the signifier of dominance has become the unexamined norm.
As Dyer (1993: 27) argues: 'In the realm of categories, black is always marked
as colour (as the term 'coloured' egregiously acknowledges), and is always
particularizing; whereas white is anything really, not an identity, not a particularizing quality, because it is everything – white is no colour because it is
all colours.' The development in the 1980s and 1990s of studies of whiteness
has a number of diverse sources (Bonnett 1996). For example, feminist writers
have begun to investigate the social construction of whiteness (Brah 1992;
C. Hall 1992; Ware 1992; Anthias and Yuval-Davis 1993; Frankenberg 1993).
The best known of recent work has been produced in the United States and
can be located broadly within materialist and differentialist positions. Roediger
(1992), in *The Wages of Whiteness: Race and the Making of the American Working Class*, provides a historical account – in a political economic tradition –
of the processes of becoming white. In contrast, Frankenberg's (1993) *White
Woman, Race Matters: The Social Construction of Whiteness*, provides an equally
insightful account, stressing the multifaceted nature of the lived experiences
of whiteness.

With work that is beginning to emerge in this area, there is the danger
of unproblematically equating whiteness with power. In this process whites
and blacks are reified in a way that does not resonate with the complexity of
contemporary conditions in Britain, as is reported in recent empirical work
with young people in multicultural cities (Mac an Ghaill 1994b; Back 1996).
For Brah (1992: 133–4) there is an urgent need to explore how and why
the meaning of these words (whiteness and blackness) changes from plain
descriptions to hierarchically organized categories under given economic,
political and social circumstances. Analysing whiteness removes it from its
normative location as transparent, neutral and disembodied. This is part of a
more general trend in culturally based theories whereby the ascendant social
category in established binaries (for example, men, heterosexuals and whites)
is becoming the new object of critical appraisal. There is much empirical
and conceptual work to be done in exploring the racialization of whiteness.
A range of questions emerges at epistemological and policy levels. How do
people become white? How is whiteness socially constructed? What material

and cultural resources are made available in how white Anglo-ethnicity is compulsively and publicly performed? It is important politically to stress within a British context that, at present, there is no coherent alternative explanation to the 'new white victims'' argument of New Right national and racial discourses. Equally significant is the elision of whiteness and European identity that is creating new barriers to citizenship for established minorities and more recent migrants and refugees in Europe, who are not included in the ascendant category.

Social inegalitarianism and cultural differentialism: the return of culture

Chapter 2 explored the recent theoretical move away from a focus on structure to one on culture. This shift has pushed the study of racial and ethnic representations, discourses and subjectivities to centre stage in political and academic debates. In what is called the 'cultural turn', critical theorists have suggested that a new politics of cultural difference has emerged in the 1980s. Exploring the changing politics of race and ethnicity highlights the increasing significance of the cultural production of new ethnic identities. A primary question arises from this more positive reading of culture; namely, what are the implications for changing conceptions of racism?

A major debate to emerge across European nation-states in the 1980s concerned the identification of what in Britain was called 'new racism'. The 'culturalization' of racism has been formulated in different ways, including what Fanon (1970) referred to as cultural racism. Most studies on contemporary forms of racism have noted that phenotypical or racial traits (i.e. biological markers) alone do not determine the differentiation of an ethnic group, but that phenotypical differences are signified through culture, religion and other markers (Guillaumin 1988). Barker (1981: 23) provided an early account of what he called *The New Racism*. He defined the character of this as follows: 'It is a theory that I shall call biological or better pseudo-biological culturalism. Nations on this view are not built out of politics and economics, but out of human nature. It is our biology, our instincts to defend our way of life, traditions and customs against outsiders not because they are inferior but because they are part of different cultures.' Here, Barker is arguing that from the early 1980s racism tended to be rationalized in terms of 'cultural differences' rather than 'cultural superiority'. The latter form of racism was clearly described by Cleeve (1982: 12–13) who in an article in the *Sunday Telegraph*, called '1938: When the British was best and the £ rode high – a vanished world', wrote that:

> There were very few immigrants in Britain and almost none of these were coloured. Naturally enough, this affected thinking about foreigners and 'coloured races'. Foreigners were queer, and they lived a long way away. And not only 'British was Best' but Britain was Best. People were fiercely nationalistic and contemptuously chauvinistic. Italians were Wops, Spaniards were Dagos. Frenchmen were Frogs. Germans were Boches

and Huns. Negroes were Niggers and Chinamen were Chinks. Indians were Wogs, Jews were Yids, Jewboys, Kikes, Isaacs. . . . Of course there were sophisticated people who were international in outlook and who recognised to be white and to be British was no automatic superiority over foreigners and Negroes but there were not enough of them to affect the general tone of the country.

New racism with its emphasis on cultural differences is described by Worsthorne (1982: 20) in another article in the *Sunday Telegraph* called 'Why not inequality?'. He argued that:

> . . . ordinary people accept wealth and privilege far more readily than they accept, say, coloured immigration, because wealth and privilege are part of the British heritage in a way that coloured immigrants are not. Everyone loves a lord. But very few like a coloured neighbour. Take a poll on the abolition of the House of Lords, and relatively few will welcome the idea. . . . But a massive popular majority will favour immigration control. Such popular sympathy or affection has little to do with any abstract approval of hereditary privilege. Almost nobody approves of titles in theory, just as no one disapproves of blacks in theory. In each case it's simply a case of liking the familiar and disliking the unfamiliar . . . since for the great body of people a sense of nation remains more precious than social justice, equality or freedom itself, none of which abstractions has any meaning except in terms of a specifically British experience.

Most significantly, with reference to understanding social and cultural transformations, new racism in a British context can be read as having its origins in the socio-economic and political crisis of the early 1980s (Centre for Contemporary Cultural Studies 1982). The restructuring of the enterprise economy and the reconstruction of British national identity and nationhood were two sides of the same coin. Critical theorists working in the new racism problematic successfully identified linkages between the redefining of a unified British culture and new forms of racial exclusion. For Gilroy (1987: 43), in his study of the cultural politics of race and nation: 'Its novelty lies in the capacity to link discourses of patriotism, nationalism, xenophobia, Englishness, Britishness, militarism and gender difference into a complex system which gives "race" its contemporary meaning.' A main element of the 'new racism' is the deracialization of race, involving the displacement of an older racial vocabulary in public arenas, in which explicit references to race are now coded in the language of culture. Solomos and Back (1996: 19) make clear the complexity of the new vocabulary of British racism for the 1990s. They suggest that what has emerged from writings on new racism is: 'that a range of discourses on social differentiation may have a metonymic relationship to racism. The semantics of race are produced by a complex set of interdiscursive processes where language of culture and nation invokes a hidden racial narrative. The defining feature of this process is the way in which it naturalises social formations in terms of a racial-cultural logic of belonging.'

During the past decade a number of questions have been raised about the conceptual value and empirical validity of the British notion of new racism. Mason (1995: 129) has compared Barker's (1981) socio-biological focus on 'the alleged naturalness of group exclusiveness' with Balibar's (1991a) emphasis on cultural incompatibility. He warns that 'this diversity in usage of what is intended to be a subtype of a generic concept of racism should alert us to a potential problem'. From a European context, Wieviorka (1994: 182–3) distinguishes between classical, inegalitarian and new, differentialist sociological accounts of racism, and argues that the suggestion that the latter form is in the ascendancy is empirically adequate as a statement of historical fact, but that it must not be taken as a general theory of racism. As he points out: 'First, culturalist or differentialist perspectives in racism are not new. It is difficult to speak of Nazism, for instance, without introducing the idea that anti-Semitism in the Third Reich was deeply informed by these perspectives. Jews were said to corrupt Aryan culture and race, and the "final solution" planned not to assign them to the lowest place in society, but to destroy them.' For Wieviorka (1995) there is only one racism, which often combines various versions of the association of cultural differentialism and social in-egalitarianism. In a British context, Hickman (1995a: 4), drawing on European literature, maintains that: 'The uncritical, and misleading, acceptance of the "newness" of cultural racism might not have occurred if the problematic of racism in Britain had been a more inclusive field of study. To take two historically and contemporaneously significant instances, both anti-Semitism and anti-Irish racism reveal that there is nothing new about cultural differen-tiation as a basis for racist discourse in this country.' She provides a fascinat-ing exploration of the political discourses about Irish migrants in the 1830s and 1840s that she finely illustrates, revealing that they foreshadowed much that was later described as 'new' in the 1970s and 1980s with reference to responses to Asian and African-Caribbean post-war migrations.

In much of the British literature discussing the origins and effects of new racism, there has been an exclusive focus on its links with the emer-gence of the New Right, which helped generate discourses and policy reforms. This is accompanied by a tendency among differentialist theorists to emphas-ize the need to examine contemporary forms of racism in specific contexts, while themselves failing to do so. This is most evident in relation to what has been omitted in 1980s accounts, namely an examination of the differen-tial impact of new racism on and among different social groups located in specific regional and institutional spaces. For example, most of these texts are marked by a lack of methodological reflexivity, which fails to explore the implications of culturally based forms of racism for middle-class occupational groups working in state institutions. Duffield (1982: 23) was an exception to this trend, providing an early development of Barker's work by examining the similarities between the 'new racism' and what he called the 'new realism' of the liberal establishment with the policy shift from assimilation to integra-tion. Although new racism depended on a pseudo-biological underpinning and new realism on a psychological and sociological base, he argued that culturalism was nevertheless the shared terrain that linked the new realism with the new racism. That is, despite apparent differences, both viewed culture

as a 'problem'. For Duffield: 'New realism and the new racism are in fundamental agreement over the terms in which black people in Britain are to be
discussed and their future decided. . . . The new realists' project is to show
how people maintain and recreate their own bounded ways of life. This is
precisely the food on which new racism thrives. The elision is achieved
because each has the other inscribed within it.' These notions of new racism
and new realism, with their shared conception of intrinsic cultural differences as primarily causal of social behaviour, were pervasive because of their
strong 'common-sense' appeal in the popular, authoritarian British state of
the early 1980s. So, for example, it could be argued that although liberal
policy makers, researchers and public-sector professionals rejected the older,
biologically based racist inferiority/superiority couplet, they operated in the
culturalist model. More recently, in a paper called *The Symphony of the Damned*,
Duffield (1996: 5) has returned to the question of new racism, arguing that it
helps to explain the West's internal crisis, as well as underpinning 'common-
sense' explanations for the external crisis of increasing political instability
and intercommunal conflicts in marginal areas of the global economy. He
maintains that:

> The external variant of modern racism developed during the 1980s.
> While having academic and political expression, it also informs most
> of the media view on ethnic conflict and state fragmentation in places
> like Liberia, Somalia, Rwanda and the former Yugoslavia. In relation to
> West Africa, this external variant has been called 'new barbarianism'.
> . . . For the new barbarianism, the anarchic and destructive power of
> traditional feelings and antagonisms is unleashed when controlling
> forms of governance or economic regulation collapse.

The reclaiming of culture by differentialist theorists has also resulted in
the suggestion of the need to move beyond the idea of a single monolithic
racism and to acknowledge the wide range of contemporary racisms, locating
them in specific socio-historical and spatial conditions (Anthias and Yuval-
Davis 1993). For example, Brah (1992: 133) argues for the need to locate different racisms within the specificity of different sets of economic, political and
cultural circumstances that have been reproduced through specific mechanisms
and that find different expressions in different societies. She adds: 'anti-black
racism, anti-Irish racism, anti-Jewish racism, anti-Arab racism, different vari-
eties of Orientalisms: all have their distinctive features'. However, as Miles
(1989: 132) has suggested, most commentators have done little to identify or
explain these new racisms. Furthermore, a major weakness of these theorists
is that while claiming that different groups have been racialized on the basis
of different signifiers of difference, they have failed to go beyond the black–
white dualism, holding on to 'colour racism' as the 'real racism'. In an
important recent collection Brah *et al.* (1999b) highlight the limitations of
this earlier work. The collection brings together research about a diverse
range of identities which are rarely analysed together, including Welsh, Irish,
Jewish, Arab, White, African and Indian. It sets out to interrogate and critique
orthodox theorization of the political processes that underpin the production of these identities. The collection enables the consideration together of:

the underplaying of anti-Semitism and anti-Arab racism in race-relations and anti-racist models; the loss and dislocation of identity but also the potential for reformulating identities afforded transnational communities; an exploration of the interrelationship between different social divisions with particular reference to gender, class and sexuality; the critical examination of differences within racialized collectivities; an exploration of ethnic majorities, including questions of whiteness; the contingent contestations that underpin Britishness and the 'sub-national' identities that constitute the hierarchical relationship that is the United Kingdom.

Contemporary forms of ethnic, national and religious exclusions

Recent social and cultural changes, involving global economic restructuring, advanced technological communications and increasing cultural exchange, have highlighted a wide range of processes of social exclusion and marginalization that have challenged older models of racism. In a British context, three main issues have been of particular significance: Euro-racism, the intensification of Islamaphobia and the arrival of new migrants, 'illegal' immigrants, refugees and asylum seekers. The re-emergence of the far right and neo-Fascist parties in Eastern and Western Europe, with the accompanying increased physical and symbolic violence against migrant and Jewish communities, and the wider dimensions of a rapidly changing world of ethnic nationalisms and religious fundamentalisms in Europe and beyond, have served to illustrate the parochialism of much British anti-racist theorizing (Alund and Schierup 1991; Balibar and Wallerstein 1991; Webber 1991; Silverman 1992). By the end of the 1990s important work was carried out that traced developments of racism in individual European nation-states (Wieviorka 1991; Ford 1992; Atkinson 1993; Wrench and Solomos 1993; Willems 1995). However, such work offers only a partial insight into the rise of Euro-racism. As Bonnett (1993: 30) makes clear: 'moves toward militant rejectionism have taken place in the context of the integration of the European Community (EC) and the emergence of pan-EC immigration, refugee and social surveillance controls'. He illustrates this with reference to former British Prime Minister John Major's desire to construct a 'perimeter fence' around Europe to protect the continent from immigrants (see Campaign Against Racism and Fascism 1991).

There have been different explanations for the phenomenon of Euro-racism. For Miles (1993: 16), the new comparative interest in contemporary European racisms was an important analytical development in the late 1980s that followed the weakening of the race-relations paradigm. He maintains that the notion of Euro-racism signals an intensification of nationalisms associated with the crisis in the nation-state in the latest stage of globalization. Although sensitive to the particularity of the political and ideological form of each nation-state, he identifies a common set of problems facing European Union societies resulting from the restructuring of capitalist economies in a period of continuing reorganization of the capitalist world economy. The politics of immigration is one such problem, with the need for EU member states 'to continue to regulate the political and ideological consequences of large-scale labour migrations that occurred during the 1950s, 1960s and early 1970s and the resulting rise of nationalisms'.

Whereas for Miles racism is conceptualized as integral to the development of capitalist societies, Wieviorka (1991, 1994, 1995) places his work in analytical frameworks that put modernity and post-industrialism at the centre of his explanation for the rise of contemporary European racisms. Wieviorka distinguishes four forms of racism located in modern social and political conditions: a universalist type, evident in conditions of colonial expansion which inferiorizes 'pre-modern others'; second, a racism associated with downward social mobility – a 'poor white' response common at times of economic recession and unemployment in modern industrial societies; third, an anti-modernist stance, which appeals to traditions of nation, religion and community, and is often directed against the Jews and economically successful Asians; and, finally, intergroup tensions that have complex relations with the conditions of modernity. Wieviorka maintains that all contemporary European societies are experiencing huge transformations that define what he calls, in the case of France, *une grande mutation*, manifested in 'the era of destructuration', that is constituted by crises in industrialism, the welfare state and national identity. For Wieviorka, these changing conditions in Europe have allowed each form of racism to develop as a space of racism, with racists taking up a complex mixture of various positions.

A major feature of Euro-racism has been increased levels of state surveillance and exclusion alongside an upsurge in popular violence against Muslims. For example, in France, the headscarf affair of 1989 helped to generate a major moral panic against Islamic people. It involved the suspension from a state school of three Muslim girls, who insisted on wearing headscarves that their headteacher judged to contravene French laws on *laïcité* (secularism), a term denoting the separation of state and religious institutions. The headteacher's decision was eventually overturned by the Minister for Education, Lionel Jospin (Silverman 1992; Hargreaves 1995). A range of reasons has been identified for the intensification of the racialization of Islam, including: that in many European societies Muslims form the largest non-European minority; that following the collapse of communism, Europe is returning to an earlier historical conflict between Christians and Muslims; that the early 1970s world recession was associated with 'greedy oil sheikhs' (Mason 1995). More recently, the Islamic revolution in Iran and the Gulf war have been represented as a direct challenge to Western, and more specifically, North American hegemony. Most significantly, the Rushdie affair is projected as illustrative of the major threat of religious fundamentalists against liberal social democratic Western societies. As Hoogvelt (1997: 182) has argued, 'In the last twenty years or so a number of apparently political and social events all over the world have led Western commentators to speak of a militant Islamic revival.' Hence, as Castles and Miller (1993: 27) point out: 'Muslim minorities appear threatening partly because they are linked to strong external forces, which appear to question the hegemony of the North[ern hemisphere], and partly because they have a visible and self-confident cultural presence.'

In a British context, Muslims have emerged as a major target of official racial discourses and increased levels of popular violence. Historically, one can trace the shift in central government political rhetoric with Sikhs represented as the 'others' in Enoch Powell's speeches during the 1960s and 1970s. At this time there was much debate in the media concerning the problem of Sikhs enforcing Sikh culture on their children and refusing to assimilate to British culture. Equally interesting is the way in which different cultural objects, here Sikh turbans, can come to signify a cultural threat to the nation. By the 1980s Muslims had become demonized as the main 'enemy within', threatening the 'British way of life'. Most recently, this was articulated by the Conservative MP, Winston Churchill: 'He [Major] promises us that fifty years from now, spinsters will be cycling to communion on Sunday mornings – more like the muezzin will be calling Allah's faithful to the high street mosque' (see Runnymede Trust 1993). As Anthias and Yuval-Davis (1993: 55) have pointed out:

> Since the 'Rushdie Affair', the exclusion of minority religions from the national collectivity has started a process of racialization that especially relates to Muslims. People who used to be known for the place of origin, or even as 'people of colour' have become identified by their assumed religion. The racist stereotype of the 'Paki' has become the racist stereotype of the 'Muslim fundamentalist'.

This racial discourse is being mediated in state institutions. For example, schools are in the process of constructing a new hierarchy of ethnic masculinities (Mac an Ghaill 1994a). For more than two decades, African-Caribbean boys have been positioned as the main disciplinary problem (Gillborn 1995). They are currently being joined by Muslim boys as the new folk devils, with corresponding negative categorization, stereotyping and moral evaluation.

The term Islamaphobia is gaining increasing acceptance as signifying that existing anti-racist discourses do not adequately address questions of cultural and religious discrimination. This has been a central argument among sections of the Muslim community in Britain, highlighted in two main issues: their campaign for government financial support for Muslim schools and their mobilizing against the publication of Salman Rushdie's book *The Satanic Verses* (see Asad 1990, 1993; Al-Azmeh 1993).[1] Modood's work has been of central importance in articulating the need to move beyond a black–white dualistic model of racism. He was specifically critical of the municipal anti-racism of the 1980s, which he located in the broader political development of new social movements, acknowledging the American influence on the shift from race relations to anti-racism with the celebration of the collective black subject. Modood (1989: 280–1) argued that in the 1980s race professionals and theorists marketed the idea:

> of an Alabama-like Britain consisting of two races, whites and blacks, and the latter as a potentially revolutionary underclass allied to feminism, gay rights, Irish nationalism and radical ecology. The politics based on these ideas, with the corollary that 'race relations' had to be redefined

as 'anti-racism', came to prominence in the wake of the urban riots of 1981 and after, and reached a peak in the heyday of Ken Livingston's rule at the GLC.

Modood's critique of anti-racism is not easily classified in conventional political divisions of left and right. In his polemical style, there appear to be convergences in his analysis with new right attacks on anti-racism. At the same time, his critique challenges both liberal racial relations and radical anti-racist theorists. His writing serves as evidence of the unsettling of liberal multiculturalists and radical anti-racists, who developed their respective positions in opposition to each other around the highly contested concept of culture. His central challenge to the hegemonic claims of the category black is part of a broader ethnic assertiveness among Muslims, which marked the end of the political high point of materialist representations of anti-racism.

A third example of emerging contemporary forms of social exclusions that have challenged older models of colour racism is illustrated by the growing importance of new migrants, 'illegal' immigrants, refugees and asylum seekers. Hooper (1997: 16), describing Italy as a death-trap for recent immigrants, highlighted the varied migrant population of modern European societies with: 'its Filipino, Ethiopian and Dominican daily helpers, its Albanian squeegee merchants, North African farm workers and Sri Lankan street vendors'. Equally significant is the social positioning of gypsies and travellers in Britain, who are currently receiving much negative media attention. There is a long history of neglect, both by the state and anti-racist movements, of the material and cultural experiences and needs of gypsies and travellers. Hawes and Perez (1995: viv) have explored the cumulative effects of this long history of neglect alongside recent changes, including Court of Appeal decisions on the definition of a gypsy, the provisions of the 1994 Criminal Justice and Public Order Act and the impact of European legislation. Acknowledging the complexity of the social location of gypsies in a new politics of cultural difference situation, they argue the case for the use of the concept ethnic cleansing to describe 'the actions and attitudes of British society to the most maligned of its minorities, the Gypsies'.

The erasure of anti-Irish racism: racism without race?

The erasure of anti-Irish racism has a long history in British sociological representations of racism and ethnicity. This includes the early race-relations problematic and continues through class-based Marxist and Weberian accounts to more recent post-colonial theories. As Hickman (1995a: 4) argues: 'In Britain . . . "race" has been socially constructed in exclusive and exclusionary ways. Just as "racial", ethnic and national discourses are about processes of inclusion and exclusion, so too the disciplines and concepts with which they are studied have their own closures which include and exclude.' In a shared sociological framework of black and white social collectivities, African Caribbeans and Asians are represented as the exclusive focus of research, albeit through caricatured representations of both groups. This reduction of racism to colour racism serves to deny the existence of anti-Irish discrimination. In this process, England's largest immigrant group – the Irish – are made culturally invisible. In turn, this serves to reinforce the categorization of racism in terms of a 'common-sense' dichotomy of 'black victims' and 'white perpetrators', which sociologists claim to oppose.

Said (1993: 284) has written that: 'It is an amazing thing that the problem of Irish liberation not only has continued longer than other comparable struggles but it is so often not regarded as being an imperial or nationalist issue; instead it is comprehended as an aberration within the British dominion. The facts conclusively reveal otherwise.' With notable exceptions, most sociological commentators have not recognized these 'facts' (Miles 1982; Cohen 1988; Brah 1992; Anthias and Yuval-Davis 1993). Their work is marked by a number of arguments that serve to 'de-racialize' the Irish in Britain, while simultaneously 'over-racializing' African Caribbeans and Asians. The arguments include: that anti-Irish racism is mainly a historical phenomenon; that the Irish as well as the Jews have historically experienced institutional discrimination but that this did not result in processes of racialization equivalent to those experienced by New Commonwealth immigrants; that the Irish experience of prejudice occurs at a cultural and therefore less serious level, such as that of anti-Irish jokes; that there may be similarities between black groups and the Irish, for example, around class location, but that the Irish are privileged as part of the white European collectivity. The dominant conceptual model in these accounts is that of assimilation, in which whiteness, Europeanness, Christianity, and belonging to the British Isles are all taken as marks of sameness and identification between Irish and British people. Mary Hickman (1995a) has produced a major socio-historical analysis that challenges this theoretical framework. This is discussed in Chapter 4 in relation to the question of anti-Irish racism and the history of the development of a racist British nationalism. She notes that the chief exceptions to the dominant assimilationist paradigm are a number of chapters in Gilley and Swift (1985), Devine (1991) and Fielding (1993).

In response to the argument of assimilation, Irish political activists and community workers have established the notion of the 'invisibility' of the Irish in Britain. From a sociological point of view, we might begin to consider this claim by asking, invisible to whom? This book argues that sociological accounts of racism and ethnicity have systematically excluded the Irish, thus making them conceptually invisible in anti-racist representations at a theoretical and policy level. However, although the Irish have generally not been represented as a legitimate racialized minority, either in the mainstream academy or by the state, there are academic and local authority sources available that serve to support the Irish community's claims concerning institutional disadvantage and discrimination. For example, Rex and Moore (1967) reported in the 1960s that the Irish were seen by other residents as responsible for the declining conditions of an inner-city area in Birmingham. A further example is found in Tomlinson's (1981: 177) study, carried out on 'educational subnormality' which concentrated on African-Caribbean and Asian students and decided not to include the Irish. Despite this omission, she reports that: 'One [psychologist] thought Irish children have similar problems to West Indian children – "they are deprived and not too bright".... Another psychologist thought that ... the educational deprivation of Irish families marked them out as the most deprived group: "You get a total lack of schooling and unsurpassed parental ineptness".' In contrast to the conceptual invisibility of the Irish among sociologists, at the level of popular culture the Irish are a highly visible minority. This was most recently illustrated in the soap opera, *EastEnders*, which presented negative stereotypes of the Irish, with which – in its social-realism style – it was assumed British viewers would identify.

During the 1970s and 1980s, Irish community workers and academics brought together a wide range of empirical evidence of the institutional and individual discrimination that the Irish experience in a wide range of Britain's institutional sites, including migration, work, health, education, policing and legal systems and welfare rights (Conner 1985; Hickman 1986, 1995b; Hazelkorn 1990; Greenslade 1992; Gribben 1994; Kowarzik 1997; Williams *et al.* 1997). Most significantly, Mary Hickman and Bronwen Walter (1997) have recently carried out a large-scale empirical study, funded by the Commission for Racial Equality, entitled *Discrimination and the Irish Community in Britain*. As this work finely illustrates, one of the major effects of the black–white dualistic model of race and racism is that it does not help us to understand the current high levels of disadvantage experienced by the Irish in Britain. Traditionally, employment for Irish men has been mainly in unskilled manual jobs and, although this pattern has changed since the war, Irish men are still disproportionately represented in this type of work. Also, the housing patterns of the Irish in Britain have been shown to be skewed towards less secure tenure categories, for example, the private rented sector, with owner-occupation rarer for the Irish than for any other group. People born in Ireland suffer disproportionately from accidents, illness and suicide and Irish men have been shown to die younger in Britain than in Ireland, with their overall health standards being lower. In the field of mental health, Irish people are overrepresented in figures for psychiatric hospital admission. However, psychiatry does not incorporate transcultural elements with an Irish perspective, resulting in misdiagnosis and mistreatment – notably of schizophrenia which is frequently diagnosed as alcohol psychosis (Williams *et al.* 1997; Williams and Mac an Ghaill 1998). This may be influenced by the traditional stereotyping of the Irish as drunkards (Greenslade 1992). The overall position of the Irish in Britain has historically been one of uncertainty as a result of the colonial legacy and the continuing political struggle in Northern Ireland, and the subsequent lack of a political settlement between Ireland and Britain. This position is well illustrated by studies that have highlighted the criminalization of the Irish community in Britain associated with the introduction of the Prevention of Terrorism Act and resulting from the Northern Ireland situation (Hillyard 1993). The general lack of social mobility for most of the older generation of Irish in Britain highlights the significance of class and age as key features of racialization. At the same time, the overrepresentation of Irish women in low-paid work in underresourced public services illustrates the gendering of racialization (Walter 1984; Lennon *et al.* 1988; Hickman and Walter 1995). A focus on these different social divisions in the community highlights the need for a multifaceted understanding of the racialization of Britain's Irish population.

As indicated previously, the recent development of the Good Friday Agreement has opened the way for a new political settlement between Ireland and Britain. The response of the British state to the Irish living in Britain has received little attention from the government, the media or academics. This will undoubtedly be a key question for future research in this area.

A study of the Irish is of particular conceptual value in critically exploring the sociology of racial and ethnic difference. First, the inclusion of the Irish may help to develop sociology so that it takes seriously a notion of multiple, decentred racisms, marked by a logic of relationality and contradiction. This, in turn, may serve to substantiate the differentialist claims of the complexity of identity formation in Britain in late modernity. There is a need to explore the different subject positions that are inhabited in various racisms. Furthermore, analysis of the interconnections between racism, class, gender and sexuality needs to take account of the *positionality* of different racisms with respect to one another (Brah 1996). Second, Irish community activists interpret the high levels of deprivation among the Irish as evidence of racial discrimination. Critically examining the causal relationship between high levels of deprivation and discrimination among the Irish in order to establish explanatory frameworks of racialization needs to occur in a more general framework of the sociology of racism and ethnicity. This would involve setting out to challenge the conceptual inflation of anti-black racism that fails to desegregate the impact of different social categories and their level of determinacy, in terms of individual lived experiences and collective institutional outcomes for all minority ethnic communities.

It is important to note that in focusing on anti-Irish racism to illustrate the limits of the black–white dualistic model of racial discrimination, we are at an early stage in providing alternative theoretical explanations. In contrast to historical, literary and cultural studies, sociological frameworks have not been developed that enable us to analyse systematically, and document coherently, the material, social and discursive production of contemporary processes of anti-Irish racism and the emergence of complex Irish ethnic identities (Fielding 1993; Foster 1993; Hickman 1993; Atkenson 1996; Kiberd 1996).[2] This is similar to the recent studies of Muslims in Britain that are used to illustrate the limits of earlier models of racism and anti-racism. For example, Modood's writing has undoubtedly highlighted the need to focus on broader cultural and religious issues, alongside colour racism. However, the work in this area remains sociologically underdeveloped. With reference to the Irish, theoretical and empirical studies are currently being carried out throughout Britain. This work has become more sustained with the establishment of Irish study centres within higher and further educational institutions, as indicated in this book with reference to the work of Mary Hickman, who is director of the Irish Studies Centre at the University of North London (see Hickman and Walter 1997, 1999).

Notes

1 It is too early to know the effect of the recent Iranian–British agreement, which is intended to restore normal diplomatic relations between the two countries. Under the agreement, President Mohammed Khatami has agreed not to send agents to carry out the fatwa that was imposed on Salman Rushdie by the late Ayatollah Ruhollah Khomeini. In return, Britain has agreed to dissociate from the book *Satanic Verses*, which Muslims have found blasphemous.
2 See also Deane (1991); Kearney (1985); J. Smyth (1993); Graham and Kirkland (1998); Gibbons (1996); Breen *et al.* (1990).

4 Globalization *and* localization: nation-making *and* citizenship

The local–global nexus, social transformations and urban restructuring

This chapter explores nation-making and citizenship within the local–global nexus of the interplay between changing racial, ethnic and national identities and social and cultural transformations. The end of the twentieth century has seen unprecedented political-economic and cultural change in the politics of race and nation in Britain, the United States and much of Europe. The rise of Euro-racism has been widely reported, with suggestions that new cultural forms of racism and ethno-nationalism have emerged in the context of globalization. These changing political conditions include: challenges to the configuration of the UK – involving the development of a new settlement between Britain and Northern Ireland, the establishing of the Scottish parliament and the Welsh assembly; a new Europe; nation-building in Africa; and conflicts in East and Central Europe and territories of the former Soviet Union. They are taking place in highly contested European national arenas in which questions about asylum seekers and refugees, immigration and what constitutes the nation-state are major debates. Equally important is the transformation of regional and institutional spaces such as restructured post-Fordist labour markets, deregulated housing markets, contracted-out health services and redesigned educational agendas. These are impacting on deracialized cultural forms of racism, the production of new ethnicities and the emergence of shifting subjectivities. It is important to examine the impact of these wider changes at a time of convergences across Europe between anti-racist and racist discourses around the new politics of cultural difference.

For Walters (1995: 1), just as postmodernism was *the* concept of the 1980s, globalization may be *the* concept of the 1990s. Social theorists emphasize the development of new information technologies, the rapid expansion of global networks of communication, and the emergence of complex global systems of production and exchange. The discourse of globalization in the 1980s may be read as a way of explaining socio-economic and cultural changes taking place in advanced capitalist societies in the post-war period.

At a general level, globalization may be understood as referring to the processes, procedures and technologies – economic, cultural and political –
underpinning the current 'time-space' compression which produces a sense of
immediacy and simultaneity about the world (Brah *et al.* 1999a). The effects
of globalization may be seen as: 'larger and larger numbers of people [living]
in circumstances in which disembedded institutions, linking local practices
with globalized social relations, organize major aspects of their day to day
life' (Giddens 1990: 79).

In a rapidly expanding literature, the different interpretations of globalization, which are inextricably linked with the movement of capital, labour,
commodities and cultural practices, can be located in a framework of materialist and differentialist positions. Materialist accounts have pointed out that
there is a long history to the increasingly global extent of the international
division of labour, new communications networks, technologies and financial
flows. During the 1970s, materialist-based world systems analysis, with its
focus on political economy, was of central importance in exploring changing
social divisions of the capitalist world economy (Wallerstein 1974; Amin 1980;
Robertson 1992). As Hoogvelt (1997: xiii), writing of this period, suggests:
'Within the Marxist structuralist tradition the evolving international state/
market nexus was analysed in terms of the dialectical development of capitalism in historical periods. Capitalism's inherent contradictions were said to
be worked out in different phases of expansion, punctuated by crises, in which
the state and interstate relations were time and again rearranged as political
structures that held in place the exploitative economic relationship between
core and peripheral economies.' Working in this framework, Sivanandan
(1989) has developed an analysis of what he calls 'new circuits of imperialism',
emphasizing that relations between the 'First' and 'Third' worlds are taking
place in the context of a global economy that is dominated by Western
multinationals and post-colonial powers. From a materialist position, current
culturalist accounts of globalization underplay Western and, more specifically,
American hegemonic power, which is setting the agenda on international
relations.

Silverman (1992: 89) has pointed out that in the 1970s the language of
'difference' and 'culture' became increasingly mobilized in the discussion of
social, economic and national questions, as well as questions of identity. A
differentialist position focusing on emerging forms of cultural hybridity among
transcultural communities and the proliferation of identities and difference,
has problematized that which sociology has taken as given, bounded, national
social formations. Cultural theorists are preoccupied with fundamental shifts
that have taken place in the direction of a global economy, with its associated,
internationally prevalent effects on patterns of lifestyles, consumption and
communication. As Carter *et al.* (1993: x) suggest, new social movements have
emerged from a 'redrawing of the boundaries – geographical, socio-symbolic,
psychic – of identity and community: and, in asserting the reality of cultural
differences and the affective investments they solicit, all have posed unmis-
takable challenges.' Hall (1991a: 33), writing from within a differentialist framework, describes two forms of globalization that are still struggling with one
another: 'an older, corporate, enclosed, increasingly defensive one which has

to go back to nationalism and national cultural identity in a highly defensive way, and to try to build barriers around it before it is eroded. And then this other form of the global post-modern which is trying to live with, and at the same moment, overcome, sublate, get hold of, and incorporate difference.'

One of the most visible effects of global changes on local urban sites is the collapse of regionally based manufacturing industries and expansion of the service sector, resulting in changing forms of incorporation, social division and spatial mobility of labour. The cumulative effects of the globalization of capital are generating new forms of consumer lifestyles. These cumulative effects include new patterns in the international division of labour, the changing nature of the nation-state and the associated crisis in Anglo-ethnicity, new labour processes and local labour markets, new educational and work technologies, increased state regulation of youth, advanced global communication systems and diverse family forms (Harvey 1989; Giddens 1990; Appaduri 1991; Jameson 1991). At the same time these changes have been accompanied by the feminization and racialization of poverty, the decline of class politics, including the contraction of the trade union movement, alongside the relative success of new social movements, such as feminism and anti-racism (Cockburn 1983; Phizacklea 1990). Post-Fordist accounts of recent occupational changes project increased social and economic polarization between professional elites and multi-skilled workers and a class of service workers employed in low-paid, part-time, non-unionized jobs (Allen 1992; Murray 1989). From a materialist position, differentialist accounts of globalization, with their focus on cultural shifts, are seen to underplay the continuing overrepresentation of minority ethnic communities within the latter occupational sector. In this view, current structurally based socio-economic changes are taking place that are very uneven in their effects on people's lives. For example, Taylor *et al.* (1996: 202), in their study of Sheffield and Manchester, question cultural theorists' preoccupation with the postmodern city that they claim has little to say about older industrial cities and the development of a highly marginalized underclass. They maintain that the new politics of cultural difference analysis with its specific culturalist understanding of globalizing reality is informed by: 'a degree of resignation with respect to the contemporary potential of reformist political or economic policies in individual "national societies"; but also with a pronounced lack of "empirical" interest in local voices, local utopias and local histories, in all of their specific and contested forms.' In contrast, Carter *et al.* (1993: ix), working in a new politics of cultural difference (differentialist) framework, argue that: 'Old divisions and loyalties based around class and geographical community may have been undermined by the globalization of markets, communications networks, networks of power and capital flows: but in their place – paradoxically both as a resistance to, and at the same time a product of those global forces – we see the development of new communities of interest and belief.' In turn, materialist theorists are more sceptical and pessimistic, particularly in relation to the emergence of communities of interest among new migrants, 'illegal' immigrants, asylum seekers and refugees, with the intensification of immigration controls and policy mechanisms across Europe (Sivanandan 1989).

Nation, state and racism

During the 1980s conceptualizations of the state were much debated from a wide range of sociological positions (Jessop 1982; Yuval-Davis and Anthias 1989). In contrast to this general sociological work on the state, the inter-relationship between racism and the state in Britain at this time was greatly undertheorized (Hickman 1995a). Solomos (1993: 2) locates this complex rela-tionship in a broader framework concerning the nature of racism in contem-porary capitalist societies, suggesting that in this context competing sociological approaches have failed to resolve two basic problems: first, the question of the relationship between racial and ethnic categorizations and economic and class determination; second, the role of the state and the political institutions of capitalist societies in the reproduction of capitalism, including the complex role of state intervention, with reference to controlling immigration, managing race relations and, more broadly, the integration of racial and ethnic group-ings into the wider society. From a different perspective, Bradley (1996: 37), in the context of her discussion of the limits of modernity and its accom-panying ideas derived from classical social theory of the nineteenth and early twentieth centuries, notes that Bauman (1992) considered the nation-state to be the spatial framework for classical sociology. She argues that: 'When discussing social divisions, those thinking in terms of nation states were drawn to consider internal divisions and inequalities (such as class and occupation) rather than external divisions and inequalities such as those of nation, ethnos and racial group. Any approach drawn from classical sociology is thus likely to privilege class as the most significant form of social division' (see Smith 1971, 1986). The legacy of this earlier history was still evident in the 1970s and early 1980s in British materialist analyses of racism.

By the end of the 1990s much appears to have changed. Ignatieff (1993: 2), in his study of Bosnia, *Blood and Belonging: Journeys into the New National-ism*, claimed that: 'The repressed has returned, and its name is nationalism.' In what Castles and Miller (1993: 2–3) call the age of migration, there is an increased interest in questions of the state, the nation and national identity. They describe how new forms of global migration and growing ethnic diversity are related to the fundamental socio-economic and political transformations of the post-Cold War epoch. Equally important, the media have popularized the emergence of ethno-nationalisms and ethnic cleansing. For du Gay (1996: 1), as identity has become a central theme in contemporary debates, 'the identity of the "modern-state" as an ostensibly "sovereign" entity has been put into question in the light of an intensification in patterns of global interconnectedness'. Hay (1996: 9) provides a rounded picture of the 'mod-ern' state, which helps make sense of the conflicting logic of a progressively integrating world market alongside the continuing central significance of new nation-states. He usefully distinguishes between three moments of stateness which he argues have tended to be elided in much state theory. First, the state as nation, that is as an 'imagined' national community. Second, the state as territory, that is as a strictly bounded sovereign terrain. Third, the state as institution, that is as a set of apparatuses and practices unified through some form of centralized co-ordination. There is a need to hold on to these closely interrelated, different meanings of the state in exploring issues of nation, nationalism, ethnic belonging and racialized exclusions. This is of particular importance, as a central limitation in earlier materialist representations was the conflation of nation and state. For Anthias and Yuval-Davis (1993: 22):

> Theorising the state, as a separate sphere both from the 'nation' and the 'civil society', is vital for any adequate analysis of nationalism and racism. Theoretical perspectives that have expanded the domain of the state to include all major ideological apparatuses, or have dispensed with the category of the state as a meaningful analytical category altogether, cannot explain struggles and differential power access of different ethnic collectivities (as well as other groupings in civil society) to it.

By the late 1990s, in exploring how the relationship between the state and the nation is organized around 'fictive ethnicities' (Balibar and Wallerstein 1991) and racialized conceptions of national identity, differentialist accounts drawing on Foucault (1977) have understood the state in a desegregated way as a complex of discourses and practices infused with power relations that are not located in one place but that are suffused throughout social formations (Westwood 1996). However, there are limitations in conceptions of a non-unitary state that focus on the diffusion of power and power-knowledges. One such limitation is that of underplaying the cumulative effect of the wide range of discourses in different state agencies that impose racial, ethnic and national divisions in the society. These limitations have been made clear in recent research on sexual politics. As Ballard (1992: 106) points out in his paper 'Sexuality and the state in time of epidemic', in which he argues for a non-determinative approach:

> the state has a prominent role both through law, which reifies dominant social values by their enforcement through the coercive apparatus of the state, and through the services and controls of the welfare state. The modes of state influence lie first, in labelling categories; second, in explicitly and implicitly encouraging or disencouraging identities and behaviour; and third, in effectively institutionalising various forms of discourse and practice.

More specifically, with reference to racism and ethnicity, for example, in terms of constructing national identity, the state with its apparatus of enforcement at its command sets the legal limits of nationality and citizenship, defining who is 'national' and who is 'alien' (Gilroy 1987; Yuval-Davis and Anthias 1989; Westwood 1996). In other words, there is a need to acknowledge the power of the racialized state and its central functions of racial regulation and order, to produce categories of inclusion and exclusion (Wallerstein 1974; Amin 1980). Traditional legislative categories have included the early twentieth-century 'Jewish alien' and the post-war 'New Commonwealth immigrant' and, more recently, 'the ethnic minority'. HIV/AIDS activism made an important contribution at a conceptual and political level in its rethinking of the nature of the state, 'maintaining a complex view of [it] as both process and institutional apparatus, with various levels and sectors of state action producing conflicting rationalities' (Connell 1990). From this position, as was illustrated in the organized oppositional response to Section 28 (Section 28 of the 1988 Local Government Act prohibits the 'promotion of homosexuality' by organizations funded by local authorities), attempts to control and repress sexuality produced the opposite effects. In arguing that the state is a complex nexus of institutional arrangements involving ideological, juridical and repressive mechanisms, race can be understood as 'occupying varying degrees of centrality in different state institutions and at different historical moments' (Omi and Winant 1986: 77). In exploring the state and racism there is a need to hold on to the complex interaction between state ideologies, institutionally based cultural representations and ethnic and national subject positions.

In turn, this opens up the question of political interventions, which is increasingly important when contemporary homogenizing technologies of state power associated with processes of Western globalization, modernization and collective consumption are represented as overly determining 'local' national responses. There is a tendency in much globalization theory to underplay the role of the state in reproducing national and ethnic ideologies and boundaries. It is suggested that recent developments have the effect of dramatically weakening the role of the nation-state. That is to say that supranational cartels, organizations and agencies of governance – for example, transnational companies, the European Union, the North American Free Trade Association, the International Monetary Fund, the World Bank – are likely to assume an increasingly central position in relation to the running of the world economy, and this is making a profound impact on social and cultural relations at the local level (Brah *et al.* 1999a). Hirst and Thompson (1996: 7) challenge this view, maintaining that what we are facing is much more a 'conjunctural change toward greater international trade and investment within an existing set of economic relations' as opposed to 'the development of a new economic structure'.

Building the (Great) British nation: social inclusions and exclusions

Smith (1993: 71), discussing the relationship between immigration and nation-building, argues that 'at a time of unprecedented global mobility, spatial boundaries may no longer be significant for what they physically contain, but they are increasingly important for who they symbolically exclude'. Despite the introduction of increasingly stricter immigration control, especially in the receiving countries of the Northern hemisphere, the scale and the velocity of the migration of people across international borders have increased dramatically in the past thirty years (Ahmad 1992; Castles and Miller 1993), with women migrants a significant proportion of these late twentieth-century population movements (Brah *et al.* 1999a). Appadurai (1991: 191–2) captures this 'new times' of shifting social collectivities in contemporary global reconfigurations that has varied forms of migration at its centre. He writes:

The landscapes of group identity – the ethnoscapes – around the world are no longer familiar anthropological objects, insofar as groups are no longer tightly territorialized, spatially bounded, historically unselfconscious, or culturally homogeneous. . . . By Ethnoscape, I mean the landscape of persons who make up the shifting world in which we live: tourists, immigrants, refugees, exiles, guestworkers, and other moving groups and persons constitute an essential feature of the world and appear to affect the politics of and between nations to a hitherto unprecedented degree. This is not to say that nowhere are there relatively stable communities and networks of kinship, friendship, work, and leisure, as well as of birth, residence and other filiative forms. But it is to say that the warp of these stabilities is everywhere shot through with the woof of human emotion, as more persons and groups deal with the realities of having to move or the fantasies of wanting to move.

However, globalization theorists, with their focus on the opening up of global markets, communication networks and capital flows, have tended to underplay the differentiated spatial mobility experienced by specific social groups as nation-states reproduce racial boundaries against both established ethnic minorities and new migrants. This is most visibly displayed in constructions of Fortress Europe. As Hirst and Thompson (1996: 31) argue, poor labour migrants are facing increasing restrictions. They maintain that:

The supposed era of globalization has not seen the rise of a new unregulated and internationalized market in labour migration. In many ways, for the world's underprivileged and poor there are fewer international migratory options nowadays than there were in the past. At least in the period of mass migration there was the option to uproot the whole family and move in the quest for better conditions, something that now seems to be rapidly closing off for present-day equivalent sections of the world's population. They have little option but to remain in poverty and stick it out.

In a British context researchers have clearly demonstrated the long history of the effects of British immigration legislation on racial and sexual exclusions (Holmes 1988; Layton-Henry 1992; Saggar 1992; Solomos 1993; Hickman 1995b; Brah 1996). Both the Conservative and Labour governments have been equally implicated in the introduction and maintenance of immigration legislation from the Commonwealth Immigration Acts of 1962, 1968, 1971, and the Prevention of Terrorism Act 1974; through the Nationality Act of 1981; to the Carrier's Liability Act of 1987 and the Asylum and Immigration Act of 1996 (see Brah *et al.* 1999a). As Mason (1995: 109) argues, 'although this was never expressed formally, the principal intention of immigration controls introduced since 1962 onwards was increasingly to exclude potential migrants who were not white'. Hence, although there are real limitations imposed on our understanding of racial difference and the wide range of ethnic diversity in Britain, resulting from the dominant black–white dualistic model that elides race, ethnicity and skin colour, this long history of racist exclusion and its accompanying ideological positioning of black

British citizens as 'outsiders' begins to justify its appeal. As Anthias and Yuval-Davis (1993: 51) have pointed out, in the shift beyond the 'colonial paradigm' that has informed immigration legislation in the post-war period:

> The introduction of the nationality Law, the increased limitations on new immigration, the growing percentage of blacks born in the UK and the greater importance of the European Community have all changed the principles of construction of these national boundaries. As before, this has been reflected in the changing categories of official statistics. The category of NCWP [New Commonwealth Countries and Pakistan] has disappeared and instead the statistics become more focused upon the division between White and non-Whites, as in the LFS [Labour Force Survey] data and the 1991 census . . . Racial boundaries rather than imperial boundaries have come, then, to be significant markers of national rights in Britain today . . . it does construct the official boundaries, and indeed the new official statistics, in terms of race and colour.

The nation-state: the self-production of a national community

Anti-essentialist understandings of national identity have been made popular by a number of commentators, including Anderson (1983), Hobsbawm (1983) and Gellner (1983), who have argued that the nation as an ideological construct of modernity is an 'imaginary community', an 'invention'. Post-colonial writers such as Bhabha (1990a) have developed this further. Employing a discursive approach to national identity he suggests that the nation is studied through its narrative address. This argument is developed within a long history of British social theorists who have spoken of the ambivalence of nationalism as 'Janus-faced' (Nairn 1977; Giddens 1985; Bhabha 1990a; Billig 1995). For example, Nairn (1977: 31) has contrasted positive forms of nationalism among movements for national liberation from colonialism, with negative forms that include European Fascist movements. Sociological accounts of nation and nationalism have highlighted the links between nationalism and racism in the development of a British nationalism in the post-war era as an exclusionary force to deny black British people a national identity and citizenship rights (Gilroy 1987; Solomos 1993). For example, Anthias and Yuval-Davis (1993: 40), positioning themselves against Anderson's (1983) argument that nationalism and racism are distinct, align themselves with other critics of British nationalism, such as Sivanandan (1982), Miles (1982), Gilroy (1987) and Cohen (1988), arguing that 'racism is an inherent part of the hegemonic Anglomorphic ethnicity in Britain'. They claim that defining elements of this link are the exclusionary and inclusionary assumptions in the construction of British nationality. Miles (1993, 1994a) has developed a more historical comparative approach in exploring nationalism and racism within Britain.

Following the emergence of what was called new racism in the late 1970s that originated in a British social and political crisis, the 1980s witnessed a 'renewed emphasis on a unified and unitary British national culture' (Mason 1995: 114). At this time the ascendant New Right political agenda occupied the moral high ground with its projected atavistic representations of a consumer-based acquisitive individualism, the patriarchal family, the strong state and a patriotic British nation (Layton-Henry 1992; Saggar 1992). As Gordon and Klug (1986: 11) have pointed out, the emergence of social authoritarians' discourses converged around the issues of race and sexuality. They maintained that: 'there is clearly an overlap in ideology which opposes black immigration on the grounds that white Britain could be swamped and one that advocates measures to strengthen the British family, both physically and ideologically, on the grounds that the moral integrity of the nation is at risk.' Gilroy (1987: 45–56) argued for the need to recognize how the languages of race and nation are articulated together. More specifically, he illustrated the power of cultural forms of racism in the 1980s in which Englishness and blackness were reproduced as mutually exclusive categories. More recently, in pointing to new emphases in racist ideologies, Bonnett (1993) suggests the emergence of new questions with reference to nation and belonging. He maintains that, 'the "racial" problematic of "why are they incompatible with us?" has been combined or replaced with "what is it to be a member of a racial minority and British?" and "what positive and negative attributes do they possess that make them less or more like us?"' (Bonnett 1993: 25). He adds: 'The second of the two newly emphasised problematics within contemporary rejectionism turns on the question "What is it to be a member of a racial minority and be British?"' (Bonnett 1993: 27).

Gilroy and Bonnett's analytical frameworks, drawing on the concept of new racism, are representative of the way in which the impact of, and responses to, post-war migration of Asians and African Caribbeans have come to be understood across the political spectrum. Such analyses are part of a wider differentialist explanation that overemphasizes an ascribed 'newness' to the emergence of New Right discourses in the 1970s and 1980s, in defining who belonged to the national community. They share a central weakness of a differentialist position; that of its ahistorical approach, which fails to address earlier migrations to Britain and other European societies. Materialist accounts of immigration make a perfunctory claim of the need to explore a wide range of migrations before returning to the main object of their analysis, that of post-war black migration. For example, Solomos (1993: 52) writes: 'Of course migrants from a variety of racial and ethnic backgrounds have con-tinued to arrive and settle in Britain, and it is important in any rounded account to look at their experiences also. For the purposes of this study, however, we shall concentrate on the politics of black immigration and settlement since 1945.' A remarkable absence in materialist and differentialist accounts is that the experiences of the Jews and the Irish are not seen as of central significance to understanding the formation of the British nation-state and the political specificities of British nationalism. As Hickman (1995a: 5) has persuasively argued, an analysis of anti-Irish racism and the experience of the Irish in Britain is particularly pertinent for tracing the historical development of a racist British nationalism. She draws on the work of Balibar (1991c), who argues that: 'in France the sharpest edge of racist discourse tends to press on populations of "Arab-Islamic" origin because a condensation or superimposition of the colonial and anti-Semitic schemas has occurred so that the imagery of cultural and religious rivalry reinforce each other.' Hickman suggests a similar argument with reference to the social position of the Irish in Britain. She maintains that: 'both the colonial racism stemming from Anglo-Irish relations and the construction of the Irish (Catholic) as a historically significant Other of the English/British (Protestant) have framed the experience of the Irish in Britain. Historically, anti-Irish racism in Britain has comprised both elements of racism . . . that is, the Irish have been constructed as inferior and, in the articulation of racist discourse with anti-Catholicism, the Irish have been constructed as alien' (Hickman 1995a: 5). She uses this socio-historical explanation of the social position of the Irish in Britain to illustrate a broader argument that challenges the new racism thesis.

Hickman makes a major intervention into contemporary debates in the sociology of racism and ethnicity with her claim that the race-relations problematic, anti-racism and differentialism are seriously flawed in working with a shared assumption of a myth of cultural homogeneity prior to the 1950s. Furthermore, this dominant sociological conception of racism converges with the way in which the state, organized far right racist groups and popular forms of racism construct the 'problem' of immigrants and who legitimately belongs to the national collectivity. Hickman suggests that the political pervasiveness of this cultural myth reflects a major limitation of British sociology of racism and ethnicity: that of the disconnection from questions of nation, nationalism and migration. She maintains that the absence of migration reflects a hegemonic assumption that Britain evolved as a nation-state without any large-scale, inward migration of people. In fact, as she points out, Britain, as a leading capitalist country, has a long history of migration in response to the ever-changing demands of capital for labour. More specifically, she argues that: 'The tension between the tendency of capitalism to develop the nation state and national cultures and its tendency from its inception to be based upon antagonistic differences based on "racial", tribal, gender, linguistic and regional particularities explains the generation of some of the differences between groups of people' (Hickman 1995a: 6). Here we see how the differentialist preoccupation with culture has served to erase the central question of how the modern state has to mobilize 'national' ideology. A particular weakness of sociologists who argue for a new racism is that they concentrate too much on one source, that of New Right political commentators, while underplaying the ideological infrastructure of the state, with its apparatus of enforcement at its command in defining who is 'national' and who is 'alien'.

Locating her work in a European tradition, Hickman develops her analysis of the myth of cultural homogeneity which assumes the assimilation of earlier immigrants – particularly from Ireland – to Britain (Balibar and Wallerstein 1991; Silverman 1992). Her analysis illustrates the rather narrow quantitative approach of much British sociology of racism and ethnicity. In contrast, European theorists, placing migration theory at the centre of their analysis, have developed broader debates around the issue of immigration as a key cultural code in the making of the nation and nationalism (Noiriel 1988; Balibar and Wallerstein 1991; Silverman 1991, 1992). For example, Balibar (1991d: 222) has spoken of how: 'we thus discover, for our part, that in present day France, "immigration" has become, *par excellence*, the name of race, a new name, but one that is functionally equivalent to the old appellation, just as the term "immigrant" is the chief characteristic which enables individuals to be classified in a racist typology.' Hickman explores the work of Silverman (1992), who argues that the reverse of the problem of immigration is the myth of assimilation. In France a mythical idea has been developed that assimilation was a constant reality until the new immigration of north Africans, which brought with it to France the alien phenomena of ghettos and ethnic concentrations. For Silverman, this concept of assimilation masks a process of racialization. He locates the development of the myth of assimilation in the context of post-war phenomena: the globalization of capital and the end of the high period of colonial expansion, maintaining that assimilation functions as a 'retrospective illusion' and as a post-war myth (Silverman 1992: 104). He explores how this redefinition of past and present immigration is a central element in the current racialization of immigration and wider socio-economic and political questions (Silverman 1992: 95). In turn this has had major disorientating effects on anti-racist movements.

Referring to the work of the historian Noiriel (1990), who has suggested that ideas of assimilation, uniformity and universality have been crucial in France for masking ethnic, regional and other differences, Hickman asks: what discourses and practices of the British state have masked the internal ethnic, regional and national differences that characterize the United Kingdom? She argues that the construction of a narrative of homogeneity around whiteness has obscured the full recognition of historical and contemporary forms of racialized exclusions. She points to the need to go beyond the black–white dualistic model – the paradigm of colour – to deconstruct whiteness. In this process we will be able to examine the experience of the Irish in Britain in the context of the problem of constructing the nation that is not reducible to colour as the only signifier of exclusion/inclusion. She refers to Balibar's (1991b) claim that every nation-state is faced with the problem of how to make the people produce themselves continually as a national community. As she points out:

> It has therefore been a main function of national cultures to represent what is in fact the ethnic mix of modern nationality as the primordial unity of 'one people'. This has been achieved by centralized nation-states with their incorporating cultures and national identities, implanting and securing strong cultural institutions, which tend to subsume all differences and diversity into themselves.
>
> (Hickman 1995a: 7)

Hickman's socio-historical approach is a necessary reminder to contemporary sociologists, particularly when postmodernists insist on the newness of cultural phenomena, that a more rounded analysis of the current dynamics of racial politics demands a rigorous investigation of historical continuities alongside structural discontinuities. In other words, the myth of British cultural homogeneity prior to the 1950s is premised on historical amnesia among sociologists (Kearney 1990).

Shifting boundaries of the British national collectivity

Much of the sociological work in this area seems to share an assumption that nationalism is a homogeneous ideology. With reference to the changing political dynamics of the British national collectivity, there is a need to highlight the complex interconnections between different social divisions and subject positions that are currently marked by 'differences of class, place of birth, ethnic origin, religion, political beliefs, gender and other factors [that] radically affect the specific kinds of collectivity ideologies different segments of the British population hold and the ways they construct their boundaries' (Anthias and Yuval-Davis 1993: 41–2). As Anthias and Yuval-Davis (1993: 41) argue:

> Exclusionary and racist ideologies were (historically) used . . . as the basis of legitimizing the domination and exploitation of other collectivities by the British empire; at 'home' ('the lower orders'); 'close to home' (racism against the Celts – especially the Irish) and then further afield, against what is known today as the Third World, that which constituted most of the British empire.

Historically, this assumed homogeneity of nationalism has contributed to the confusions and contradictions that surround the elision of Britishness and Englishness, at both a theoretical and popular level. These confusions and contradictions have been, and continue to be, differentially experienced by the English positioned at the centre and those who exist at what is referred to as the 'Celtic Fringe' in the British state (Hechter 1975; Hickman 1995a; Kiberd 1996). Presently one of the most dynamic political impacts on the changing boundaries of the British nation-state is the challenge to the configuration of the UK, involving the development of a new settlement between Britain and Northern Ireland, and the establishment of a Scottish parliament and a Welsh assembly. Recent theoretical and empirical work has begun to explore ethnic majorities, including questions of whiteness, and the contingent contestations that underpin Britishness and 'sub-national' identities that constitute the hierarchical relationship that is the UK (Brah *et al.* 1999a and b). Emerging out of this work is a focus on the Anglo-ethnic majority as a main object of inquiry. This needs to become a central area of interest for British sociology of racism and ethnicity in current conditions of 'post-colonialism'. Hall (1991b: 22) argues that one of the best-kept secrets of the world is that Englishness, represented as a stable, homogeneous, and unitary category, is not that in relation to its own territory:

> It was only by dint of excluding or absorbing all the differences that constituted Englishness, the multitude of different regions, peoples, classes, genders that composed the people gathered together in the Act of Union, that Englishness could stand for everybody in the British Isles. And that is something we are only beginning to see the true nature of, when we are beginning to come to the end of it.

As Hickman (1995a: 3) suggests, this process has never been a secret for many Welsh, Scottish and Irish people living in Britain and Ireland. However, for much of the history of the field of inquiry it has remained hidden from the ethnic majority, including most English sociologists who maintain a sense of cultural indeterminacy about their own Anglo-ethnic status which serves to protect it from critical investigation (see Samuel 1989).

Social positioning in relation to dominant ideological forms of British nationalism also needs to address the effect of location on a sense of national and regional belonging and the relation between the two. Most particularly, the past twenty years have witnessed the development of a strong British state and the weakening of civil society. This has included reducing the power of local government, the decline of trade unions and a systematic derision of public institutions by central government and a powerful tabloid press alongside attempts to remove the gains of new social movements, such as those of feminism and anti-racism. Of particular significance was the Conservative government's attempts to remove political mobilization against the state. During the 1980s, Irish nationalists, blacks, women's groups, trade unionists and church officials were all represented as part of the 'enemy within'. This New Right project has had very different effects on different regions of the country, including reinforcing a 'rich' South–'poor' North divide in the United Kingdom. Of specific material and symbolic significance has been the juxtaposed portrayal of the ascendancy of 'The City' (London) and the rapid decline of the 'overindustrialized' North, large regions of which have experienced severe feelings of social dislocation, cultural exclusion and spatial immobility at a time when there is much political rhetoric of building 'a new Britain at the heart of Europe'. Central to these 'new times' is the state's recomposition of the working class, some of whom are experiencing a second and third generation without work. New exclusionary state practices in regulating and overdisciplining this section of the population are reproducing such social groups as 'outside' the nation-state. As outlined in Chapter 1, in revisiting the relationship of the politics of race and social class at the beginning of the twenty-first century, these highly alienated social groups need to be at the centre of sociological inquiry.

Race, nation and racism – place, space and time

The histories and geographies of social closure and cultural exclusion are defining elements of the politics of race and nation. Earlier materialist theorists acknowledged the significance of spatial and temporal dimensions in their accounts of racism. For example, issues such as territory, neighbourhood and belonging are attributed importance in explaining the micro-politics of local places. The racialization of place and time has a long history, including the nineteenth-century experiences of the Jewish diaspora, migration of the Irish, post-war New Commonwealth migration and in the 1970s and 1980s, minority communities' residence in urban spaces. A continuing feature of nationalist discourse has been an imagined 'golden age' before the Jews, the Irish and the blacks 'took over our area', illustrating the way in which memory plays a key role in processes of racialization (Cohen 1988, 1993). Earlier anti-racist studies argued that place-specific localities were of major significance in the racialization of British politics, from the Notting Hill riots of 1958 to the Brixton, Handsworth, Toxteth and Moss Side 'riots' that occurred between 1981 and 1985. Similarly, high-profile media accounts of the New Right's demonization of 'black muggers' and 'Muslim fundamentalists' have cata-logued the 'multicultural colonization' of Britain's inner-city spaces, such as Brent, Bradford, Dewsbury, Manchester and St. Paul's, Bristol.

Materialist-based anti-racist accounts have concentrated on the social reproduction of racism and have tended to provide unidimensional under-standings of place that underplay intersubjective dynamics and the complex-ity of local productions of racial, ethnic and national identities (Billig 1995). In these explanations, the conceptualization of place provides little sense of an active, historically contingent process, which represents a multilayered lived context combining doing (social action) and being (identity resource). Solomos and Back (1995: 40) have described the diverse ways in which dis-courses of race are contextualized and situated in specific localities. As they maintain: 'notions of race and ethnicity intertwine with myths of territory, locality, neighbourhood and identity to produce mythologies about the role of spatially defined "others"'. There is a need here for empirical work that investigates the specificities of inter-ethnic interactions. For example, inner cities in large conurbations are often occupied by both an older, white British working-class population and a younger generation of minority ethnic com-munities. Anti-racist theorists have tended to concentrate too much on the social positioning of minorities and to underconceptualize the responses of the white Anglo-ethnic majority, whose behaviour it is assumed can be read off from the oppositional binary structure of a black–white dualism in which 'whiteness' speaks power and 'blackness' speaks powerlessness. Anti-racist texts have often presented the interaction between such social collectivities as a simple story of a racist older white generation drawing on the legacy of imperial images and local understandings of racism. Such representations fail to capture the complex articulation between and within different sets of social relations and divisions, and the associated complex tensions and alliances in local neighbourhoods. A further limitation in these accounts is the failure to address the constitutive dynamics of subjectivity in relation to a sense of local belonging in the context of a plurality of differences. In short, a real sense of the local political players and the messiness and unpredictability of political life is missing. The search for a new settlement among the different political traditions in Northern Ireland is a useful reminder of the complexity of developing a way forward that combines community differences that are circumscribed by complex social relations of domination and subordination that need to be worked out at the local level of neighbourhoods, as well as at local and central government levels.

A way forward for sociology is to make geographies and histories of contemporary racisms, ethnicities and nationalisms more systematic and rigorous by engaging with social and cultural theory that is currently being developed from a multidisciplinary base (Harvey 1989; Soja 1989; Jameson 1991; Lefebvre 1991; Carter *et al.* 1993; Massey 1994). Jackson and Penrose

(1993a), drawing on such work, have brought together an edited collection on *Constructions of Race, Place and Nation*. In it, they argue that:

> By demonstrating the existence of a plurality of place-specific ideologies of race and nation rather than a monolithic, historically singular and geographically invariant racism or nationalism, the constructedness of place is revealed through its capacity to be moulded according to the dictates of particular racisms and nationalisms ... particular notions of 'race' and nation are articulated by different groups of people at different times and at different spatial scales, from the global to the local.
>
> (Jackson and Penrose 1993b: 12–13)

Importantly, they add that in each case the idea of race or nation is part of a broader set of ideologies and social practices. Recent sociological studies, drawing on differentialist representations of racism, marked by ambivalence, contingency and contradictions, have placed temporal and spatial issues at the centre of their work (Westwood 1990; Keith 1993; Back 1996).

One of the main limitations of more recent sociological work is that it remains in an anti-racist framework underpinned by a black–white dualistic model. Hence, the increased interest among contemporary social scientists in place and time has been highly selective. This has been illustrated recently in Solomos and Back's (1995) study *Race, Politics and Social Change*. In a review of the book, Cashmore (1996: 136) writes: 'Its context is that happy hunting ground for race researchers, Birmingham. Rex and Moore reported on the devilry afoot in the 1960s with their *Race, Community and Conflict*. In the 1980s, I set my tape recorder to work with Birmingham residents to try to unravel the logic of racism. Now [in 1996] Solomos and Back return to the scene to explore, in their words, "the political ideas and values of politicians and activists about race".' As Cashmore points out, their empirical research was carried out in the city of Birmingham. However, the city's largest ethnic minority group, the Irish, are absent from the text. More specifically, Solomos and Back have excluded the specificity of place indicated in the high-profile campaigns mobilized by the Irish community in Britain around the imprisonment of the Birmingham Six and the Guildford Four. This absence is an example of the process of 'over-racializing' particular black ethnic groups and their areas of residence, while 'de-racializing' the location of white ethnic minorities in the British nation-state. In this way, sociologists have reinforced the invisibility of state criminalization of the Irish community in Britain as a key process of contemporary racialization. In contrast to most of the academic work in and on Britain, Anderson (1993: 96), with reference to state responses to minority groups, moves beyond the black–white dualistic model in her account of the multiplicity of constructions of one of Australia's Aboriginal settlements. She explains that:

> Australia's indigenous peoples have been defined within a racialized universe that for two hundred years has facilitated their dispossession and legitimated their specialized treatment by the state and its agents. The nature of relations has differed considerably by region, just as they have prompted variable modes of accommodation, adaptation and

resistance on the part of the Aborigines. This unevenness of Aboriginal oppression and resistance points to the need for further place-specific studies in the historical geography of colonialism and postcolonialism, studies that would get past reiterating a universal black/white alterity and seek to contribute to a more regionally sensitive fund of knowledge.

Citizenship, identity and the politics of cultural difference

If globalization was the concept of the 1990s at an international level, citizenship was the 'big idea for the 1990s' at a national level (Taylor 1991). Government Citizens' Charters have reconstituted the citizen as being primarily a consumer with particular rights in the sphere of collective consumption. As Mason (1995: 115) argues: 'By contrast with the stridently nationalist conception of British citizenship which was openly promoted in the 1980s, by the 1990s all political parties were offering rather different and, they argued, enhanced conceptions of citizenship. The emphasis . . . was upon citizenship as an expression of the contract between an enabling state and individuals who were free to choose and direct their own destinies.'

Until recently, academic debates on the meaning of citizenship were much influenced by Marshall's (1950) theoretical framework in terms of the progressive attainment of universal standards. He suggested a number of categories of citizenship; those of civil, political and social rights, the attainment of which ensured full membership in the national political community. As indicated by the title of Marshall's earlier work, *Citizenship and Social Class*, the primary focus of this evolutionary model was the gradual incorporation of previously excluded social classes (Mason 1995). Presently, both the concepts of citizenship and national identity are highly contested (Parekh 1991; Turner 1993). For example, Parekh (1995: 255) argues that: 'National identity is not a substance but a cluster of tendencies and values, that it is neither fixed nor alterable at will, and that it needs to be periodically redefined in the light of historically inherited characteristics, present needs and future aspirations.' Of strategic significance here has been new social movements that have illustrated the limitations of class reductionist accounts that underplay the wide range of identities that both differentially position and are taken up by social collectivities in relation to the rights and duties of citizenship. Feminist research has been important in highlighting the limits of earlier analysis on citizenship and the politics that it informed for the lives of women within public spaces and their participation in the body politic (Yuval-Davis and Anthias 1989; Walby 1994).

As Hall and Held (1989) argue, discourses on race, nationality and immigration have provided the most dynamic arena in which contemporary conceptions of British citizenship have been discussed. Anti-racist analysis in the 1970s and early 1980s successfully established that there was a 'different reality' experienced by black British citizens. Marshall's work assumes that in the nation-state there is an overlap between membership of the national collectivity and citizenship of the state (Anthias and Yuval-Davis 1993: 30). A main site for anti-racist mobilizations, as pointed out above, has been immigration legislation and political discourses of exclusion that serve to question the legitimacy of black minorities' claim to British citizenship. Alongside the black communities' struggle against racial barriers imposed by immigration controls and nationality laws, they have experienced various forms of institutionalized racism that have denied them equal access to the rights and benefits that citizenship confers on members of the national collectivity. Another major issue raised by anti-racist research and community activism has been the question of representation of ethnic minorities in the political process. For example, a number of studies have shown that blacks are underrepresented at national and local levels of government. More recent work has provided 'evidence of growing involvement and interest in institutions of mainstream politics and attempts to gain access to political representation' (Solomos and Back 1995: 208).

Debates in Britain around black people's belonging to the nation have been constructed in terms of an assimilationist view of citizenship which demands cultural conformity in exchange for conferment of citizenship against a multicultural position that maintains that cultural distinctiveness is a necessary condition of developing civil, political and social rights (Mitchell and Russell 1994: 138). By the late 1990s these debates, although unresolved, appear somewhat limited and dated. As Solomos and Back (1995: 210), in the context of the globalization of patterns of migration, argue: 'In a context in which patterns of migration, settlement and the development of ethnic communities have substantially transformed the social and political structures of these societies [West European], the meaning of citizenship and national identity is being rapidly transformed.' In the past, much sociological literature focused on the failure of central government to 'grant' citizenship *from above* (Turner 1990). Presently, a major issue across European societies is the mobilization of ethnic minorities, particularly around demands for conceptions of equality that allow the expression of cultural and religious identities (Balibar and Wallerstein 1991; Brubacker 1992; Campani 1993). In a British context this self-organization has been represented by anti-racists as a form of regressive fundamentalism. From a broader political perspective, Yuval-Davis (1992: 280) has argued that: 'The rise of fundamentalism is linked to the crisis of modernity, to a general sense of despair and disorientation, in which there is no clear moral order.' In this context, the Anglo-ethnic majority's discontents are displaced on to ethnic minorities and, more specifically at the present time, on to the 'demonized' Muslim community. An alternative reading of the development of ethnically or religious-based organizations is to see them as a continuation of the long history of the black community's struggle to 'win' a sense of citizenship *from below*. Nevertheless, a major argument remains for a more inclusive conception of citizenship as the new politics of cultural difference engages with the increase in essentialist and absolutist conceptions of ethnic difference in racialized communities.

For Hall and Held (1989: 176), a contemporary politics of citizenship has to come to terms with the challenge posed by 'difference', for example in 'the diverse communities to which we belong, the complex interplay of identity and identification in modern society and the differentiated ways in which people now participate in social life'. They argue that the 'diversity of

arenas in which citizenship is being claimed and contested today is essential
to any modern conception of it because it is the very logic of modern society
itself'. Mercer and Julien (1988: 97) capture this more complex cultural form
of politics in their discussion of the positive political significance of inner-
city riots in opposition to the 1980s Tory hegemony:

> For us, 1981 was a profoundly empowering moment, mobilising ener-
> gies and abilities to challenge our conditions of existence. The feeling
> of empowerment came from the collective identity we constructed for
> ourselves as black gay men, enabling us to overcome the marginality
> we experienced as black people and the individual isolation we felt as
> gay people. Politics is about making connections practically, with the
> forming of alliances between different social groups, and at a cognitive
> level with the recognition of diverse categories of race, class, gender,
> ethnicity and sexuality in articulation of power relations. The gay black
> group enabled us to start a conversation between ourselves, making
> connections between patterns of our common experiences to recognise
> the structures responsible for the specificity of the oppression in the
> first place.

As illustrated above in contemporary discussions conceptualizing modern forms of British citizenship, the social and political position of established
ethnic minority communities has been a highly dynamic arena. The experiences of these racialized groups across Europe in terms of social closure,
political exclusion and spatial immobility are of high symbolic significance
in testing nation-states' collective self-image as modern democracies. By the
end of the twentieth century a restructured Europe sees new political developments, divisions and realignments that have produced the emergence of
other racialized social groups, such as new migrants, 'illegal' immigrants and
asylum seekers, who are currently at major risk because of their lack of civil
rights and hence their inability to organize politically (Sivanandan 1990c).
As Anthias and Yuval-Davis (1993: 152–3) have argued:

> Migrant workers and refugees from Third-World countries in Britain
> have no settlement rights, are vulnerable to being declared illegal im-
> migrants and being deported, and are therefore exploited economically
> and harassed in very similar ways to 'guest workers' in other European
> countries. The move towards a Single European Act in 1992 and the
> removal of movement restrictions among the members of the European
> Community is going to intensify even more the process of polarization
> between those who are settled and have legal rights in Britain and
> therefore in Europe, and those who are going to continue to be under
> continuous threat of harassment and deportation. And the division
> between those two categories of people is not necessarily going to be a
> colour line.

As demands increase for the harmonization of more stringent immigration and asylum policies across Europe, difficult issues remain for reconcep-
tualizing notions of inclusive citizenship. As Silverman (1992: 2) argues, in
the context of European integration and the need for anti-racist movements

and movements for human rights to think differently about rights, it seems that it is easier to harmonize controls than it is to harmonize rights. He suggests that in order to develop effective international co-operation between anti-racist movements, there is a need to explore the different national models within which rights have been historically formulated, which act as barriers to harmonization today. This is particularly difficult at a time of increasing social dislocation for large sections of indigenous populations in de-industrializing societies and an accompanying identity crisis in ethnic majority groups. The growing political influence of far right racist movements and, more specifically, the disorientating impact on anti-racist mobilizations of the way, for example, the Front National in France has used New Right discourse to deny its racist and Fascist core adds to the urgency of understanding the changing dynamics of racialized political processes in modern societies (Lloyd 1994). These issues are further examined in the next chapter in exploring the crisis of anti-racism, and ethnic minority mobilization at local and national levels.

Part **III**

'COMING TIMES': *the* STRUGGLE *for* RACIAL EQUALITY *and* ETHNIC MINORITY MOBILIZATIONS

5 Anti-racism *and* ethnic minority community mobilization

Representing racial difference: multiculturalism, anti-racism and the new politics of cultural difference

Chapter 5 critically explores the politics of anti-racism and ethnic minority mobilizations. Until recently in Britain, multiculturalism and anti-racism provided the main arena for those on the political left in which questions of racism, ethnicity and cultural difference were debated. As suggested in earlier chapters, a key element of anti-racism was to define itself against what was seen as multiculturalism's politically divisive focus on ethnic difference. Currently, the new politics of cultural difference (differentialism) is challenging anti-racism, claiming that it has underplayed the significance of culture, while at the same time highlighting anti-racism's cultural essentialism. It is pointed out that anti-racists' dismissal of ethnicity on the grounds that it underplays racist power relations was conflated with the denial of what is a critical, lived category for minorities. There is a danger that what became a limited debate between multiculturalists and anti-racists is being displaced by an equally limiting debate between essentialist and anti-essentialist accounts. A main argument of this chapter is that, in exploring contemporary social and cultural transformations, the new politics of cultural difference does not have to be seen as displacing an earlier anti-racist politics. Rather, the politics of difference as part of 'new times' provides an opportunity to re-read 'old times' in a way that strategically enables us to rethink the underconceptualization of British anti-racism. More specifically, it is suggested that the new politics of cultural difference, in making problematic the grand narratives of political-economic analyses of racism do not have to result in questions of representation, culture and difference erasing the 'big questions' around social reproduction, state regulation and institutionalized-based exclusions. As Rattansi (1992: 41) reminds us: 'Political and cultural questions of representation were always implicit in the older conception of the "black struggle". Now they have to be reassessed in a context where older socialist and antiracist certainties no longer hold.' For Rattansi, there is now a need to move beyond both multiculturalism and anti-racism.

The issue of representation may be seen as the starting point of any politics of identity. Brunt (1989: 152) maintains that there are two questions that need to be addressed in relation to the issue of representation. The first is 'how our identities are represented in and through the culture and assigned particular categories'; the second is 'who or what politically represents us, speaks and acts on our behalf'. She suggests that, in answering these two questions, we get a sense of how we both 'make sense' of the world and get a sense of our 'place' in the increasing range of identities made available to us. Bonnett (1993: 14), in his book *Radicalism, Anti-Racism and Representation*, draws on Spivak's (1988b) critique of political radicals' self-representation in their construction of the 'Third World' subject, to provide a productive re-reading of British anti-racism in Britain. Setting out to make visible three particular acts of interpretation, he argues that:

> Through distinct rhetorics of 'racial', national, cultural and political identity, each of the modes of representation I will be discussing – 'racial' rejectionism, multiculturalism and anti-racism – has constructed different rationalities of 'racial' difference, different definitions of 'racial' minority and majority identities and what divides them. These rationalities have been used to construct different subjects to 'speak for'. In the case of 'racial' rejectionism the subject has been the 'natural law' and/ or the 'authentic' white Briton. Multiculturalists, by contrast, have often claimed to be speaking for 'other' cultures, whilst anti-racists have positioned themselves as a conduit for 'the Black voice' and 'Black' resistance. By showing how rejectionists, multiculturalists and anti-racists interpret visible minority and majority identity I aim to critically explicate their disparate rationalities of 'racial' difference and claims to speak in the name of particular groups and ideals.

Drawing on the above arguments, this chapter critically examines academic and political representations of anti-racism and ethnic minority community mobilization in the context of an increasingly complex politics of location.

The crisis of anti-racism in late modernity

A main issue for *Contemporary Racisms and Ethnicities* is to explore philosophical, political and policy questions around contemporary representations of racisms and ethnicities in the context of rapid transformations in late modernity. In the 1970s anti-racism provided a strategically important critique of the liberal race-relations problematic that underplayed the importance of racialized structures of power at the level of economy, state and civil society. Anti-racism was highly successful in providing an alternative public language involving new conceptual frameworks, symbols and values that served to disrupt the socio-historical legacy of an imperial society. In turn, the anti-racist problematic now finds itself critiqued, both externally from the New Right and internally by the new politics of cultural difference. The development of a state of crisis in the anti-racist movement in the late 1980s and early 1990s may be seen as 'a product of both its own rationalities and a confrontation with a powerful political antagonist. Although these points of crisis are not necessarily complementary they have combined to produce a period of considerable retreat and intellectual self-doubt' (Bonnett 1993: 45–6). Lloyd (1994), writing of the current crisis in anti-racist movements in the UK and France, locates her argument in a more general thesis concerning the fragmentation of the left with reference to the Enlightenment-derived universalism that underpins established conceptions of anti-racism. She suggests that anti-racist organizations, being unable to overcome the contradictions of universalist and particularist/differentialist positions, have found it increasingly difficult to respond to the New Right, which has turned these positions to its own advantage by arguing that it is universal human nature that explains the fundamental incompatibility of different national cultures.

There is much confusion concerning whether there is a need to move beyond an anti-racist stance, particularly with reference to issues of difference, culture and diversity. And, if there is such a need, how is it to be done? and who is to do it? One of the most difficult issues for 'coming times' – inherited both from 'old times' and 'new times' – is the question of what can be done in political and policy terms to address current modes of racism. In changing contemporary socio-economic and political conditions a number of issues add immediacy to the question of developing an effective political position. First, the increased visibility of the growth of racist ideologies, and extreme right and neo-Fascist movements across Europe and beyond (Balibar 1991b; Silverman 1992; Wrench and Solomos 1993). Second, the move from 'simple' to 'complex' inequalities, including recognition that large sections of the white British working class are experiencing increasing levels of social exclusion and marginalization. Third, the emphasis renewed in the 1980s on a unified and unitary British national culture and an accompanying crisis in Anglo-ethnicity. Fourth, a popular, media-led argument, embedded in racial and national discourses, that equal opportunities and anti-oppressive initiatives have gone too far, resulting in the white British ethnic majority as the 'new victims in their own country' of a 'politically correct' anti-racism.

What is anti-racism? Theoretical underdevelopment and conceptual inflation

Over the years a wide range of definitions of anti-racism and multiculturalism have emerged from different theoretical and political positions. These more subtle divisions between and within anti-racism and multiculturalism, including the ways in which versions of both are often combined in practice, are examined elsewhere and are not addressed here (Bonnett 1993; Gillborn 1995). I am concerned specifically with exploring the question of anti-racism and minority group mobilization in the context of both historical and contemporary social and cultural transformations. I shall focus on materialist and differentialist (new politics of cultural difference) positions, which are two of the most dynamic contributions to current debates. As with the term racism, anti-racism continues to be a highly contested term, with a wide range of

definitions. This has resulted in different meanings being conceptually conflated. Anti-racism has become overladen with these multi-meanings and
this has contributed to its becoming a catch-all phrase. Such an expansive
use of the notion of anti-racism was encouraged by developments in local
politics which became the main site of public debate about anti-racism once
it had shifted to the local political arena (Miles 1982; Ball and Solomos 1990;
Solomos and Back 1995). In the search for a more conceptually rigorous and
consistent approach, it is necessary to desegregate different levels of meaning: distinguishing between policy and practice, the theoretical from the
political, individual experience from that of the social collectivity, and state
policies from popular mobilizations against racism. Taguieff (1991), writing of
the crisis of the anti-racist movement in France, suggests a useful distinction
between three types of anti-racism: an economic reductionist-based approach,
a demonological stance and a rationalist pedagogical conception of anti-
racism. His work begins to engage with the changing dynamics of racial
difference in the contemporary conditions of a de-industrializing society
in which the Front National has developed racist discourses that find an
increasing resonance with those experiencing extreme forms of social dislocation as well as more broadly at a time of national uncertainty in the
context of late modernity.

It was suggested in Chapter 1 that anti-racism was of central significance during the 1980s in helping to shape contemporary representations of
racism. Equally important, during this period, representations of anti-racism
were constructed in relation to dominant conceptions of racism. These have
been explored throughout earlier chapters. Most significantly, it was argued
that representations of racism privileged post-war New Commonwealth immigration and settlement as the dominant paradigm (Hickman 1995a). This
involved the construction of a specific hierarchy of fixed racialized identities
that displayed predictable signs, most specifically colour, as the central marker
of difference. Counter-discourses were developed, involving a new vocabulary that included emerging concepts of oppressed black communities, institutionalized racism and the collective black subject. During the 1970s and
1980s critical theorists developed materialist-based conceptual frameworks
and empirical studies, in which they concentrated on particular sections of
selected 'non-white' groups, namely African Caribbeans and Asians. In turn,
these theoretical limitations have circumscribed an understanding of British
anti-racism. This has served to legitimize the exclusion of other ethnic groups
from ethnic monitoring, anti-racist programmes and local authority resources.
By the 1990s, British anti-racists' contradictory stance is highly visible in
relation to anti-Semitism and anti-Irish racism. Across Europe and Britain,
there is much evidence of the increase in anti-Semitism, which, conceptually,
the anti-racist paradigm with its exclusive focus on colour racism is unable
to address (Atkinson 1993; Willems 1995; Gilbert 1996). At the same time,
anti-racists, both in conceptual and policy terms, continue to ignore the
political mobilization of the Irish in Britain around issues such as the British
state's political and military occupation of Northern Ireland, community
campaigns for recognition of ethnic status, and struggles against the criminalization of the Irish in Britain (Hillyard 1993; Hickman and Walter 1997).

Bonnett (1993: 37), in his critique of the rather simplistic notions of local authorities' anti-racist approaches during the 1980s, has suggested that two central tendencies can be identified: an individualistic strand focusing on racism as caused by personal prejudice and misinformation and a second approach that sees racism as an integral part of British social, economic and political life. There has been a wide range of criticisms of these approaches that were combined within the 'race awareness training' programmes set up by radical local authorities (Sivanandan 1985; Wetherell and Potter 1992). Although the American influence has been signalled in these criticisms, there has been a failure to locate this influence within the wider American cultural hegemony operating in Britain that has served historically, and continues at the end of the twentieth century to distort an understanding of the 'peculiarities of the English', with reference to anti-racist politics and minority group struggles (Katz 1978). This historical overvalorizing of American theory and policy may be contrasted with the theoretical and political disinterest by British anti-racist theorists in European accounts of racism and anti-racist mobilizations. During the 1970s and 1980s discussion of anti-racism tended to be overly inward-looking, with a primary focus on a national and increasingly nationalist British perspective. Although American racial politics are still influential in helping to maintain a black–white racialized dualism, more recently, with the re-emergence of the far right and neo-Fascist parties in Eastern and Western Europe, the success of the Front National in France, and the increasing visibility of refugees and asylum seekers, these changes have impacted on British academic and political anti-racist accounts (Sivanandan 1989; Miles 1993; Wieviorka 1995). Theorists are currently more sensitive to the wider dimensions of a rapidly changing world of ethnic nationalisms and religious fundamentalisms in Europe and beyond (Alund and Schierup 1991; Silverman 1992; Rattansi 1994). This comparative perspective highlights the specificity of British anti-racism, which has been defined in a narrower way than in Europe, where there has been a particular concern with the role of anti-racist social movements and organizations as well as with the ideologies that they articulate (Wrench and Solomos 1993; Lloyd 1994).

In trying to work through the confusions that surround anti-racism, there is a need to place academic, political and popular representations of anti-racism in a broader framework, which holds on to the global–local nexus of social and cultural change. However, when anti-racism is located in such a framework, there is a tendency to overemphasize in a linear way one dimension of the interrelationship, highlighting how anti-racism has been shaped by socio-political issues. Such an approach is an advance on much of the work in this area. However, it is too limited and limiting a perspective. The range of critiques of anti-racism from the political right and left needs to be placed in the context of anti-racism's history in Britain. Recent theoretical work on the new politics of cultural difference speaks of the crisis of anti-racism, with the emergence of many cultural forms of racisms, new ethnicities and the fragmentation of the collective black subject. However, what is understated in these texts is that this crisis is of such significance precisely because anti-racism itself emerged in Britain in the 1980s as of central political significance for both the political right and left. In the context of wider social and cultural transformations, anti-racism became a constitutive element of the changing forms of racialization of contemporary social and political relations (Cambridge and Feuchtwang 1990a; Anthias and Yuval-Davis 1993; Solomos and Back 1996).

New Right critiques of anti-racism: British national belonging

Unlike much of the political left's uninterest in questions of culture and difference, during the 1980s a defining aim of the New Right was to project culture as of key political importance. Whether it was Margaret Thatcher's 'understanding of how people might feel swamped by increasing numbers of outsiders' or Norman Tebbit's 'cricket test' remark, whether children of immigrants would support the English cricket team or that of their 'home' countries, the New Right cultural restorationists were centrally concerned with the issue of what constituted Britishness and who legitimately belonged to the British nation. They were posing the 'interesting national questions' that resonated with a wide range of constituencies, as in an earlier period Enoch Powell claimed to speak for 'the forgotten British people'. The New Right's position can be contrasted with the mainstream left, which defensively responded in terms of vague conceptions of a social-democratic, welfarist and multiethnic citizenship. The main political and theoretical challenge to this Tory 'high moral' discourse, which has been underreported, came from new social movements including radical women's, black, lesbian and gay movements. For example, Liz Kelly (1992: 22) offered a radical critique of the legacy of the 1980s nationalist enterprise culture that involved, she argued, a recomposition of the English social landscape with the resulting repositioning of minority social groups.

> What the last decade has demonstrated is the skill of small groupings within the Conservative party to exploit local controversies, generate enormous media support and have MPs then respond with speedy legislative fixes – a number of these local controversies have been initially located in education and have focused on sexuality and race. Each of these interventions has fed a specific construction of family and nation that lies at the heart of the New Right philosophy: their creation of a 'traditional way of life', which they then become defenders of. This spurious unity requires the exclusion, or at least the de-legitimation, of those who represent an alternative set of values: those outside the white 'Persil' family – e.g. single women choosing to have children, lesbians and gays; Black families that seek to maintain some of their own cultural values; those who represent sectional interests. . . . The success of this ideological strategy is evidenced in the increasing acceptance of the view that equal opportunities programmes promote 'minority' interests, when in fact, if successful, they would benefit the majority of the population who are not white, male, heterosexual and able-bodied.

The development of 'anti-anti-racism' by the New Right can be read as part of a larger political project of protecting British cultural heritage. In this discourse, anti-racism was seen as a major threat – in Palmer's (1986) words, an 'assault' – to the social and moral order of society. This involved the Tory government replacing the post-war consensus with a new political agenda, in which earlier representations of British culture, nation and belonging were invoked and reworked for the 1980s as key discursive resources to challenge what would later be named as the left's 'political correctness'. In his article, 'A dirty war: the New Right and local authority anti-racism', Gordon (1990: 188–9) outlines the success of central government in providing a contemporary 'common-sense' explanation, in which 'racialized outsiders' were located at the centre of national political life at a time of rapid social change. He describes the New Right's analysis, which combined intellectual and popular accounts in successfully linking, in the public consciousness, anti-racism and the ideological baggage of the far left. Although, as he shows, many of the New Right's allegations against local authorities' anti-racist interventions were untrue, nevertheless they helped:

> to secure support for government policies and influenced others and helped achieve a number of victories: the abolition of the Greater London Council, a pioneer in municipal anti-racism and a hate figure of the New Right; the restriction of local authority powers to pursue contract compliance policies; the abolition of the Inner London Education Authority; and the restrictions on the curriculum and local education authority powers represented by the Education Act 1986 and the Education Reform Act 1988. And to these might be added the fiscal restrictions, such as rate-capping, and the replacement of rates by the poll tax.

Such an analysis begins to signal that by the late 1980s the New Right was more aware than the left of the wider cultural importance of what race, cultural difference and anti-racism had ideologically come to signify. A key feature of the British New Right policy in the 1980s was to rework critiques of social democratic institutions constructed by progressive theorists, such as Marxist accounts of social reproduction. This added to the left's confusion about how to respond to 'new times'. The Conservatives were highly successful in projecting themselves as modernizers with their ideological appeal to the principle of universality. In contrast, the left was projected as a group of reactionaries holding on to old social practices, which privileged the political establishment, such as local authorities and the trade unions, and special-interest groups, such as minority ethnic communities. Although we have moved beyond the high point of New Right ideology, the left has not recovered from the political success of the former's hegemonic position in setting a national populist agenda.

Many commentators have noted the unpopularity of anti-racism, pointing to its alienating oppositional stance. However, owing to the paucity of research in this area it is difficult to test the accuracy of this claim, particularly with reference to practice (Feuchtwang 1990a and b). As Gillborn (1995: 79–80) notes: 'Given our current state of knowledge, it is difficult to arrive at any secure judgement about the overall success or failure of antiracism.' More specifically, it is difficult to identify the acceptance or rejection of anti-racism by different social groups among ethnic majority or ethnic minority communities. In contrast to its theoretical underdevelopment, anti-racism has attained a high profile in the British media. The influential tabloid press and broadsheets, in their different linguistic registers, often cite anti-racism as an illustration of the imported American notion of 'political correctness' that they position themselves as challenging. This adds further difficulties in attempting to gain a clear perspective on the possibilities and limitations of anti-racism as part of a wider British political process.

Two events in particular hold important symbolic value for the media, which have consistently represented anti-racism as 'having gone too far', namely that of the Rushdie affair and Burnage High School, where an Asian student was killed by a white peer in Manchester. It is important to con-textualize the media hysteria that surrounded these events, which have had different disorientating effects on anti-racism. The media's contribution to the construction of the Rushdie affair can be read as a high point in the pervasiveness of the development of anti-Islamic discourses within the nexus of the state, institutional sites and popular consciousness. The Rushdie affair opened up anti-racists' ambivalences and contradictions in relation to ques-tions of minorities' culture and ethnicity. The Burnage Report, emanating from anti-racists, was presented as a public vindication of the tabloids' long-established stance on defending public institutions, such as state schools and social work, from 'loony left' extremists. The tabloid press projected anti-anti-racism as resonating with the wider concerns and anxieties of the white British majority. At the beginning of the twenty-first century the left has not constructed a coherent alternative position to that of the right in relation to these events. This is highly significant as both could be said to have signalled the end of materialist-based anti-racism developed in the 1980s (Gilroy 1992).

Left critiques of anti-racism: fragmentation and the absence of culture

By the late 1980s anti-racism in Britain had experienced increased fragmenta-tion, with major challenges from within its own constituencies, as part of a broader political context of the contemporary implosion of 'progressive' social categories. Solomos and Back (1996: 117–18) explain the difficulties involved:

> From the perspective of contemporary political debates the attempt to develop political strategies around the notion of anti-racism has proved problematic. At a conceptual level there has been a notable lack of clear conceptualisations of the political and social objectives of anti-racist movements or their limitations. At the level of policy and practice there has been both confusion and hostility to the attempt to institu-tionalise a bureaucratic framework for implementation of anti-racist policies, in relation to such areas as education, social welfare, adoption and training.

A number of arguments against the limitations of materialist-based anti-racism have been explored above. Most importantly, it was argued that anti-racists had constructed a version of the black collective subject while underplaying key elements such as cultural and religious identities, which politically did not fit into their secular framework. A critical concern here is the question of the conceptual adequacy of materialist conceptions of anti-racism to address new cultural forms of racism. For example, as Gilroy (1992: 53) illustrates: 'Apart from the way that racial meanings are inferred rather than stated openly, these new forms are distinguished by the extent to which they identify race with the terms "culture" and "identity", terms which have their own resonance in antiracist orthodoxy.' More specifically, the new politics of cultural difference has developed critiques of anti-racism, which are marked by varying forms of reductionism and essentialism, in which complex and multifaceted phenomena are framed within mono-causal explanations.

Cohen (1992: 77–8) provides one of the most conceptually sophisticated critiques of materialist versions of anti-racism. His work is grounded in theory-led empirical work with young, white, working-class men and police trainees. It was carried out soon after the publication of the Scarman Report (1981) on the Brixton riots in south London and explores their responses to racist material. In his paper, ' "It's racism what dunnit": hidden narratives in theories of racism', Cohen uses the students' accounts to construct a typology of models explaining racist discourse. A main argument is that in telling only part of the story these accounts are reductionist and limited. Drawing on the work of Levine *et al.* (1987), Cohen identifies two main types of reduction in his students' explanations of racism: that of radical holism and methodological individualism. Radical holism involves the actions or attitudes of particular individuals or groups and the meaning of particular events being explained as the expression of an overdetermining social totality, such as 'capitalist society', 'patriarchy', or 'the white power structure' – which supervenes in every case. On the other hand, he claims that methodological individualism: 'seeks to desegregate all larger institutional and historical entities into the practices and relations of individuals or groups who compose or inhabit them' (Cohen 1992: 78). Cohen maintains that holistic and individualistic explanations of racism have different political implications. Holistic explanations are evident in accounts of institutional racism and individualistic explanations underpin deficit models of working-class culture. However, the two are not mutually exclusive and he cites the equation, racism = power + prejudice, that was widely adopted in the anti-racist movement – including in the influential Inner London Education Authority's policy statement during the 1980s – as evidence of such a double reduction.

Shifting from earlier materialist representations of anti-racism to the deconstruction of racialized and ethnic identities in the new politics of cultural difference highlights the need to examine the concept of power in relation to the interplay between social structure and subjectivity. In the social sciences power has tended to be conceptualized in terms of either the actions of individuals or institutional agents, or the effects of structures on systems. This has been reflected in theoretical debates about social oppressions that have tended to adopt a dichotomized approach, emphasizing either psychological-based processes of personal prejudice or institutional social structures. Henriques *et al.* (1984) have shown the limitations of this individual–society dualism – a classic Western cultural case of individuality versus sociality – with its implicit assumption that individuals could live outside society or that society is not composed of individuals. This split has manifested itself in the area of racial differentiation in terms of earlier arguments between multiculturalist and anti-racist positions. The latter emphasized the explanatory power of racism as a single overarching structure of domination between blacks and whites. Historically, this radical perspective has provided an important political challenge to mainstream liberal and conservative theory which failed to make power relations problematic. However, in this approach, racial oppression is often understood in terms of what the dominant group 'does' to the subordinate group. It has tended to stress external social structures and the accompanying one-dimensional view of power as repressive. Furthermore, there has been a failure to theorize the interconnectedness between different forms of oppression, and the complex social subject. In a decompartmentalized policy approach there has been a tendency to conceptualize race/ethnicity as having something to do with black people, gender as something to do with women, and sexuality as something to do with lesbians and gays. From the position of the new politics of cultural difference there is a need to go beyond such additive models with their hierarchies of oppression. Holding on to the tension between earlier and more recent accounts, we need to think of complex sets of oppression in terms of how they operate in specific regional and institutional spaces, and in terms of a politics of difference located in material relations of dominance and subordination (Fanon 1970; Parmar 1989).

One of the most unexpected developments in moving beyond simple oppositional racial polarities has been an increasing awareness of the convergences across Europe between anti-racist and racist discourses (Taguieff 1988, 1990; Guillaumin 1995). The shift from more certain times is illustrated in the British literature on anti-racism in which different theorists have commented on 'unexpected' similarities between the political right and left. For example, Gillborn (1995: 74) speaks of Modood's language echoing the New Right's attacks on attempts to address racial inequalities critically. Similarly, Gabriel (1994: 188) writes: 'Both Gilroy's critique and neo-liberalism have converged in their opposition to institutionalised anti-racist politics and have thus served to legitimise the arguments for market solutions to questions of race and ethnicity.' Interestingly, Gilroy (1992: 50), in his development of a new politics of cultural difference position, was one of the earliest theorists, referring to what he called 'ethnic and cultural absolutism' as characteristic of anti-racist discourses, to suggest that both racists and anti-racists in Britain tended to work with similar conceptions of cultural exclusivity. He pointed out that:

> For all its antipathy to the New Right's new racism, the common sense ideology of antiracism has also drifted towards a belief in the absolute nature of ethnic categories and a strong sense of the insurmountable cultural and experiential divisions which, it is argued, are a feature of

racial difference. I have argued elsewhere that these ideological failures have been compounded. Firstly by a reductive conception of culture and secondly by a culturalist conception of race and ethnic identity (Gilroy 1987). This has led to a position where politically opposed groups are united by their view of race exclusively in terms of culture and identity rather than politics and history.

Although these more recent convergences are beginning to be acknowledged, what remains underreported is that one effect of the dominant anti-racist black–white dualistic model is that it converges with the British state's construction of the problem of immigrants and racism as narrowly constituted and of recent origin (Hickman 1995a: 4). As Dafydd Elis Thomas (1985: 7), a former Plaid Cymru MP, has suggested: 'The unspoken discourse of the "multi-cultural" debate is the one that goes to the heart of the nature of British society, and the British state itself. Diversity and plurality has to be seen as "recent". To admit otherwise is to admit that the whole history of Britain internally as well as externally has been about imperialism, racism, colonialism, linguistic and political domination.'

As is explored above, a number of commentators have addressed the issue of the crisis of anti-racism at ideological and policy levels. What is underreported in these overly rationalistic accounts are individuals' complex personal and collective emotional investments in anti-racism. Within the socio-political discourses of the late 1970s and the early 1980s anti-racism had a central place in helping to shape for the political left and the right, a collective sense of who they were culturally. Both right and left, from their different positions, displaced their own wider internal political discontents on to anti-racism. Anti-racism during this period may be read as a major cultural code that spoke of either social disruption (for the right) or modernization (for the left) of an old imperial society, in which an alternative image of the future was not available. For the left, emotional investment in the dominant, social democratic project was damaged by the collapse of the post-war social order. The left's collective identity, which represented a legacy of 1960s class-based politics, was developed in a political framework that took for granted the rational and progressive unfolding of history as premised in the Enlightenment project. More specifically, the left's commitment to socialism, the trade union movement and the welfare state represented major strategic vehicles of attaining social justice and equality in the modernist era. At a time of the long Conservative hegemony at the centre, local politics emerged as a highly productive place for progressive political forces. As Solomos and Back (1996: 108) have argued: 'the notion of anti-racism became a symbol of wider debates about the role of policies initiated by radical left local authorities, trade unions and other organizations to promote the idea that they were committed to a positive programme to tackle racialized inequalities.' In this context of a descending class politics, anti-racism was in the ascendancy, providing a cultural space for left activists in which to practise progressive politics.

Cohen (1992: 63) has suggested the need to explore the way that 'images or metaphors which are applied to define racism by analogy hold the key to understanding people's emotional investment in antiracist positions'. He adds that it is just as necessary: 'to be aware of the role which desire, displacement and fantasy play in our practices, as it is in relation to the perverse ideo-logic of racism itself'. Different subject positions and accompanying complex investments in the anti-racist project were taken up by different social groups. Of particular significance was the self-positioning of the white British new middle class, for whom anti-racism provided a moral stance from which to distance themselves from what they defined as an intrinsically racist British culture, which was unable to cast off its imperial past. Equally significantly, as Cohen (1992: 76) suggests: anti-racism provided space that enabled 'certain individuals to dominate the group in the name of an "imagined community" of race or class which they either claim or are made by others to represent'. Ultimately, for the left, too much was demanded of anti-racism during the 1980s, which was imbued with the major symbolic moral responsibility of creating a new social order and new political subjects that would build an enlightened civic sensibility in Britain. Current critiques of antiracism from the left remain partial in erasing critical psychological and psychodynamic explanations of the possibilities and limits of anti-racism, thus overstating the social while downplaying the psychic, resulting in a unidimensional explanation. Here there is an assumption of an a priori superiority that anti-racist 'facts' are theoretically more adequate and efficacious explanations of racialized relations than the logic provided by 'common-sense' feelings about race and racial difference. Institutional spaces are re-created as pre-Freudian landscapes in which there is an absence of individual intention, structure of feeling, emotional responses, repression, displacement and irrationality (Freud 1933; Fanon 1970; Lacan 1977). We are returned to a Kantian world in which it is assumed 'that our lives can be lived by reason alone and that through determination . . . we can struggle against our inclinations, to live according to the pattern that we have set ourselves through reason' (Seidler 1990: 219). We need to go beyond earlier overly rationalist critiques of antiracism by the right and the left that employed a positivist epistemology (Taguieff 1991).

Shifting geographies of anti-racism: complexity, heterogeneity and location

Theoretical critiques of anti-racism in the 1980s, from the political left and right, tended not to be grounded in the complexity and heterogeneity of anti-racist practices. For example, there was little sensitivity to the question of shifting geographies of racist and anti-racist practices. Gilroy's (1987, 1992) early critique has been of particular significance with his generalized rhetorical claim of 'the end of British anti-racism'. While indicating that he was focusing on specific forms of anti-racism, he underplayed the question of regional context; namely, the municipal anti-racism of 'radical' Labour-controlled local authorities, with a specific focus on the Greater London Council (Troyna and Williams 1986; Gillborn 1990). This question of context needs to be located in a broader political and academic trend, marked by a strong regional bias that is built into these influential texts, which project on to the rest of Britain the political effects of London-based radical local authority policies. During the 1980s social theorists, policy makers and their critics colonized understandings of what was going on in Britain with reference to racism and anti-racism. At this time local authorities were a key site for the development of anti-racism. As Solomos and Back (1996: 104) have pointed out: 'One of the key changes in Britain in the last twenty years has been the way that central and local government have taken on a public commitment to anti-racism and multiculturalism.' The shared ethnicized map of the political left and right served to 'over-racialize' localities where there was a predominance of African-Caribbean and Asian people while simultaneously 'de-racializing' predominantly white areas occupied by the Anglo-ethnic majority. This was finely illustrated with reference to the 1985 riots which took place in the Birmingham area of Lozells. Given the high visibility in the racialized British imagination of the neighbouring area of Handsworth as 'black', the riots were reported as taking place there (Mac an Ghaill 1988).

Just as theoretical critiques of anti-racism have disconnected from lived relations in a range of local communities, which is explored below, in turn anti-racist practices in institutional arenas have disconnected from changing theoretical positions. There has been little interest among anti-racist activists in debates about the ontological status of racism or the suggested shift from biological-based explanations of racism to new cultural forms. This double disconnection is evident in two of the central sites of anti-racist practice, namely education and social work. Anti-racism in English schools can be explored as a microcosm of the movement's limitations in the 1980s. Here we see an example of the conceptual inflation of racism and the resulting limitations of anti-racism which does not address the historically specific nature of racist practices in specific public institutions. Anti-racist practice in schools, as with teaching more generally, is undertheorized. Philosophically, teaching belongs to a long British empiricist tradition of 'getting on with it'. The New Right has worked with and increased this general tendency, in which technical rationality continues to provide the dominant epistemology of practice. In this broader context, there is not a theoretically clear analysis of what anti-racism *means* or what it is for, but rather assumptions about what it does *not* mean. That is, anti-racism does not mean a mono-cultural curriculum; it does not mean an assimilationist stance or an over-concern with a multicultural defined ethnicity. At the same time, this can be seen as part of an established hierarchical division of academic labour in which the academy develops theoretical frameworks that professionals implement or, in more recent language, 'deliver'. Hence, there is a tendency that once anti-racism has been established as an institutional problem, the analytical work is assumed to be completed and there is a reductionist attempt to deliver the best anti-racist policy. The test of anti-racist policies is not their theoretical rigour, internal consistency or comprehensiveness, but rather an instrumentalist concern with whether they work. Furthermore, they frequently remain at an idealist level that fails to address the necessary material conditions for countering racism in specific institutions of civil society. It is assumed that public institutions such as education, training or social welfare can compensate for

wider racialized barriers in the economy and the state. In the overly politi-
cized atmosphere of the 1980s, partly explained by the extremely hostile
conditions in which it operated, British anti-racism tended to take up a
strong moral rhetorical stance that served to mask its theoretical and conceptual underdevelopment (Macdonald *et al.* 1989; Gillborn 1995). As Cohen
(1992: 79) has argued in relation to the limits of anti-racist essentialisms:
'they tend to be strong on moral denunciation but weak in their inclusiveness
and weight of explanation. This inevitably reduces their strategic purchase
on racist practices.'

Minority ethnic group mobilizations – social and cultural transformations

As Lloyd (1994: 228) has pointed out in her comparison of anti-racism in
France and the UK, in the latter 'through the implementation of the Race
Relations Acts, especially the 1976 Act, the state has played a leading role in
the developing anti-discrimination, multi-ethnic and "anti-racist" policies'
as part of a wider state policy of integration and control. She argues that:
'The growth of a "race relations industry" armed with a carefully tuned set of
policies for different ethnic groups has in the UK eclipsed the role of association.' One of the main controversial and unresolved issues of the 1980s is
the relationship between forms of anti-racism developed by the local state
and minority ethnic group mobilizations and protest (Gilroy 1987, 1992;
Cohen 1993). As Bonnett (1993: 52) argues, 'the anti-racist mode of representation constructs a monolithic black subject, a construction that constrains
a propensity to conflate "racial" and political categories.' He suggests that
this gives rise to two problems: namely, the isolation of anti-racism from the
wider community and an inability to respond to minority groups' assertion
of cultural and religious identities. There are a number of interrelated concerns
here. First, there was a tendency for minority mobilizations to be subsumed
within local authority anti-racist initiatives, with terms such as black and
anti-racism being appropriated and incorporated into bureaucratic structures
that appeared as further barriers to minorities' attempts to secure equality.
Second, an unintended consequence of local government-funded strategies
targeted at community organizations was 'the exacerbation of tensions and
conflicts both within a given minority ethnic community, and between such
communities and local majority communities, while serving to amplify the
boundaries around particular groups' (Jeffers *et al.* 1996: 124). Third, there
was a failure to link anti-racist mobilizations with minority communities'
histories of protest. Lloyd (1994: 229) describes the fundamental divisions,
including sectarianism and unwillingness to listen to black anti-racists within
the white left that emerged in anti-racist/anti-Fascist organizations in the
1970s. She adds that: 'Contemporary debates between the Anti-Racist Alliance,
Anti-Nazi League and Anti-Fascist Alliance are reproducing those of the 1970s
without apparently trying to draw lessons from them, but also with the new
dynamic of a much stronger challenge from black leadership'. Fourth, the concentration on African-Caribbean and Asian post-war immigrants' experiences

of racism – the colonial paradigm – resulted in the homogenization of these groups, which in turn served to underplay the differing impact of social and cultural change on each community, as well as erasing the dynamic interaction of class, gender and generational differences in each community.

In drawing attention to these limitations we begin to reconnect that which has become disconnected; anti-racism and minority community mobilizations, in the context of the interplay of changing concepts of racism and anti-racism with broader social and cultural transformations. In turn, this may help to provide a clearer understanding of the politics of British anti-racism. A main focus becomes the location of British anti-racist politics in a wider European framework that places the changes of late modernity at the centre, enabling us to identify the complex and changing politics of cultural difference (Cohen 1992; Rattansi and Westwood 1994). An exploration of European anti-racisms is particularly important in identifying the differing histories of origin and political developments of different nation-states. Key historical symbolic moments in different societies provide a map that helps us to read at a local level the specificities of the political development of anti-racist movements across Europe (Alund and Schierup 1991; Silverman 1992; Willems 1995). The experience of Nazism and the Holocaust has provided an important point of reference for the articulation of anti-racist perspectives in European societies in the period after the Second World War (Arendt 1973). In Britain there has tended to be a more complex picture, with the adoption of a wide range of historical influences. These have included external reference points, such as the 1960s black civil rights movement and black power in America, and the black South Africans' political struggles during the 1970s and 1980s, as well as significant internal symbolic moments, such as post-war Commonwealth immigrants' attempts to gain 'racial' equality. However, much contemporary work on anti-racism is marked by historical amnesia. As Solomos and Back (1996: 109) maintain: 'from a historical perspective, the anti-slavery and anti-colonial movements have played a crucial role during the past two centuries in shaping our understandings of "race" and racism.' One element of the productive tension between materialist-based accounts of anti-racism and the new politics of cultural difference accounts involves a re-reading of earlier academic representations of the political mobilizations of minority ethnic communities in Britain. This is particularly salient with the increased divisions among anti-racist forces, the lack of clarity of the political implications of decentred accounts of power and the fragmentation of racialized identities.

History of black mobilization and protest in Britain: materialist accounts

Early materialist theorists were highly critical of the dominant race-relations representations of the 1970s, which did not address the question of the political structure of the black community. For materialists, behind this apolitical stance was hidden an appeal to national homogeneity. So, for example, Carby (1980: 2) attacked the assumed nationalist consensus of official reports and documents. She maintained that: 'Inherent contradictions and conflicting interests . . . within and between racial, sexual and class groupings are contained by and subsumed under an apparent unity of interests.' Equally importantly, a major ideological division was created by state policy, race-relations researchers and public sector professionals that posited a generational division between the 'rural and passive first generation' of black immigrants and the 'rebellious urban second generation'. The intergenerational rebellion of young blacks was primarily attributed to those of African-Caribbean origin. Allen (1982: 146), who challenged the caricatured images of 'first generation' blacks, argued for a historical analysis of the black community's political activity and its resistance to racism. She was particularly critical of the portrayal of 'passive' blacks who were in fact involved in the national struggles for independence in their countries of origin. Images of 'rebellious' first-generation black workers are to be found in the early literature on race-relations, for example Banton (1955), Patterson (1963) and Davidson (1966). Hence, their response to racist practices could not be reduced to the Nottingham/Notting Hill riots of 1958. But a reading of much of the 1970s literature indicates that this history has been erased.

This erasure was taken up by a number of predominantly black theorists who addressed themselves to the question of the continuity of the black community's resistance to racism since their arrival in Britain. Sivanandan (1982), at the influential Institute of Race Relations, provided one of the most comprehensive historical analyses of the black community's political structure and resistance to racism. He traced the move from resistance to open rebellion in the early 1980s and located within this process the growth of unity between African-Caribbean and Asian struggles. Sivanandan detailed the early individual and collective uncoordinated and separate strategies that were adopted in the workplace by the black communities during the 1950s. Also of importance in uniting the black communities against racialism was the anti-colonial struggle. For Sivanandan, the 1962 Immigration Act marked a shift away from the earlier experience of colour prejudice to that when prejudice was institutionalized in the power structures of society, that is, a shift away from racialism to racism. In response to such a change, the black struggle in the workplace and community was strengthened. At work, there was increased pressure for self-representation and, in the community, self-help groups flourished. Of particular significance was the development of the linking of anti-racism and anti-imperialism. The black struggle in Britain was increasingly informed by the black struggles of the past and the present, including those of Gandhi, Nehru, Nkrumah, Nyerere, James, Williams, Du Bois, Garvey, the ongoing struggles in Vietnam and 'Portuguese Africa' in Guinea-Bissau and Cape Verde, and the struggles for Black Power in the United States (Sivanandan 1983: 3).

Sivanandan next analyses what he called the defensive struggles of the 1970s, following the passing of the 1971 Immigration Act, with its intention to stop all black immigration. He stressed how the fight against racism strengthened the class struggle through a series of industrial disputes in the early 1970s, including the most publicized of the strikes at Mansfield Hosiery Mills (1972), Imperial Typewriters (1974) and Grunwick (1976). Black political organizations, such as the Black People's Freedom Movement and the Black Workers Movement, were of particular significance to these disputes as trade union racism expressed itself in terms of lack of support. By the mid-1970s, young people were at the forefront of the black struggle, with a growing number of African Caribbeans identifying with the 'popular politics of Rastafari' and the emergence of Asian youth organizations and defence committees, for example, the formation of the Southall Youth Movement, following the killing of Gurdip Singh Chaggar. Equally important to the black community's resistance were the women's struggles 'at the factory-gate, on the streets, in the home, at the schools and in the hospitals' (Sivanandan 1983: 32). Speaking later of this period, when the black infrastructure began to erode under the pressure from Urban Aid programmes and the creation of a 'class of black collaborators', Sivanandan (1983: 4) describes the strategic position of women in the black struggle. He records that: 'It was only the black women's movement that continued from the 1970s and into the 1980s to hold together the black infrastructure. It was the women, both Afro-Caribbean and Asian, who were to continue to collate the struggles, to connect with third world issues, to publicise and organise and, above all, uphold the unity between Asian and Afro-Caribbean communities' (see Bryan *et al.* 1985).

Sivanandan argued that, during the 1970s, there was a shift from a concern with 'immigration control to induced repatriation' and, with the passing of the 1981 Nationality Act, Britain was becoming a 'pass law society'. It was against this background, with increasing repression from an authoritarian state, that black resistance developed into open rebellion in 1981, beginning in Brixton and spreading throughout urban areas of Britain. Joshua *et al.* (1983), in examining the 1980 'Bristol riot', argued that this was not a recent phenomenon, but rather that 'collective racial violence', understood politically 'as an expression of political struggles and aspirations of the black communities settled in Britain' (Joshua *et al.* 1983: 1), was an integral part of the history of black settlement in Britain throughout the present century. For Sivanandan and Joshua *et al.*, the primary cause of that resistance was racial subordination. They saw the black community's response as a non-revolutionary strategy to gain power in the existing social framework and to challenge the increasingly racist role of the state. They stressed the collective nature of the resistance as evidence that in the black community there was a shared understanding of racism that expressed itself repeatedly in terms of a rational form of violence.

From a present-day perspective in developing an understanding of the politics of racial inequality and social change, Sivanandan and Joshua *et al.*'s work remains of central importance in demonstrating that black resistance to racism is not a static phenomenon that can be understood in the abstract, but rather that it has assumed distinctive forms in particular historical periods, while also illustrating continuity of the black community's struggle. These accounts are also important in challenging the erasure of this struggle. From this perspective, liberal concessions to the black community during the 1970s and early 1980s, with the plural integrationist shift towards a minimal acceptance of their culture, can be seen not to have been automatically given by the state. Rather, the cruder methods of the assimilationist model, for example that of the policy of 'dispersal', were eventually abandoned because of the resistance, both formal and informal, of the black community. This materialist-based work is a useful reminder of the necessity to acknowledge that minority communities themselves are central agents in developing political strategies to attain racial equality. Ironically, an unintended effect of local state anti-racist initiatives in the 1980s was to displace minorities to the margins of policies that were designed to benefit them. These materialist accounts are also of importance in highlighting the strategic need for community mobilization among established migrants to align with recent migrant workers and refugees whose limited civil rights may reduce their ability to ogranize in an anti-racist movement. For Sivanandan (1990b: 22): 'the joint struggles of refugees, migrant and black groups in Britain not only help to sustain the links between racism and imperialism and between racial oppression and class exploitation, but have also been at the forefront of the attempts to build a network of European groups against a new European racism.'

Class, race, cultural politics and community

As explored in Chapter 1, the relationship between class and racism in the 1970s and early 1980s was a central dynamic force in conceptualizing the politics of racism and social change (Rex 1973; Rex and Tomlinson 1979; Centre for Contemporary Cultural Studies 1982). During this period much of the literature that addressed itself to black working-class political activity tended to locate it within social democratic forms (Heinemann 1972; Miles and Phizacklea 1977, 1979). Such work, focusing on the divisions between and within ethnic groups, concluded that although high levels of support for the Labour Party and trade union membership were to be found among the black community, the racial divisions in the labour movement forced blacks back into ethnic associations, and a resulting contrast was made between the 'passivity and emphemerality' of West Indian political associations and 'the more cohesive formal and informal Asian organisations' (Wallman 1979). Miles and Phizacklea's (1977: 492) research during this period on black minority ethnic groups in Britain distinguished between three main modes of political mobilization: class unity, with its emphasis on common socio-economic interests for ethnic minority and majority groups; ethnic organization, involving separate forms of ethnic mobilization; and black unity, in which there was organization across ethnic lines. Finding little hope for the implementation of the class unity or black unity process, they pessimistically concluded that this resulted in the ethnic organization process being of primary political significance for the black community in Britain.

Miles and Phizacklea challenged the dominant race-relations construction of the analytical problem around black political activism in terms of the relationship between class and race. For them, race has no analytical value, therefore this interpretation posed a false dichotomy (Miles 1982). In turn, a main theoretical challenge to Miles and Phizacklea came from the Centre for Contemporary Cultural Studies (1982). The work of CCCS was developed in the context of what they identified as the changing politics of race and nation in the 1970s/early 1980s. Most significantly, at this time there was a resurgence of the National Front, which was involved in highly public and systematic violence against black people. It was also a time in which different sectors of the black community were politically active in different arenas in defending their communities. Small (1994: 77) describes the wide range of black responses: 'Black people have developed cultures and communities of resistance from attempting institutional change from within, to community level organising, from ideological and cultural resistance to physical resistance, collectively and individually.' These struggles were not reducible to the traditional class analysis of the workplace. This was most visible in relation to the 'urban riots' of 1980, 1981 and 1985 (Solomos 1988). A main strength of Miles and Phizacklea's position, which is more evident from a contemporary perspective, was to warn against the political and conceptual limits of mobilizing around the notion of race. A major weakness, as the Centre for Contemporary Cultural Studies (1982) argued, was that Miles and Phizacklea, along with other Marxists, could not explain the internal dynamics developing among minority communities, and more specifically the construction of collective identities spoken through race, community and locality (Gilroy 1987).

Gilroy (1981: 212) was highly critical of materialist studies which, following the approach of Castles and Kosack (1973), concentrated their analysis on the work situation. He accused Phizacklea and Miles (1980) of imposing their own Eurocentric models of political activity on to blacks. Furthermore, he argued that their quantitative methodology failed to make explicit what was specific about black political struggles, that is the relationship between such struggles and the wider black community. For Gilroy, the community was a vital analytical concept, with its linking of waged and domestic labour for an understanding of the black community's political structure and activity.

> Localized struggles over education, racist violence and police practices continually reveal how black people have made use of notions of community to provide the axis along which to organize themselves. The concept of community is central to the view of class struggle presented here. For it links distinct cultural and political traditions, which have a territorial dimension, to collective action and consciousness and operates within the relations of economic patterns, political authority and uses of space.

The intervention of the Centre for Contemporary Cultural Studies (1982) was important in challenging the hegemony of class analysis as a sufficient explanatory framework for understanding black political mobilization. Here we see a shift from ideology to culture as the dynamic political element. For example, Gilroy (1982: 210) maintained that cultural forms of resistance were of primary significance to the specificity of the black struggle. For him, race was not reduced to the old questions of ethnicity or custom but rather racist and anti-racist ideology and black resistance were seen as elements of class conflict. As he pointed out: 'the politics of black liberation is cultural in a special sense: Coons, Pakis, Nig-nogs, Sambos and Wogs are cultural constructions in ideological struggle. Cultures of resistance develop to contest them and the power they inform, as one aspect of the struggle against capitalist domination which blacks experience as racial oppression. This is a class struggle in and through race.' In later work, Gilroy (1987: 38) further developed this line of analysis. Arguing for the political significance of the concept of race in black people's lives, he moved towards the notion of race formation. As he suggested: race formation 'refers both to the transformation of phenotypical variation into concrete systems of differentiation based on "race" and colour and to the appeals to spurious biological theory which have been a feature in the history of "races" . . . (and to) the release of political forces which define themselves and organize around notions of "race". The concept supports the idea that racial meanings can change, can be struggled over.' With the current, more general use of this term it is not always clear if race formation is intended to displace class formation at an explanatory level, or whether it is continuing to signal the ongoing ambivalent relationship between race/racism and class.

Changing ethnic minority mobilizations: racial fragmentation and community representation

There is a tendency in the politics of cultural difference accounts to overstate the limitations of materialist analysis in emphasizing the homogeneity of the black community. In fact, earlier critical literature records a range of industrial disputes in which class divisions in the black community were highlighted. For example, the *Race Today* (1976: 123), describing the adoption of the political strategy of community self-defence, argued that living in Britain had different meanings for different sectors of the black community.

> Neither is the Asian community of one mind. A middle class has developed within. . . . For this group, Britain is experienced as quite a different place from those who have nothing to sell but their labour power. . . . Until recently all appeared to be running smoothly. The concentration of attacks had the effect of tearing the veil from the surface, bringing to the fore what the different sections stand for. The middle class Asians do not want to fight. They prefer appealing to government ministers and the police to calm things down. Pressing on them are the mass of Asian families who have been facing the attacks on the ground. The latter stand for the mobilisation of the strength and the power of the community in mass meetings, mass demonstrations, and vigilante groups.

There has been a long debate about the assumed unitary class position of Asians and African Caribbeans in Britain that has included a critical discussion about the position of the black middle class (Miles 1989; Sivanandan 1990a). For example, Sivanandan (1990a: 125) argued that: 'There is no such thing as a black-qua-black movement any more. There are middle-class blacks fighting for a place in the (white) middle-class sun and there are workless and working-class blacks fighting for survival and basic freedoms.' This informed his response to what was a major debate in the 1980s, the question of black sections in the Labour Party, which he critiqued for serving the self-interest of middle-class blacks (see also Gilroy 1987).

More recently, in discussing ethnic minority political mobilizations, there has been a shift away from materialist-based accounts of differentiated class responses to that of the fragmentation of racialized identities. Most of this work, which continues to operate in the dominant black–white dualistic model, has focused on the responses of Asians and African Caribbeans to the different-iated impact of racism on their communities. For example, African Caribbean groups have mobilized around their collective experience of racism in the education system and the criminal justice system, particularly campaigning against the 'Sus' laws that were criminalizing the young. (Under the provi-sion of the Vagrancy Act of 1824, police were able to arrest an individual 'on suspicion of loitering with intent to commit an arrestable offence'. During the 1980s black people were over-represented in being 'picked up' under what came to be called the 'Sus' laws. After much resistance by the black community, 'Sus' was abolished in 1981.) Asian groups have been more actively involved in defending their communities against violent attacks, racial harassment on housing estates, and in organizing campaigns against deportations and other issues arising from the racial and sexual discriminatory effects of immigration laws. Brah (1992: 133) writes of this more complex picture, pointing out that:

> The stereotypic representations of African-Caribbean and South Asian communities have been substantially different. The gendered discourses of the 'Nigger' and the 'Paki' in post-war Britain represent distinctive ideo-logies, yet they are two strands of a common racism structured around colour/phenotype/culture as signifiers of superiority and inferiority in post-colonial Britain. This means that African-Caribbean, South Asian and white groups are relationally positioned within these structures of representation. By their behaviour and actions they may reinforce these structures or alternatively they may assume a political practice which challenges these different strands of anti-black racism.

Knowles and Mercer (1992), working from within a politics of cul-tural difference framework, explore the possibilities of developing an anti-essentialist and pragmatic feminist and anti-racist politics of mobilization against the vagueness of the enemy of state racism and white power. They provide an interesting discussion of the limits of materialist accounts in which oppression is simply read off from 'experience'. They are critical of work such as that of Carby and Bourne for its emphasis on the inscription of racism and gender inequality in processes of capitalism, colonialism and patriarchal social systems, which Knowles and Mercer see as producing overly functionalist arguments. Knowles and Mercer maintain that racism and sexism should be viewed as a series of effects that do not have a single cause. Brah (1992: 138) has responded to this critique, in which she wishes to hold on to the product-iveness of materialist and the politics of cultural difference positions. She accepts the limits of the materialist position, that the level of abstraction of categories such as capitalism and patriarchal relations do not lend themselves to clear guidelines for political organization and that racism and sexism are not monocausal phenomena. However, she argues that she cannot see how conceptualizing racism and sexism as a series of effects produces a more useful strategic political action. Brah suggests that: 'The main issue is not whether we should jettison macro-level analysis of gender or racism in relation to capitalism, colonialism or state socialism in favour of empirically grounded analysis of the concrete manifestations of racism in a given local situation, but how each is overdetermined by, and also helps to determine, the others.'

Another key contentious issue of these changing times is the question of claims to community and community representation. Eade (1989: 2–3), in his book *The Politics of Community*, provides a useful background to understanding the political representation of Britain's minority communities, which he argues has tended to be explored largely in terms of the interests of minority ethnic group leaders. He refers to the work of Saifullah Khan (1976), who questioned the validity of ethnic minority leaders' claims to represent 'their community'. She suggested that categories such as the 'Pakistani community' were in fact a result of the interplay between community leaders and outsiders, such as state agencies, the media and academics. Both Eade and Khan stress the need to place the question of community in the arena of wider political representation. In a more recent discussion Anthias and Yuval-Davis (1993: 190) critiqued the concept of community in the context of identity politics. Donald and Rattansi (1992: 5) welcome the productiveness of the rethinking of culture in recent theory and political practice, which they argue 'undermines the claims and comforts of community, understood in terms of normative identity and tradition, whether of nation, religion, ethnicity or the black experience'. They suggest that what Gilroy refers to as 'black expressive cultures' in Britain has posed a key question: 'How might it be possible in unpropitious times, to create a radically pluralistic culture for a post-modern society like Britain?' (Donald and Rattansi 1992: 5).

Solomos and Back's (1995) empirically grounded study, *Race, Politics and Social Change*, in examining the changing political landscape of local urban politics, makes clear how difficult it is to answer this key question. They bring together the interplay between a changing British nation-state at the local level and the changing dynamics in minority groups. Exploring African-Caribbean and Asian political mobilizations at the level of local communities and mainstream politics, they illustrate the important role that these groups have played in helping to shape political discourses and to influence policy agendas. They also draw attention to the growth of contemporary forms of black nationalism and ethnic absolutism in minority communities. Their study provides a clear insight into the radical shift from earlier class-based analyses of the earlier 1980s to the multidimensional elements of the mid-1990s, in which a range of cultural spaces have been opened up in minority communities, particularly in terms of collective investments in racial, ethnic and religious identities. For Solomos and Back, contemporary politics of race and ethnicity are not reducible to a simple process of exclusion or inclusion. Rather, they see the need 'to analyse the possibility of change by taking into account the actual historical and political context within which specific struggles over access to political power and influence take place' (Solomos and Back 1995: 213). As they argue, such a sensitivity will enable us to understand the possibilities for transformation and the limits of reform.

Beyond the 'colour line': Irish and Muslim political activism

In Chapter 3 I explored how recent cultural changes, involving global economic restructuring, advanced technological communications and increasing cultural exchange, have highlighted a wide range of processes of social exclusion and marginalization that are claimed to have challenged older models of racism. At the same time, these new conditions call into question older, anti-racist conceptual frameworks, based on a black–white dualism, for understanding contemporary forms of political activism carried out by minority ethnic communities. More specifically, recent Irish and Muslim mobilizations illustrate the limitations of our understanding of the politics of race and nation in Britain.

The erasure of the Irish from theoretical and empirical studies is one of the main failures of British sociology of racism and ethnicity. The undertheorized social position of the Irish community in Britain has been accompanied by processes of 'de-racialization' which add to the difficulty of making sense of their political mobilization. Earlier race-relations studies, such as Rex and Moore (1967), in their perfunctory treatment of the Irish, assumed that the whiteness of the Irish had resulted in their assimilation into British society. Implicit in this appraisal was an assumption that the Irish would wish to assimilate or believed that they could. As pointed out in Chapter 4, a more recent study by Solomos and Back (1995) carried out in Birmingham continued this long sociological uninterest in the Irish. This study set out to examine the political mobilization of ethnic communities in the city at a time of ethnic revival among the Irish, following years of suppressed public cultural affirmation dating back to the pub bombings in 1974 and the violent reactions of the local indigenous population. This increased cultural recognition is reinforced by romanticized stereotypes and highly sexual portrayals of the Irish in the media. The commodification of Irishness as a central signifier of sociability is most overtly illustrated by the ubiquitous Irish theme pubs that have spread across Birmingham and other urban areas.

The Irish community has its own history of migration and incorporation into the British state, particularly with regard to labour and housing locations, and experiences of the state and civil society, including immigration, the courts and the police. At the same time the Irish have developed their own forms of accommodation, contestation and resistance (O'Tuathaigh 1985; Swift and Gilley 1989; Hickman 1995b). These strategies are exemplified most graphically in long political campaigns – such as those against the imprisonment of the Birmingham Six and the Guildford Four – which form part of the wider contestation of state criminalization of the Irish community. Irish community groups in Britain, such as the Irish Representation in Britain Group, are lobbying the Office for National Statistics for inclusion of the Irish as an ethnic minority in the 2001 Census. The Irish community across Britain is developing counter-discourses to anti-Irish racism that are not derived from discourses of anti-black racism (Williams *et al*. 1997; Williams and Mac an Ghaill 1998).

In response to the denial by British academics and policy makers of anti-racism, there are risks for the Irish of adopting limited defensive strategies. First, as is the case in many anti-racist narratives that juxtapose a moral binary of immigrant 'goodies' and British/English 'baddies', there is a danger of adopting a 'roots approach' that simply inverts the existing racial dualism while serving to romanticize the Irish experience in England. At the same time there is a danger in a critical account of making an appeal to an authentic Irish community on the basis of their shared experience of British racism, which subsumes differentiated experiences around gender, sexuality, age, geographical location, as well as travellers and 'first' and 'second' generation (Mac Laughlin 1995). For example, contesting the pathologization of Irish males inherent in media representations of 'Paddy' underplays the specific gendered experiences of women, who form the main population of the Irish community. Furthermore, as Hickman and Walter (1995: 5) maintain: 'invisibility does not protect Irish women in Britain from racism. Indeed, they are often more exposed since their productive and reproductive roles connect more firmly to British society.'

There are political difficulties in providing critical 'insider' accounts of racialized groups. However, as Enloe (1989: 62) has argued:

> many nationalisms that have rearranged the pattern of world politics over the last two centuries have been patriarchal nationalisms. They have presumed that all the forces marginalised or oppressing women have been generated by the dynamics of colonialism or neo-colonialism, and hence the pre-colonial society was one in which women enjoyed security and autonomy. Thus simply restoring the nation's independence will ensure women's liberation. . . . Repeatedly male nationalist organisers have elevated unity of community to such political supremacy that any questioning of relations between women and men inside the movement could be labelled as divisive, even treacherous.

Similar assumptions are to be found among racialized social groups in their mobilization against British racism. In a study of Irish young male migrants in Britain I found that the masculinity of Irish nationalist politics is displayed by a wide range of cultural signifiers, including the pervasive playing of the national anthem at public gatherings and the obligatory response in terms of a military-style stance; the high visibility of the Irish flag, the tricolour, in the Irish community in Britain, the consumption of traditional Irish music, recalling the sacrifices of male Irish heroes; the celebration of male literary figures; and, more recently, the celebration of the ubiquitous Irish football team, although it is managed by an Englishman (Mac an Ghaill 1996a). Most significantly, the militarization around the armed struggle, encapsulated in the Irish Republic's national anthem (translated as *The Soldier's Song*), serves symbolically to reproduce a public collective consciousness of what it means to be an Irishman. In turn, this historical legacy is a central element that informs the production of specific masculine subjectivities among Irish young men. It should be noted that this version of Irish nationalist politics may be read as the adoption of a rather atavistic and essentializing stance around national difference. Nevertheless, it is also a potentially powerful political mobilizing force in a nation for whom a 'normal mode of citizenship' is that of immigrant status. In exploring how Irish young men in Britain come to inhabit a range of masculine subject positions, it is necessary to examine the changing sexual politics in Ireland. In the above male fantasy narrative, women tend to be written out. However, this is not to suggest that women do not contend this culturally internal marginalization and exclusion at home and in Britain. For example, there has been a rapid growth of Irish women's groups that have been very successful in publicly challenging the prescriptive sexual politics of the Irish state and the Catholic Church. Irish society has been rapidly transformed in the past thirty years, but what is underreported is that feminism has been one of the major social forces bringing about this change (Smyth, A. 1993; Walshe 1997).

In contrast to the conceptual invisibility of the Irish in sociological texts, the increasing racialization of Muslims in Britain and across Europe has made them highly visible (Safran 1987). Modood (1992) has written of the new ethnic assertiveness among Muslims, which is particularly evident among sections of the younger generation. His work has become a key reference point in challenging reductionist anti-racist accounts, which he sees as preoccupied with colour racism while failing to acknowledge the centrality of cultural and religious concerns for Asian minorities (see Brah 1996). For example, he (Modood 1992: 272–3) argues that: 'Authentic "antiracism" for Muslims . . . will inevitably have a religious dimension and take a form in which it is integrated to the rest of Muslim concerns. . . . I believe that we are slowly learning that our concepts of racial equality need to be tuned not just to guaranteeing that individuals of different hues are treated alike but also to the fact that Britain now encompasses communities with different norms, cultures and religions.' Two main issues that have highlighted the cultural and religious specificities in the Muslim community have been campaigns for state-sponsored schools and mobilizing against the publication of Salman Rushdie's book *The Satanic Verses*. The argument for separate schools has combined issues of racism in education, evident in the response to ethnic-minority languages, increased violence against Muslim students and the failure of the state education system to meet the cultural and religious aspirations of many Muslims (Gabriel 1994). Of particular concern is that whereas Muslims have been refused state-sponsored schools, Catholic, Church of England and Jewish religions have been granted them. Most recently, central government has approved the first state funding for Muslim schools. The secretary of state for education and employment has accepted applications from the Al Furqan primary school in Sparkhill, Birmingham, and the Islamia primary school in the London Borough of Brent, to gain grant-maintained status with full public funding (Carvel 1998: 7).

The Rushdie affair has rightly been claimed as a key moment for the British left, and most notably anti-racists, in challenging the old certainties around questions of multiculturalism and anti-racism with black minority ethnic groups claiming the right to cultural difference. The Rushdie affair opened up anti-racists' ambivalences and contradictions in relation to minorities' culture and ethnicity. On the one hand, anti-racists have promoted the need to include minority cultures. On the other hand, from their Enlightenment-informed, secular universalism, ethnicity was seen as a pre-modern cultural form that it was assumed *would* and *should* disappear in an enlightened Britain, free from racism. Yuval-Davis (1992: 281), noting the erasure of women's responses to the Rushdie affair and the Gulf War of 1990–1, commented that the Rushdie affair has produced in Britain a preoccupation with fundamentalist issues that has caused great confusion both in the left and the right. For example, she argues that: 'those who uphold the fashionable "identity politics", in which the organising principle is around legitimising people's differences and uniqueness in the public as well as in the private spheres, could not challenge what was claimed by fundamentalist leaders to be the essence of their "cultural difference"' (see p. 81, note 1).

The end of anti-oppressive politics?

This is a difficult period for anti-racist politics, with the shift from 'movement' politics to 'lifestyle' politics. It is marked by the resurgence of racial violence across Western and Eastern Europe, new cultural forms of racism, which see the convergence between discourses of racism and anti-racism, the deracialization of policy and the implosion of progressive social categories as part of a broader disillusionment with Enlightenment-based values of progression, social justice and universalism. Lloyd (1994: 238–9), in her discussion of the crisis of anti-racism in the UK and France, argues that in a broader European context it may be necessary to construct a new framework at the end of the twentieth century. She maintains that:

> if the basis of universalist ideas of equality, liberty and fraternity cannot be transposed to contemporary struggles, and are unable either to confront racism (which they largely predated) or inspire people, then as Balibar argues, we need to 'transform what we mean by universalism' (Balibar 1989: 21). This involves fundamental changes in our understanding of citizenship and political participation, which is on the agenda for anti-racists because of Fortress Europe. . . . Finally, this entails a realization that what has been criticized recently as 'universalist' was in fact highly particularist, and that those values of humanism, liberty, equality and fraternity will have to be fundamentally rethought if they are to provide a new basis for a European and international anti-racism.

The past decade in Britain has also witnessed the privatization of morality with which the public, collectivist stance of anti-racism is not in tune. At the same time, there is a general alienation from parliamentary politics. As Brunt (1989: 150) has argued: 'The way to characterise the present situation of Britain entering the 1990s is in terms of a gaping disparity: a tiny minority of various strands of the British Left and progressive movement busy rethinking and reviewing its politics while the vast majority of the British people continue to anathematise the very idea of being involved in politics of any sort.' At the end of the 1990s these trends are continuing.

Young (1993: 123–4), writing in an American context, has provided a productive way forward that moves beyond the limits of an anti-oppressive (anti-racist) problematic, while suggesting the complex interrelation between social positioning and subjective identity formation. In her paper that explores how political actors conceive group difference and how they might best conceive it, she writes that:

> Historically, in group based oppression and conflict difference is conceived as otherness and exclusion, especially, but not only by hegemonic groups. This conception of otherness relies on a logic of identity that essentialises and substantialises group natures. Attempts to overcome the exclusion which such a conception generates usually move in one of two directions: assimilation or separation. Each of these political strategies itself exhibits a logic of identity; but this makes each strategy contradict the social realities of group interfusion. A third ideal of a single polity with differentiated groups recognising one another's specificity and experience requires a conception of difference expressing a relational rather than substantial logic. Groups should be understood not as entirely other, but as overlapping, as constituted in relation to one another and thus shifting their attributes and needs in accordance with what relations are salient. In my view this relational conception of difference as contextual helps make more apparent the necessity and possibility of political togetherness in difference.

Contemporary Racisms and Ethnicities critically explores materialist accounts of an anti-racist problematic. It is particularly concerned with the limitations of an anti-oppressive position as a conceptual framework and its failure to capture the dynamics of local English institutional sites that are experiencing and producing major social, economic and cultural change. In this way, I locate an anti-oppressive analytical position, promoted by specific earlier versions of socialism, feminism, anti-racism, gay and lesbian rights, as theoretically incomplete. At the same time, there continues to be a need to identify structural relations of social power and the resulting patterns of collective social justice. A key issue for theorists is whether we can identify differentiated forms of social power without relinquishing forms of structured oppression. In other words, holding on to the tension between a politics of redistribution and a politics of difference. The development of policies aimed at reducing inequality requires a more sophisticated conceptual framework accompanied by a more empirically grounded critique. This is explored in the concluding chapter. Producing more coherent analyses in the sociology of racism and ethnicity demands an understanding of the tension between identity politics (a materialist anti-racist position) and the new politics of cultural difference (differentialism). I agree with Gamson (1995: 400) when he argues that: 'The problem, of course, is that both the boundary strippers and the boundary defenders are right.' He suggests that a distinction between the two approaches can be understood as one of identity building and identity blurring.

Conclusion: 'coming times': re-making policies – re-making ethnographies

Beyond the black–white oppositional structure: beyond a categorical sensibility in changing times

In this final chapter the main arguments presented throughout the book are drawn together, exploring continuities and discontinuities in the interplay of contemporary social and cultural changes, with shifting ideologies, discourses and representations of racism and ethnicity. A generation of theory was developed in the 1980s in the context of the ascendancy of New Right discourses on Britishness, the nation and cultural belonging. We are now in a period of its descendancy that was most graphically signalled by the collapse of the Conservative government. However, the Labour government is continuing the 'old Conservative tunes', with its emphasis on the inevitable political-economic logic of late capitalism as the grand metaphor of the global market continues to shape how we live our lives. Notions of globalization, modernization, social inclusion and self-empowerment are invoked in the reinventing (rebranding) of a changing Britain for the new millennium. These concepts are not explicitly defined but may be read as class and racially coded terms, in which the 'new poor' – such as lone parents, job-seekers and the long-term unemployed, located in inner-city areas, as part of the working class – are being reconstituted in response to the needs of the permanent revolution of late capitalism. What is underreported here is the constitution of the 'new poor'. Minority ethnic communities are overrepresented among these marginalized groups, alongside new migrants, 'illegal' immigrants, asylum seekers and refugees (Sivanandan 1990b).

An alternative progressive and coherent framework to the politically conservative social democratic project has not been developed for 'coming times'. In this context it appears difficult, at both a conceptual and political level, to construct a socio-historical account of the achievements and limitations of anti-racist policy and practice. *Contemporary Racisms and Ethnicities* highlights the need for future work to develop English-based accounts of anti-racism involving an understanding of a temporally and spatially specific range of racisms, informed by the principle of ethnic inclusiveness. This is not to suggest the adoption of a reductionist English approach in which inclusiveness is understood primarily as a technical task of simply 'bringing in' other minority ethnic groups and the Anglo-ethnic majority. At the beginning of the twenty-first century, there is an urgent need conceptually to rethink questions of racial difference and ethnic belonging in broader frameworks of civil rights and social justice, within which an inclusive concept of English citizenship can be developed and practised. In turn, this needs to inform and be informed by political and policy interventions in specific institutional arenas that resonate with a wide range of constituencies and the way that they live with a plurality of differences (Mercer and Julien 1988; Connolly 1991; Parekh 1991; Young 1993).

In much anti-racist literature there has been a concentration on racialized differences between oppositionally located blacks and whites, rather than on the complexity of changing formations of multiple racisms and new ethnicities. In such work, there tends to be a certain unitariness and rigidity in the projected social collectivities, with little indication of their historical and geographical specificity. In other words, there is a theoretical underdevelopment of the relational status of these racialized/ethnic cultural forms as part of a broader relational logic of shifting social and cultural boundaries. At the same time, there is little awareness of the possibility that under different conditions cultural claims and affiliations might change. A particular claim of this chapter is that dominant forms of anti-racism are failing to make contact with a younger generation, of ethnic minority and majority status, who are located in the changing morphology of urban sites. This younger generation have inherited an older imperial language of race and empire alongside a new language of de-racialized forms of racism, anti-racist discourses, and a local racial semantics that is produced in their 'home-based' neighbourhoods. They are in the process of negotiating and renegotiating new cultural forms of ethnic belonging, marked by hybridity and sycretism among diasporic groups in multicultural arenas (Hewitt 1986; Jones 1988; Back 1996). This is occurring in the context of rapid social and cultural transformations that are mediating and being mediated through a wider institutional and regional socio-economic restructuring of the nation-state. At the same time, as is highlighted in European studies of racism, there is a growing convergence across Europe and beyond between anti-racist and racist discourses, with their claims to fixed notions of cultural difference and appeals to the naturalness of wishing to live 'with your own' (Silverman 1992; Lloyd 1994).

Throughout the book I have explored how differentialist (the new politics of cultural difference) theorists have sought to challenge the limitations of materialist-based anti-racist representations. More specifically, differentialist accounts have highlighted the multiple, fluid and contradictory readings of social relations in arguing the need to go beyond the categorical sensibility that deploys the oppositional structure of the black–white dualism as an overarching explanation. However, a major limitation of differentialist accounts is that they tend to be overly abstract, failing to connect with the lived reality of people's individual and collective experiences. There has been little empirical research in institutional sites to test these claims. Furthermore, in emphasizing new ethnicities and cultural forms of racism, there has been a tendency to overstate contemporary discontinuities, positing a fundamental break with the past that serves to underplay historical and structural continuities. A materialist position highlights these continuities through a conceptual framework that speaks of social reproduction of racist ideologies, state regulation of immigration, institutional mechanisms of racial exclusion and hegemonic cultural capital. In arguing for holding on to the productive tension between materialist and differentialist positions, alongside the latter's psychoanalytic inflections, a way forward is to draw on these different social and cultural analytical tools in exploring questions of multiculturalism and anti-racism in local institutional sites. In this chapter, I focus on two underexplored elements in differentialist texts: policy making and empirical research. The second part of the chapter examines a number of emerging themes that have arisen from theory-led empirical studies with which I have been involved. I begin by exploring the changing nature of policy making in the suggested shift from 'racial inequality' to 'social exclusion'.

Policy arena: the politics of anti-racism, class and the market

Discussion of an anti-racist problematic in relation to policy needs to be historically contextualized in terms of its origins and its achievements. Social differentiation was a key theme of sociology from the early post-war period to the 1970s, with questions of class inequality a major shared concern for policy makers, researchers and public sector professionals. However, in practice the primary focus was on specific groups of socially non-mobile, white working-class males. In response to this, feminist and anti-racist theorists and community activists argued against the degendering and de-racialization of differentiated experiences and outcomes in institutional sites, including schools, social services and labour markets. During the 1970s and 1980s sociology shifted from a primary focus on social class to explore the differentiated collective experiences of women and Asians and African Caribbeans. At the same time, gender and race moved centre stage in local authority anti-oppressive policies (Weiner 1994). In the 1980s critical analysis of public-sector policy highlighted the internal philosophical divisions in the New Right project, which included the neo-Conservative emphasis on direct management and the neo-Liberal emphasis on market forces. For example, a number of writers argued that the origins of the National Curriculum were informed by the neo-Conservatives' hostile response to equal opportunities, which they perceived as threatening the traditional cultural heritage of the British 'way of life' (Mac an Ghaill 1994a). Gillborn (1995: 29) has effectively captured the significance of the New Right's political intervention in developing de-racialized policy discourses in public-sector institutions. As he argues: 'Deracialized notions of culture, language, heritage and the nation construct a policy terrain in which race equality is effectively removed from the agenda.' This was enacted with the implementation of the Educational Reform Act (1988), which can be read as a specifically deracialized piece of legislation, promoting a race-blind curricular approach.

This response was part of a wider project that aimed to construct an alternative to the post-war social democratic settlement, with its underlying values of egalitarianism and collectivism. Metcalf (1985: 11) provides the political and ideological background to the 1980s shift from the 'soft' welfare state to the 'harder' new realism of market economics. He writes:

In the popularization of a monetarist economic policy on both sides of the Atlantic, care has been taken to present these strategies as being proper to the competitive instincts of red-blooded American and British males. The call goes out to kill off lame ducks, to foreswear compassion. It is asserted that in the market-place only the fittest should survive, and that a hard, lean industrial sector is necessary. Appeals to machismo and to disdain soft emotions are quite naked, as politicians of the radical right pour scorn on the need to care for the less fortunate, on the whole idea of the welfare state.

Central government restructuring and restratification in the 1980s involved an ideological shift in official reductionist representations of public-sector institutions, which were projected as having no intrinsic value (use value) but rather as commodities that realized their value in the marketplace (exchange value). This commodification of the public sector was developed alongside the rise of managerialism. Technical rationality provided the dominant epistemology of practice and central government's predilection for technological views of public sector work inevitably created conditions under which a critical approach to professional development became impossible. Multiculturalist and anti-racist policy initiatives were influenced by this shift. Working in managerialist frameworks, their emphasis was on technicist explanations and solutions. Thus, by the late 1980s radical anti-racist interventions were severely limited.

The academic and political anti-racist work of the 1980s continues to be important in contributing to explanations about the continuing asymmetrical racialized power relations operating in British society. It is also of strategic significance in providing counter-discourses that are employed in naming racialized practices as significant in shaping social experiences (Mirza 1997). However, a central weakness in what developed as a hierarchy-of-oppressions approach was that, by the 1990s, the anti-oppressive problematic had limited explanatory power. A major strategic flaw of the mainstream left was its failure, albeit in a hostile environment, to conceptualize adequately, a comprehensive and inclusive rationale for local-authority anti-oppressive initiatives. The failure to develop an alternative social vision contributed to the ascendancy of New Right popular authoritarianism, with its invidious media-orchestrated attacks on progressive local authorities. Unintentionally, it served to reinforce the 'common-sense' view that 1970s and 1980s policies, developed in response to the demands of new identity politics of race, gender, sexuality and disability, were displacing policies on class, and were primarily concerned with minority interests and needs (Mama 1992: 80). A central weakness of much of this work was a failure to think through how race-specific institutional mechanisms of differentiation articulated with social-class divisions. It served to reinforce a common-sense binary social logic of an 'us' (gender, sexual, racial, ethnic, able-bodied majorities) and a 'them' (women, gay, lesbian, black, disabled minorities). State institutions, such as schools, social services and training agencies, were offered disparate policy documents that failed to address the complex and contradictory articulation of different forms of oppression. The Macdonald Report (Macdonald *et al.* 1989) pointed to such a complexity, suggesting that white, working-class people should not be excluded from taking responsibility for anti-racism. In other words, the ethnic majority need to be included in the development of anti-oppressive policies, which are informed by an anti-essentialist under-standing of the relations between and within ethnic minority and majority social collectivities. Equally importantly, anti-oppressive policies in the 1980s failed to acknowledge the complex, multifaceted nature and historical con-textual contingency of the mediation of these oppressions in British state institutions. These institutions are themselves sites of contradictions, ambigu-ities and tensions located in a severe long-term economic and industrial decline in 'post-colonial' conditions (Wieviorka 1991).

From policy discourses of 'race equality' to policy discourses of 'social exclusion'?

It is suggested that we have shifted from the 'simple' policy discourses of racial inequality (1950s/1960s), with their focus on selection, socialization and social mobility, through local authority anti-racist initiatives (1970s/1980s) to the 'complex' policy discourses of social exclusion and the de-racialization of policy (1990s/2000s). This new social complexity and its critique of a limited race-equality approach is often illustrated by reference to claims that 'Asian'/'Indian' students are achieving better academic results at school and higher levels of entry to university than white students. A similar argument is presented in relation to the increasing 'success' of girls alongside the 'underachievement' of boys. In response, two main political explanations are developing. First, the dominant response, that these findings are evidence of equal opportunities having 'gone too far' and serving to alienate young, white people or, in the latter case, boys. The second response is to dismiss these findings as part of a wider political project that is defensively acting against the gains of anti-racism and feminism. These responses need to be placed in the context of the New Right's dismantling of anti-racist policies in civil society which were developed by progressive local authorities (Weiner 1994; Mac an Ghaill 1996b). The Labour government, in its projected reform of the welfare state, has signalled that it does not intend to restore earlier political gains in race- and gender-equality initiatives. At central and local government levels, policy makers and officials are rhetorically appealing to the principle of what has become the catch-all term – social inclusion – as race-equality units are being closed down.[1] Ironically, during the 1980s, local authorities were responsible for the development of the amplification of ethnic differences and strong boundary maintenance between groups by encourag-ing competition between minority communities for limited public resources. We are now returning to a policy of racial inexplicitness by subsuming the needs of ethnic minorities under the more general categories of urban deprivation and social marginalization. However, the political rationale for moving to more inclusive policies is difficult to challenge at a time of increased complexity of multidimensional social exclusions in inner cities. There can be no simple return to an earlier policy agenda of 'special needs', which was informed by a conceptually flawed analysis, underplaying the complex map of multiple, fluid and contradictory interconnecting sets of social divisions between and within the ethnic minorities and the ethnic majority (Bock and James 1993). Of equal importance, minority political mobilizations – for example, among the Irish and Muslim communities – have highlighted the exclusions of specific groups who were made culturally and religiously invisible in earlier anti-racist policy initiatives.

Much of the work carried out from a differentialist position in the sociology of racism is marked by a theoretical lack of interest in, or a disciplinary parochialism to, theoretical work on state policy making and, more specifically, the restructuring of the welfare state. For example, in relation to the critique of the limits of local authority anti-racist interventions, there is little evidence of engagement with broader theoretical work on the impact of policy reformation in public-sector arenas which might help to develop new productive frameworks (Savage and Robins 1990; Cutler and Wain 1994). More specifically, in exploring anti-racist policy and practice, there is a general overemphasis on change in examining contemporary state reforms. However, in such accounts the notion of change becomes the unexplored focus that is asserted rather than demonstrated or elaborated. A main argument of *Contemporary Racisms and Ethnicities* is that cultural theorists need to recover the history of earlier materialist accounts and, in the process, re-read 'old times' texts as providing dynamic understandings of racial conflict and social change, particularly with reference to debates around the class–racism couplet. This will enable us, from the perspective of late modernity, to engage with the historical and structural continuities alongside the social and cultural discontinuities in current policy reforms.

A renewed theoretical interest in decentred cultural forms of class analysis needs to engage with the main argument of recent cultural theory that class-based communities have been displaced by consumerized lifestyles (see Baudrillard 1981; Featherstone 1991; Kumar 1995). One of the major advantages of revisiting class analysis is that it will give a critical edge to discussions employing discursively produced 'common-sense' constructs – such as choice, effectiveness and standards – alongside the more recently developed notion of social inclusion, in relation to access by minority ethnic communities to scarce public resources and public spaces. Most significantly, it will serve to make visible the ideological claims that the market as a neutral mechanism can best distribute scarce goods and services; that is, that the market can best 'deliver' high-quality services for all consumers of public goods. For Ranson (1988: 15) there is a need to remake civil society, after twenty years of erosion of public institutions. In this context, he persuasively argues that:

> Within the marketplace all are free and equal, only differentiated by their capacity to calculate self-interest. Yet, of course, the market masks

its social basis. It elides, but reproduces, the inequalities which consumers bring to the marketplace. Under the guise of neutrality, the institution of the market actively confirms and reinforces the pre-existing social order of wealth and privilege.

Gabriel (1994: 188) describes how differentialist critiques of anti-racist policy have coincided with the New Right's dismantling of the welfare state and the promotion of new consumer identities in public and private spheres. He analyses the political impact of markets in the 1980s on cultural constructions of race and social practices defined in racial terms. This is clearly illustrated with an example of the commodification of state schooling and the reconstitution of parents as consumers. This is a most apposite critique at a time of the 'white flight' of middle-class parents from inner-city schools. Gabriel indicates the pervasive influence of global markets on the movements of peoples and capital as well as products of labour and capital: 'from McDonald's fast food to tourism in the Third World to the export of African-American film and music and its "consumption" by young people in Britain'. He argues for the need to examine the impact of markets in their institutional contexts, concluding that his own case studies illustrate the limitations of the market as a mechanism for contesting racist cultural forms and inequalities, while failing to provide the means for genuinely radical and alternative forms of cultural expression.

Such arguments are particularly salient in relation to the need to move beyond critiques of the New Right hegemony and critically to examine market-based social democratic alternatives. Coward (1996: 11) cogently captures the political impact, in the context of a de-industrializing society, of the erasure of social class and the disappearance of the working class as a primary political subject. She highlights the limited response of a 'progressive' electoral politics position that appears to read the current more complex and obscure class structure as a sign of its disappearance (Lukes 1984).

> In all the talk about Tony Blair's 'stakeholder society' one concept has been striking in its absence: the working class. . . . Some time ago, the Labour Party turned its back on the concept which gave it its name. The linguistic shift to the classless, genderless, investor citizen has long seemed inevitable. New Labour may soon become 'No Labour' or even 'The Leisure Party'. . . . The working class has been written out of the script partly because no one knows what it is any more. The forms of employment practised by the working class – heavy industrial labour associated with the productive base have disappeared. The corresponding growth of the service and finance sector, increase in dual income families, casualisation and unemployment blur old economic categories.

As outlined in Chapter 1, in arguing for the need to revisit social class, this does not suggest a return to the old social democratic policy solutions underpinned by the old sociology of class. There is an urgent need for fresh theoretical frameworks and empirical research that includes social class as a central explanatory variable of differentiated institutional outcomes both *between* and *within* ethnic minority and majority communities. This involves re-engaging with earlier non-determinist sociological accounts of the class–racism couplet, as well as engaging with developments in social and cultural theory (Harvey 1996). At the same time there is a need to employ a more systematic sociological approach to spatial and temporal issues which sensitizes us to the wide range of established and emerging racialized exclusions and ethnic forms of belonging in specific contexts (see Bhavnani and Phoenix 1994). Equally importantly, psychoanalytical theories have provided new ways of thinking about the interconnections between subjectivity, difference and diversity. Such work enables us to move beyond essentialist accounts with their monodimensional perspectives to an understanding of the multidimensional social subject, which is now explored.

A younger generation: English-born minorities in a multicultural/multiracist city

For young people living in multicultural urban settings, we have moved beyond the era of post-war colonial migration to that of English-born ethnic minorities such as Birmingham Irish, Leicester Asians, Liverpool Chinese and London African Caribbeans. This marks a shift from the old certainties of colour as the primary signifier of social exclusion to more complex processes of regionally and institutionally based inclusions and exclusions. However, at conceptual, political and policy levels, the ongoing narrative of the post-war immigration of Asians and African Caribbeans is still being told in an older language of race and empire. This language is not able to grasp the generational specificities of emerging inter-ethnic social relationships and their engagement with a different racial semantics. Differentialist accounts have made an important theoretical contribution in providing new frameworks that enable us to make sense of new ethnicities, decentred subjectivities and syncretic cultures around the politics of race and nation. A main claim of this work on racial difference is that we cannot simply read off social relations from fixed oppositional categories of blacks and whites. However, there is little sense of what this might mean in specific institutional arenas.

Empirical work with young people emphasizes that their lived experience and explanations of racial difference are ahead of an older generation of anti-racist theory. Of course, this is usually the case. However, there appears to be an increasing gap between both 'older' and more recent social and cultural theory and the lived experience of youth cultures in English multicultural cities. As Back (1996: 4–5) suggests: 'There is little in the cultural studies literature that attempts to describe the cultural dynamics of new ethnicities at the level of everyday life.' Against the general uninterest of recent cultural theory in empirical work, there are a number of qualitative studies that have provided fascinating insights into the changing cultural dynamics taking place between inter-ethnic groups in multicultural cities. The most influential of these include: Jones (1988) *Black Youth, White Culture: The Reggae Tradition from JA to UK*, a study carried out in Birmingham, and two London-based studies, those of Hewitt (1986), *White Talk, Black Talk: Inter-Racial Friendship and Communication Amongst Adolescents*, and Back (1996), *New Ethnicities and Urban Culture: Racisms and Multiculture in Young Lives*. These studies suggest that to develop sociological perspectives that engage comprehensively with the range of theoretical representations of emerging ethnic identity formations, there is a need for a continual referral to social relations in institutional contexts. The hard work of theory-led empirical investigation makes clear the productivity of young people's own accounts, not only by testing theory but also providing alternative avenues of inquiry. In this way, the challenge centres not so much on underlying different representations of identity formations, for example in materialist and differentialist positions, but on a need to address more fundamental issues of the processes involved in identity formation.

There is a long tradition of cultural studies work on youth cultures being read as overly optimistic. Critics question the potential for class- and ethnic-based male youth cultures to serve as a harbinger of social change. A focus on youth styles and cultural resistances tells only part of the story. What is often missing from such texts is the new social condition in which young men and women are living. The political-economic legacy of 1980s globalization for large sectors of young people is that of a post-school anticipation of a condition of dependency on low-skilled central government training schemes, as surplus youth labour in late-industrial capitalism. Young people are now part of a generation whose transition into adulthood as workers, citizens and consumers is in the process of being reconstituted as a result of high rates of unemployment, the deregulation of youth labour markets and punitive legislative changes that have led to the withdrawal of financial state support for young people. Historically, rites of passage in industrial societies have tended to be rather ambiguous processes, lacking the collective rituals, structures and support found in traditional societies. However, more recently, young people – collectively and individually – are constructing their identities in a climate of rapid socio-economic change which has led to a major fracturing in the process of coming of age in England. For example, Willis (1985: 6) speaks of: 'how the young unemployed now find themselves in a new social condition of suspended animation between school and work. Many of the old transitions into work, into cultures and organisations of work, into being consumers, into independent accommodation – have been frozen or broken.' These transitions are further shaped and differentiated by sets of power relations around class, race, ethnicity, gender, sexuality and disability, which have contributed to a decade in which forms of material and social inequalities have greatly increased (Westergaard 1994). In short, we are witnessing highly disorganized and fractured post-compulsory school transitions, with large sectors of ethnic minority and majority working-class young people learning not to labour.

The traditional sociological concern with young people's transition from school to work has assumed that the preparation for the site of production is the primary institutional space in which the formation of young people's identity takes place. Postmodernists have developed conceptual frameworks in which they argue for the need to shift away from class-based sites of production to a wide range of consumerized lifestyles, underpinned by individualization and risk, in order to understand the complexity of contemporary identity formations (Beck 1992). Engaging with recent cultural theories, Furlong and Cartmel (1997: 4) have examined the meaning of the impact of social changes on young people's lives. They argue that: 'while structures of inequality remain deeply entrenched, in our view one of the most significant features of late modernity is the epistemological fallacy: the growing disjuncture between objective and subjective dimensions of life. People's life chances remain highly structured at the same time as they increasingly seek solutions on an individual, rather than a collective basis.'

Institutional sites, such as the family, education and workplace, appear to be secret gardens to many contemporary cultural theorists. Carrying out research with young people in the context of state institutions, and exploring the interplay between the formation of subjectivities and social destinies, is a helpful safeguard against unduly optimistic academic accounts of the meaning of youth cultures and social change. Schooling may be seen as a key institutional arena in which the changing nature of racialized difference is performed in the making and remaking of ethnic and national identities among English-born minorities and the ethnic majority. As Gilroy (1992: 55) suggests: 'crime has been displaced recently at the centre of race politics by another issue . . . now it is the classrooms and staffrooms of the inner city school which frame the same conflict and provide the most potent terms with which to make sense of racial difference.'

Over the past decade a number of theorists have explored the question of schooling, race, culture and difference (Gillborn 1990, 1995; Donald and Rattansi 1992). During this time I have carried out empirical studies in multicultural urban schools (Mac an Ghaill 1988). The following material was collected during a three-year ethnographic study between 1990 and 1992 and reported in *The Making of Men* (Mac an Ghaill 1994a), which was a theory-led empirical investigation of the social construction and regulation of masculinities and sexualities at a secondary school in the West Midlands. Much social science research on education appears to conflate and normatively ascribe differences to what is understood as the 'empirical' and the 'theoretical'. However, what constitutes the 'empirical' and the 'theoretical' can be understood as an effect of a mutually informing relationship, containing the impossibility of neutral description (Lather 1986). More specifically, I have found that recognizing the highly ambivalent relationship between the 'empirical' and the 'theoretical' is productive in developing reflexive research accounts that continually problematize 'what is going on' with reference to the new politics of cultural difference. In this way, the following empirical material is used as a device to examine different readings of social relations in a specific institutional arena, that of state education, which is conceptualized as a post-war representation of the modernist project. At the same time, it is used to explore the productive tensions between materialist-based, anti-oppressive and differentialist positions.

White Englishness, class, generation and masculinity: the production of Anglo-ethnic identities

There is a growing body of evidence that points to the contradictions, ambivalences and resistances in popular cultures of racism among white youth (Billig 1978; Hewitt 1986; Cohen 1989; Rattansi 1992; Mac an Ghaill 1994a; Gillborn 1995; Back 1996). This work challenges materialist accounts that continue to project white racism as a homogeneous social phenomenon. Until recently, materialist-based anti-racist policies tended to focus exclusively on black people. In this way, white ethnicity was made absent from critical analysis. There is an urgent need to deconstruct whiteness in terms of identity formation *and* racialization (Brah 1992). I decided to make white, English, young men the object of my research, not only in terms of racial responses to others but also by focusing on the problematic nature of white Anglo-ethnicity for a dominant majority in a 'post-colonial' era (Cohen 1997). What emerges from this approach is the range of fractured and contradictory white English male subject positions that are inhabited in relation to race, racism and culture. More specifically, I found that in exploring the young men's construction of dominant white English ethnicities from within their own cultural logic, I began to trace the links between institutional life in education and training sites, youth cultural participation, consumption patterns *and* emerging nationalist identities and masculine formations (Parker *et al.* 1992).

Hollands (1990: 171–2) provides one of the most sophisticated accounts of white working-class forms of racism in urban institutional sites, emphasizing the fragmented and diverse responses, influenced by age, gender and more specific intra-class identities. Having delineated a number of working-class transitions into work among young trainees, he set out to explore the different forms of white racism they have adopted. He draws on Cohen's (1986a and b) anti-racist work in schools, in which he distinguishes between three main class codes: an aristocratic code of 'breeding', a bourgeois/democratic variant which provides a scientific reading and a working-class, proletarian code with an emphasis on inheritance of labour power and territoriality. The last position, while also invoking bourgeois and nationalistic variations, is taken up primarily by the manual labour lads. He explains how Britain's economic decline disproportionately affects this group, resulting in their stronger self-interest in maintaining a 'white identity', even though black people are not responsible for the crisis. In contrast, the liberal position, with its more subtle and middle-class appeal, was more likely to be adopted by upwardly mobile young men. Finally, he suggests that a left-labourist perspective of racism was being developed by a group he called the politicos. Cohen and Hollands' conceptual frameworks are helpful in aiding us to understand how racialized white English masculinities are being set up by young, white, working-class men.

In contemporary urban spaces, highly complex racialized maps of inter-ethnic relations are being constructed, from which individual racial behaviour cannot simplistically be predicted or read off from an anti-racist, black–white dualistic model. During my research, white male students illustrated the generational and intra-class specificity of nationalist and racist discourses, challenging conceptions of a unitary working-class inheritance (Cohen 1986a).

These young men, who have diverse values, understandings and feelings as well as local cultural knowledges that they 'bring with them' into public sites, can be seen as active makers of Anglo-ethnic identities. A major flaw in much multicultural and anti-racist work, exemplified in the 'positive images' approach, has been a failure to conceptualize the complexity of youth identity formation. In this process, public institutions can be seen as crucial cultural spaces in which material, ideological and discursive resources are consumed, serving to affirm hegemonic masculine ethnicities while producing a range of subject positions that young men come to inhabit. Most importantly, the subjectivities of these young men are multiple and result in their offering diverse and inconsistent explanations of racism, misogyny, homophobia and heterosexism that are not passively inherited in a unitary or total way. Located in local ethnic, gender and sexual peer group cultures, different sectors of young men actively select from a range of socially oppressive constructs and in this process make their own individual and collective meanings (Gramsci 1971). For example, among working-class students, white, socially non-mobile 'lads' tended to adopt a proletarian stance, showing more continuity with their parents than other peer groups, with particular reference to their fathers' arguments that 'blacks had taken our jobs' and 'taken over our area'. They appealed to varying forms of what Cohen (1988) refers to as the 'nationalism of the neighbourhood', emphasizing the need 'to defend our territory'. White, English, socially mobile young men, adopting a more liberal perspective, challenged this interpretation, claiming that black people could not be held responsible for mass youth unemployment. A number of interrelated elements can be noted here. African-Caribbean and Asian students' orientation to school and associated masculine identities were of particular salience for the white, English, young men's responses to them. Also important, as John, a white macho lad makes clear below, is that, unlike their fathers' generation, these young men have grown up with Asian and African-Caribbean young people. This is not to imply that such day-to-day contact necessarily leads to a decrease in white racist perceptions or an increase in predictable liberal practices. However, the point to stress is that the institutional inter-ethnic social and discursive relations played out among the young men has a historical contingency in a *multicultural* as well as *multiracist* society, with its own internal set of social dynamics (Hewitt 1986; Jones 1988; Back 1996).

John: I used to be a right little Nazi.
MM: How come?
John: Probably my dad the most. He just hates blacks and Asians. He always has. My mum is always telling him not to be so bad.
MM: So how did you change?
John: I don't know. You hang around with them all the time. Like the ones in our gang, they'd do anything for you. I mean we just stick together. We always get into trouble together. Like the teachers always pick on us, so we stick together more.
MM: What about the black and Asian kids you don't hang around with?
John: Well, they're all the same as the white pricks, sucking up to the teachers. You couldn't trust one of them. Our Asian mates say themselves that the Asians are the worst, the slyest. But they go their way and we go ours, innit?
Mark: Some of the bad nutters here are the Asian kids. But really they're just as bad as the white kids in the bottom classes and the blacks. They just stand around threatening people, especially the little kids. They have to be tough all the time, causing trouble,

you know. But probably a main difference is that there's always been more Asians in the top classes. So you hang around with them more. We've got more in common, to talk about and that. The bright ones have more in common. It's not really about colour. Like we're all friends in the top set and hang round together.

Currently, much anti-racist thinking has failed to engage with broader theorizing about contemporary social and cultural transformations. Rather, there is a continuing reliance on earlier materialist theories that explain white racism in terms of a predictable racial superiority. For example, there have been few attempts either to locate explanations in the new global conditions of late capitalism characterized by time-space compression, or to investigate the impact of the restructuring of de-industrializing urban regions on relations between and within ethnic majority and minority communities. Rather than feelings of superiority, in dislocating inner-city areas of mass youth unemployment and fragmented family lifestyles young, white, English people are reporting feelings of cultural inferiority (Wieviorka 1991). A key issue among white, working-class, English young men and women in inner cities, as part of a wider crisis in Anglo-ethnicity, is their claim that schools are racist in favouring African Caribbeans and Asians while discriminating against whites. In response to this, teachers maintain that the white students' comments are a result of their racism. During my research I asked head teachers what educational principles informed their schools' anti-racist policies. They argued that it is important in a multiethnic community that the curriculum addresses students' diverse cultural needs. I found evidence in the selection of curriculum material of positive representations of minority cultures, particularly those of African Caribbeans and Asians. However, there appeared to be little awareness of the needs of other ethnic groups, including the high proportion of Irish students who often constituted the main ethnic minority group in schools in the West Midlands. Of equal significance was the failure to address white, English, working-class students' cultural needs. Asking the teachers about this absence, they replied by asking me: have white, English, working-class students got any culture? These comments highlight the conceptual limits for public-sector professionals working in an anti-racist problematic in which white racism is assumed to be a homogeneous social phenomenon and in which the representation of blacks and whites is juxtaposed in a 'simple' framework of oppressed and oppressors. The defining characteristic of the white, English, working-class as a social collectivity is their 'whiteness'. From within this reductionist black–white dualistic model of oppositional structures, 'whiteness' speaks power and 'blackness' speaks powerlessness. Hence, public-sector professionals are unable to respond to white, working-class accounts of feelings of exclusion except to read it as further evidence of a racist stance that is seen as structurally pre-given. Anti-racist policy informed by a principle of exclusivity is unable to address the ethnic majority's current experiences, concerns and anxieties.

This projection of the Anglo-ethnic majority's fears illustrates the complexity of dealing with racialized institutional spaces in English inner cities at the end of the twentieth century. White, English, young people are appropriating the language of racialized oppression in the specific context of compulsory state schooling, in which they feel that those in authority are culturally excluding them. In talking with their teachers, the teacher responses make clear the dominant institutionalized response to white, working-class young men in terms of a class cultural deficit view. Here we see the success of new social movements' development of anti-racism and anti-sexism in providing political minorities with counter-discourses to name their collective experience of hostile, unsafe and exclusionary public spaces. They are in a position to provide, to themselves and to others, an alternative explanation of their own experiences of alienating institutions. White, English, working-class young people are unable to draw on similar discursive resources to name their experience of social class alienation and marginalization. Hence, their class-based experiences come to be spoken through the language of racism. This is an interesting variation on Stuart Hall's argument in the 1980s that, for black people, class worked through the modality of race. These tensions and contradictions are likely to increase during the next decade within the wider political picture of a discursive shift in the media from the 'racial problems' of social minorities to those of social majorities as the 'new victims'.

The Real Englishmen: in search of a national(ist) identity

Much has been written by social scientists about white, working-class, male youth cultural forms of racism. White, middle-class young men have remained invisible. In my own research a most interesting subcultural group of white, English, middle-class male students was identified. They called themselves The Real Englishmen. Their name served as a triple signifier, with reference to their parents' political positions on gender, sexuality and ethnicity, which were highly problematic intergenerational issues for them. They were in the process of constructing a positive Anglo-ethnic identity. At times their talk of nationality and cultural belonging appeared obsessive. They explained the significance of their name with reference to white Anglo-ethnicity. More specifically, they were developing a young masculine identity against what they perceived as their parents' denial and suppression of English nationality and nationalism. They pointed to the need for a local sense of ethnic belonging that older generational notions of internationalism and Europeanism failed to provide. Furthermore, they highlight that an older generation's preoccupation with colour as the primary signifier of difference and differentiation prevents their parents from engaging with what for the young men are the 'real' contemporary mechanisms of exclusion that operate through culture. The Real Englishmen, in their defence of what they saw as a declining English masculine ethnic identity, nostalgically appealed to the demise of 'English culture'. Interestingly, their understanding of culture was a mixture of recent cultural studies and older English Literature meanings, to which they, as middle-class young people, had access.

    Adam: It's like we can't be English, English men, be proud of being English. I argue about this with my dad all the time. He just

> dismisses it, saying it's all constructed and we should all be
> internationalists.
>
> *MM:* Why is it important to you?
>
> *Adam:* Because it's unfair. All the Asian kids and the black kids, they
> can be Asian or black. They can be proud of their countries.
>
> *MM:* Do you think of yourselves as racist?
>
> *Adam:* No. No. That's what the teachers try and tell you, they try and
> force on you if you say anything, try to make you feel guilty
> like them. But we're not talking about colour. We're talking
> about culture.
>
> *Richard:* English culture. And if you talk about the English flag or what-
> ever, anything to do with Englishness, they call you a little
> Fascist.

In my discussions with them, parents often either conflated race and
ethnicity or subsumed the latter under the former. They displayed a contradictory response to ethnic difference, acknowledging the ethnicity of
minorities but refusing to concede their own ethnic majority status. Some of
the parents spoke of their sons going through a phase, as part of a broader
adolescent search for an adult male identity.

> *Mr Stone:* Adam reminds me of myself. Just trying out different things.
> He's very bright and the younger generation should challenge
> the older one. Adam and his friends at this age have very
> strong feelings. At times they try to shock us as parents.
> Quite healthy for young men. It's part of the process of
> their gaining their own independence.
>
> *Ms Taylor:* You see them identifying with the Union Jack and talking a
> lot about English nationality. It's all tied up with the Falk-
> lands fiasco that ignited new forms of extreme nationalism
> in this country. Some of the parents wonder if we've pro-
> duced little Fascists. But they'll come out of this surer of
> themselves. At other times, like when we visit Europe, Ben's
> very much at home as a European.

Who are the English? is a key question for British sociology of racism
and ethnicity in conditions of 'post-colonialism'. In many ways, the question of the identity of the English has been a central question in an earlier
colonial period (Spivak 1986). However, for much of the history of the field
of inquiry it has remained hidden from the ethnic majority. For many English people, from different political and ideological positions, it remains
submerged beneath questions of the 'special needs' of minority ethnic groups,
represented as either problems or victims. Critical theory reminds us that
this is familiar ground in exploring relations between dominant/subordinate
social collectivities where the focus is exclusively on the lives of the latter.
It might be suggested that English sociologists, albeit from a progressive position,
have tended to remain in this limited and limiting conceptual framework, in
which the lives of white, English people remain unexamined. In other words,
they maintain a sense of indeterminacy about their own Anglo-ethnic status
that serves to protect it from critical investigation. There are interesting

epistemological and methodological questions here about who is in a position to answer the question: who are the English?

Ethnic minorities know a lot about the English, because they have to in order to survive. Reflecting on this, I am reminded that in teaching situations many English students and academic peers find it difficult to cope with discussions about Englishness. There are a range of objections that they employ in an attempt to curtail such talk. These teaching situations are often full of tension, defensiveness and anger. However, this might be a starting point, where we might begin a productive discussion about the meaning of racial, national and ethnic difference. In other words, there is a need to move beyond a conceptual framework that begins with making minorities the object of inquiry. A key issue that emerged during my research was the question of what constitutes white, Anglo-ethnic identity. More specifically, I became interested in the constitutive cultural elements of dominant modes of white, English subjectivity that informed male students' learning to perform 'being English' in different institutional arenas. These elements consisted of contradictory forms of inherited imperial images, new cultural forms of racism and anti-racist counter-discourses that were marked by contextual contingency, ambivalence and anxiety. It is becoming evident that Anglo-ethnic identity is a highly fragile, socially constructed phenomenon. The question that emerges here is: how does this fragile construction become represented as an apparently stable, unitary category with fixed meanings? It is suggested that schools, alongside other state institutions, attempt to administer, regulate and reify unstable ethnic, racial and nationalist categories. Most particularly this administration, regulation and reification of ethnic, racial and national boundaries is institutionalized through the interrelated material, social and discursive practices of staffroom, classroom and playground micro-cultures. In turn, white, English academics, with their own self-representations, have added a further ideological layer of mystification, reinforcing the reification of the Anglo-ethnic majority.

This younger generation of white, English men raise a critical issue that is often absent from anti-racist programmes: the question of how English ethnicity fits into the complex configuration of inter-ethnic interpersonal relations at an institutional level in civil society. Furthermore, implicitly they raise questions about whether we can begin to construct contemporary forms of progressive English national identity to counter the New Right's appropriation of the discourse of nationality with its projected atavistic representations of the strong, exclusionary British nation-state. In such a process it may be possible to work through the question of why 'there ain't no black in the Union Jack' (Gilroy 1987). Hall (1992b: 258), writing of shifts in black cultural politics, refers to this title and suggests that: 'Fifteen years ago we didn't care, or at least I didn't care, whether there was any black in the Union Jack. Now not only do we care, we must.' In the context of the increasing criticism directed at materialist-based, anti-oppressive initiatives, such as anti-racism and feminism, these young men as a gendered, sexual and ethnic majority embody central contradictions in providing a critique that may help to point a way forward. Most significantly, they raise key questions about the assumptions of cultural fixity involved in processes of inclusion and exclusion that underpin anti-racist academic and political representations.

A second aspect of the white, new, middle-class, English, young men's responses to their education in an inner-city comprehensive school involved their accounts of how the 'local' institutional micro-politics of power translated into practice. Their parents believed in comprehensive education as a means of overcoming social class divisions. This informed sending their sons to the local inner-city secondary school. The students were ambivalent about their parents' choice; on the one hand, they preferred the choice of the local comprehensive to the elitist grammar school. However, the students' negative experience of their schooling included being bullied by white and black working-class male students, who perceived them as 'non-proper' boys. When they complained to their parents and teachers about this, they felt that they were ignored. With reference to inter-ethnic student conflict, parents and teachers, working in a materialist anti-racist position, argued that only whites could be racist, and hence the abuse the students received from African-Caribbean and Asian male students was dismissed. The students were also critical of their teachers and parents for generalizing across generations about responsibility for the historical legacy of colonial forms of white racism.

> *Thomas:* It's the same as the anti-sexist stuff. Our parents are always on about anti-racism and all this. And it's the same here. I always remember when we first came here and we were doing paintings and we suddenly realized you got more marks if you did multicultural ones.
>
> *Ben:* The teachers and our parents, when they talk about racism, always say white people mustn't be racist to blacks. That's fine. But they won't say anything when Asians and black kids are racist to each other.
>
> *Adam:* And how come they keep on saying that racialism is really bad but we've had a load of hassle from black and Asian kids? The ones in the lowest sets the most, the nutters, and no one says anything about that. Well, why is that OK?
>
> *Adam:* But no one asks about us. The older generation don't ask what it's like for us who have to live with a lot of black kids who don't like us. No one says to black kids, you have to like the whites. They'll tell them to fuck off.
>
> *MM:* Do you think that it's the same thing for you and for black kids?
>
> *Richard:* Well that's what the teachers come back with: only whites can be racist. It's crap, all the imperialist stuff. But the younger ones, we didn't cause that, did we?

Presently, there is a danger of the above discussion being read as support for the 'white flight' from inner cities, as white, middle-class parents search out 'good' schools for their children (Cohen 1993). However, alternative readings are possible of a younger generational response to an inherited legacy of anti-oppressive reformation, which they would argue has positive as well as negative effects. These young people point out that these issues are far more complex than their parents 'rationally imagined'. Without wishing to generalize from this particular class fraction, they provide important criticisms – from the inside, as it were – of a cultural world that progressive educators, underpinned by new social movement theory, have attempted to construct. The young men point to the internal contradictions of the complex interrelationship of different forms of social divisions. More specifically, they graphically illustrate that the attempt to address one aspect of multi-oppressions may have unintended consequences for other aspects. Anti-oppressive frameworks tend to display little sensitivity to the ways in which, in particular social contexts, such as work, training, educational or leisure sites, inter-ethnic relations exist at the intersection of a range of social relations and come to 'speak' these, often in unpredictable ways. Here we see that power relations of subordination and resistance need to be understood as being actively *produced* as well as *reproduced*, marked by a relational logic of shifting boundaries in specific public institutional spaces.

Shifting inter-ethnic tensions and alliances: cultural investments and sexual subjectivities

Rattansi (1992: 27) has outlined the contextual contingency of racialized discourses, arguing that shifting alliances and points of tension may emerge from different arenas. He writes:

> The ambivalences generated for many white youth by the attractions of Afro-Caribbean, Afro-American and African musical forms, and their admirations for some aggressive forms of Afro-Caribbean masculinity, have resulted in alliances in particular schools and neighbourhoods between white and Afro-Caribbean youth against Asian youth, while in some schools where black–white conflicts remain submerged the dominant form of racist insult occurs between different ethnic minority groups, for instance Asian and Afro-Caribbean or Cypriot and Vietnamese.

In my research I found similar shifting inter-ethnic tensions and alliances were present in a highly contingent and continually changing situation. For example, there was no fixed pattern of white or black inter-ethnic response in the different year groups. Rather, different student subgroups assigned high status to particular individuals or peer groups in which different hierarchies of ethnic masculinities were competitively negotiated and acted out. During the research period this was highlighted in relation to English-born, Asian, socially non-mobile 'lads' who racially insulted year seven students who had recently arrived at the school from Pakistan. Here we see the lived complexity of shifting processes of racialized inclusions and exclusions. The English-born Asian 'lads' drew on older hierarchies of ethnic masculinities in which low status is ascribed to 'feminized' Asian boys. At the same moment, their public performance in distancing themselves from this ascribed social category is circumscribed by a shift from colour to that of cultural difference as a signifier of racialized exclusion. In this specific institutional space contradictory discourses of exclusion positioned the new arrivals as not belonging to the 'local community' of the school and surrounding neighbourhood. Similar practices of exclusion were experienced by Arab and Vietnamese students.

Student inter-ethnic relations were a mixture of race-specific elements and a broader range of social and psychic phenomena located in the school and linked to other social arenas. These involved specific emotional invest-ments and cultural attachments around popular cultural forms such as music and sport, which were of central significance to their creative explorations of the shifting contours of cultural and political identities among and between ethnic minority and majority young people (Gilroy 1987). As in the work of Hewitt (1986) and Back (1996), these young men were involved in construct-ing new syncretic versions of transculturally based identities. This is a long way from the fixed ethnic categories of much anti-racist and multicultural discourses on the racialization of institutional arenas. Below, sixth-form stu-dents explain the inter-ethnic student complexity and ambiguity in operation at their secondary school.

Carlton: Like all the stuff we read on blacks in schools don't even begin to get at what is going on. They talk of blacks, Asians and whites and then ask them what they think of each other. It's crazy. Like here with black culture, the kids' language, cussing and that, their cool movement, the hairstyles, the music and the clothes, you see the Asians and the white kids really getting into it, deeply into it, right. But at the same time some of these Asians and whites will have racist views about blacks. And it's the same with the blacks about the others. Its really a mix-up and difficult to work out, you know what I mean?

Rajinder: You see there's a lot of sexuality in there. The African Caribbeans are seen as better at football and that's really im-portant in this school for making a reputation. And it's the same with dancing, again the black kids are seen as the best. And the white kids and the Asians are jealous because they think that the girls will really prefer the black kids. So, the race thing gets all mixed up with other things that are import-ant to young kids.

Carlton: It's all a mix-up round here with young people. They are making their own culture, really that is what is going on. You can't even call it black culture, like as though it comes from Africa or Jamaica. You see it more in London but it is happen-ing here in its own way. Places have got their own rhythm. In music and talking and acting, the way you act, there are all these different styles – black, Asian and white – that come together. Even when all the American stuff comes in, it works different in Birmingham and even different in different places in Birmingham.

Rajinder: A lot of kids say they're into this particular style or music. But most of them are picking up bits from here and there. Its like on the scene [gay] you see fashions that then are taken up among straights, who would die if they knew where they came from. But that's the way it is, whether blacks or gays are hated at one level, at another level most people are into this mixed-up culture. Like when kids go back to India, they find out they're not 'proper' Indians. In a lot of parts of England, they're not 'proper' English people. But here in our local area we are making a new generation. So, in some ways it is no good talking about blacks and whites but I don't mean we have just become a mixture. It's really difficult to talk about because we are living it. But when we think about it like now, you can see there is something going around here that is really alive, that is really new coming out from our living together.

Carlton: That is true. You can't talk about it, not really. You can't express it because we have not got a language to discuss it. But you do feel it, especially when you go away from here [Birmingham].

Fanon (1970: 160) has suggested that: 'if one wants to understand the racial situation psychoanalytically . . . as it is experienced by individual consciousness, considerable importance must be given to sexual phenomena'. As Rajinder suggests, the complexity and contingency of the student inter-ethnic relations in the research school appeared most visible in relation to sexuality. This was made most explicit by the macho lads. The white macho lads adopted a range of contradictory racial and sexual discourses. At one level, there was a strong public masculine identification with the Asian and African-Caribbean macho lads. The peer group constructed a hierarchy of sexual prowess in which they positioned themselves as the most successful with young women. This self-representation was worked out against conformist students, who they publicly derided for their assumed sexual inexperience. At another level, individual white macho lads privately spoke to me, with more confidence outside school, of the African-Caribbean macho lads' perceived heterosexual success with young white women as illegitimate. At other times, female students from the research school were labelled as 'slags' if they were seen with African Caribbeans or Asians from other schools, who were constructed as 'monstrous others' (Fanon 1970).

Jim: Some of the white girls at that school let themselves be treated like doormats by the black kids. And some of them even go off with the 'Pakis'.

Similar contradictions operated with the African-Caribbean, socially non-mobile 'lads' who combined a public solidarity with the white macho lads and privately a general criticism of white men's sexuality. They positioned themselves as sexually superior both to white and Asian students and to conformist black students. More specifically, they spoke of themselves as the main producers of popular style which they claimed made them attractive to young women. This could not be read simply in terms of youthful boasting. The African Caribbeans appropriated discursive themes from dominant, ambivalent white student representations in which black, male students' behaviour was oversexualized. As with white, male teachers, this consisted of contradictory cultural investments of desire and envy in a highly exaggerated ascription to the black, socially non-mobile 'lads' of stylish resistance, sporting skills and 'having a reputation with girls'.

In order to enhance and amplify their own masculinity, Asian, African-Caribbean and white, socially non-mobile 'lads' were overtly sexist to young women and female staff, and aggressive to male students who did not live up to their prescribed masculine norms. They adopted a number of collective social practices in their attempt to regulate and normalize sex/gender boundaries. The black, socially non-mobile 'lads' were particularly vindictive to African-Caribbean academic students who overtly distanced themselves from their anti-school strategies. In response, the African-Caribbean 'lads' labelled them 'botty men' (a homophobic comment). As Mercer and Julien (1988: 112) point out, a further contradiction in subordinated black masculinities occurs 'when black men subjectively internalise and incorporate aspects of the dominant definitions of masculinity in order to contest the conditions of dependency and powerlessness which racism and racial oppression enforce'. Ironically, the African-Caribbean 'lads', in distancing themselves from racist school structures, adopted survival strategies of hyper-masculine heterosexuality that threatened other African-Caribbean students, adding further barriers to their gaining academic success. Consequently, this made it more difficult for academic African-Caribbean students to gain social mobility via a professional job and the associated middle-class mode of masculinity. At the same time, white teachers' social positioning of black males as aggressive was reinforced (Gillborn 1990).

Conclusion: 'coming times'

Contemporary Racisms and Ethnicities has argued for the need to see the work of the remaking of conceptual frameworks, policies and ethnographies as central to the sociology of racism and ethnicity for 'coming times'. The term 'coming times' was developed among an early group of post-colonial political activists, intellectuals and poets in the emerging Republic of Ireland in the 1920s. We can only speculate as to what they would make of the current relative positions of new Ireland and old Britain, both in terms of the restructured, high-tech Republic and the incomplete new settlement in the North (Miller 1998). O'Toole (1997: 10), writing of the Dublin summit of the European Union in 1996, which was the 75th anniversary of the Anglo-Irish treaty under which the Irish State was established, describes the way in which:

> Britain was so obviously an inconsequential and edgy presence on the margins while Ireland, holding the presidency, was at the centre of things, comfortable and confident. For centuries, England was phlegmatic, assertive and businesslike, while Ireland was unsettled, uncertain, fretful about its national identity and place in the world. Now the roles have been reversed: it was in England (and also, of course, Scotland and Wales) that questions like nationality, sovereignty and identity were sites of confusion and contest, while the Republic of Ireland seemed, in 1996, to have gone beyond all that.

The Anglo-ethnic majority – including most sociologists – find it difficult to place a de-industrializing British nation-state in conditions of 'post-colonialism' at the centre of their explanation of the politics of nation and race. This book suggests the need to address the displaced anxieties of the ethnic majority in the context of class, regional and sexual politics, as a central object of sociological inquiry in the twenty-first century.

Contemporary Racisms and Ethnicities focuses on the mutual interplay of changing representations of racisms and ethnicities with wider social and cultural transformations. The book argues the need to produce local understandings of how people live with a plurality of differences. The last chapter has explored one institutional site, that of schooling, which is seen as a post-war representation of the modernist project, a project that currently appears to be in crisis. It has focused on shifting inter-ethnic tensions and alliances involving complex investments and sexual subjectivities. This is not to privilege this institutional space nor to suggest an undifferentiated category of youth as a source of social change. This younger generation – both ethnic minority and majority – displays a wide range of responses to life in a multicultural and multiracist society. Most importantly, these young people signal the need to move beyond earlier studies of post-war immigrants and their children – the colonial paradigm – to a focus on established minorities and their British/English-born children. A new vocabulary is actively being developed among this younger generation that is a constitutive element of 'coming times' in Britain. It does not provide a clear picture of the future, nor does it translate easily into a political programme or policy approach. Further work is needed on restructured labour markets and collective consumption in civil society that will provide a more comprehensive understanding of the impact of global capitalism, de-industrialization and the weakening of the welfare state in opening up spaces for racism and anti-racism (Wieviorka 1991). Importantly, such studies will highlight the socio-historical continuities and discontinuities between social inegalitarian and differentialist forms of racism at a time of convergence between racist and anti-racist discourses across Europe. In turn, this may enable us to develop a language to engage with issues of racial difference and how we might contribute to the transformative nature of racism in wider frameworks of social justice, civil rights and citizenship. *Contemporary Racisms and Ethnicities* may be read as an attempt to jostle the imagination of the reader, by providing some more metaphors for living life, some more complexities to disturb old routines, some more politics to disrupt the functions of the past and some more views to punctuate the now-crumbling view of a unified social order (Plummer 1992: xviii–xix).

Note

1 The Macpherson report challenges this general trend, highlighting the issue of institutional racism.

Guide *to* further reading

In *Contemporary Racisms and Ethnicities* I have sought to provide a critical and engaging account of what is going on in this area. In so doing, I have drawn on a wide range of books and articles. In this guide I want to suggest what I feel are some of the most helpful texts for further reading with reference to specific chapters. As well as these texts, journals are of particular importance, in providing the most up-to-date debates about racism and ethnicity at a time of rapid change. There are a number of excellent journals from which to select. My own selection includes: *Social Identities, Journal of Ethnic and Migration Studies, Ethnic and Racial Studies, Patterns of Prejudice, Sage Relations Abstracts,* and *Race, Ethnicity and Education.*

Chapter 1 Changing academic and political representations of race, ethnicity and racism

This chapter covers a wide range of earlier British debates on ethnicity, race and racism. A main point that was made here was the need to re-engage with this important literature. Some of the most interesting and influential texts of 'old times' include: Benedict 1943; Banton 1967, 1987; Rex 1970; Castles and Kosack 1973; Hall *et al.* 1978; Hall 1980; Miles 1982; Sivanandan 1982. Some of the best theoretical overviews of the 1970s and 1980s are: Rex and Mason 1986; Cohen and Bains 1988; Miles 1989; Anthias and Yuval-Davis 1993; Gabriel 1994; Solomos and Back 1996. Studies of local areas and institutions are found in: Rex and Moore 1967; Rex and Tomlinson 1979; Mac an Ghaill 1988; Gillborn 1990; Mirza 1992. Ethnic minority feminist texts on Britain, both 'old times' and 'new times', have tended to be underplayed in much of the race-relations and anti-racist literature. See Carby 1982; Parmar 1982; Amos and Parmar 1984; Walter 1984; Bryan *et al.* 1985; Hickman 1995a; Mama 1995; Mirza 1997.

Chapter 2 Racialized subjects: culture, identity and difference

The terms culture, identity and difference continue to be widely debated across different perspectives. Many of the texts in this area are difficult to engage with. It may be best to start by looking at the edited collection by Woodward (1997) which provides clear definitions of the concepts developed by contemporary cultural theorists. The suggested shift from 'old times' to 'new times' is captured in Centre for Contemporary Cultural Studies 1982; Gilroy 1987. An exploration of the complexity of culture, identity and ethnic formations can be found in Hall 1991a, 1992a and b; Said 1993. For further reading on notions of diaspora, hybridity and syncretism see: Spivak 1988a and b; Bhabha 1990a; Apter 1991; Gilroy 1993; Young 1995; Brah 1996. Wetherell and Potter (1992) provide an excellent account of discourse analysis of racism in their study of how Pakeha (white New Zealand settlers) make sense of their history towards the Maori minority. Psychoanalytical perspectives can be found in: Fanon 1970; Henriques *et al.* 1984; Gilman 1985; Cohen 1987; Bhabha 1990a; Greenslade 1992; Mama 1995.

Chapter 3   Rethinking racisms and ethnicities: rethinking the black–white dualism

The focus of this chapter is an examination of the theoretical shift beyond the black–white model of racism towards one in which cultural and religious identities are foregrounded. Said (1978) is a major influential study of the 'other' in colonial and post-colonial discourses. For feminist accounts of whiteness, see Brah 1992; C. Hall 1992; Ware 1992; Anthias and Yuval-Davis 1993; Frankenberg 1993. Roediger (1992) has written a fine historical account of whiteness. Further material on new racism can be found in Barker 1981; Centre for Contemporary Cultural Studies 1982; Gilroy 1987; from a European perspective, see Fanon 1970; Balibar 1991a; Hickman 1995a and b; Wieviorka 1995. Accounts of contemporary forms of racism in Europe can be found in Alund and Schierup 1991; Balibar and Wallerstein 1991; Webber 1991; Wieviorka 1991; Silverman 1992; Ford 1992; Atkinson 1993; Wrench and Solomos 1993; Willems 1995. Some of the best work on anti-Irish racism is: Hazelkorn 1990; Greenslade 1992; Gribben 1994; Connor 1985; Hickman 1995a; Hickman and Walter 1997; Kowarzik 1997; Williams *et al.* 1997.

Chapter 4   Globalization and localization: nation-making and citizenship

This chapter explores nation-making and citizenship in the context of the interplay between changing racial, ethnic and national identities and social and cultural trans-formations. In an expanding literature on globalization Walters (1995) provides an excellent introduction. Other key texts include: Wallerstein 1974; Amin 1980; Hirst and Thompson 1996; Hoogvelt 1997. There is a long history of critical writing on immigration legislation on racial and sexual exclusions, including Holmes 1988; Layton-Henry 1992; Saggar 1992; Solomos 1993; Hickman 1995a; Brah 1996. On national identity see Anderson 1983; Gellner 1983; Hobsbawm 1983; and on nationalism see Nairn 1977; Sivanandan 1982; Giddens 1985; Gilroy 1987; Cohen 1988; Bhabha 1990a; Billig 1995; on migration see Ahmad 1992; Castles and Miller 1993; on the British national collectivity see Hechter 1975; Anthias and Yuval-Davis 1993; Kiberd 1996. Questions of race, space and place are covered in Cohen 1988, 1993; Westwood 1990; Anderson 1993; Jackson and Penrose 1993a; Keith 1993; Solomos and Back 1995; Back 1996. Interesting texts on citizenship include Parekh 1985, 1991; Mercer and Julien 1988; Hall and Held 1989; Brubaker 1992; Silverman 1992; Campani 1993; Lloyd 1994.

Chapter 5   Anti-racism and ethnic minority community mobilization

This chapter is concerned with anti-racism and minority ethnic community mobil-izations. There is a broad critical literature on anti-racism which includes: Macdonald *et al.* 1989; Cambridge and Feuchtwang 1990a; Cohen 1992; Gilroy 1992; Bonnett 1993; Lloyd 1994; Gillborn 1995. For further reading on the growth of racist ideologies and extreme right and neo-Fascist movements across Europe and beyond, see Balibar 1991b; Silverman 1992; Wrench and Solomos 1993; and for material on anti-racist movements across Europe see Taguieff 1988, 1990; Alund and Schierup 1991; Silverman 1992; Guillaumin 1995; Willems 1995. Minority ethnic group mobilizations are discussed in Gilroy 1987; Cohen 1993; Lloyd 1994. The history of black mobilization can be found in Banton 1955; Patterson 1963; Davidson 1966; Allen 1982; Carby 1982; Sivanandan 1982, 1983; Joshua *et al.* 1983. On questions of class, race, cultural politics and community see Rex 1973; Miles and Phizacklea 1977, 1979; Rex and Tomlinson 1979; Wallman 1979; Centre for Contemporary Cultural Studies 1982; Solomos 1988; Eade 1989; Knowles and Mercer 1992; Small 1994. Historical and contemporary accounts of Irish mobilization can be found in Jackson 1963; Curtis 1968, 1971; L. Curtis 1984; Williams and Mac an Ghaill 1998; Hickman and Walter 1995; Mac Laughlin 1995; Williams *et al.* 1997. On Muslim mobilization and religious identities, see Asad 1990, 1993; Modood 1992; Al-Azmeh 1993; Brah 1996.

Conclusion: 'coming times': re-making policies – re-making ethnographies

This chapter focuses on questions of policy and ethnography. On questions of living with difference, see Mercer and Julien 1988; Connolly 1991; Parekh 1991; Young 1993. There are a number of interesting texts available on policy such as Brah and Deem 1986; Jenkins and Solomos 1987; Macdonald *et al.* 1989; Williams 1989; Solomos and Ball 1990; Savage and Robins 1990; Mama 1992. Detailed accounts of contradictory popular cultures of racism among white youth can be found in Billig 1978; Hewitt 1986; Cohen 1989; Rattansi 1992; Mac an Ghaill 1994b; Gillborn 1995; Back 1996.

References

Ahmad, A. (1992) *In Theory: Classes, Nations, Literatures*. London: Verso.

Ainley, P. (1993) *Class and Skill: Changing Divisions of Knowledge and Labour*. London: Cassell.

Al-Azmeh, A. (1993) *Islams and Modernities*. London: Verso.

Allen, S. (1982) 'Confusing categories and neglecting contradictions', in E. Cashmore and B. Troyna (eds) *Black Youth in Crisis*. London: Allen and Unwin.

Althusser, L. (1971) *Lenin and Philosophy and Other Essays*. London: New Left Books.

Alund, A. and Schierup, C. U. (1991) *Paradoxes of Multiculturalism: Essays on Swedish Society*. Aldershot: Avebury.

Amin, S. (1980) *Class and Nation*. London: Heinemann.

Amos, V. and Parmar, P. (1984) 'Challenging imperial feminism', *Feminist Review*, 17, 3–19.

Anderson, B. (1983) *Imagined Communities: Reflections on the Origin and Spread of Nationalism*. London: Verso.

Anderson, K. J. (1993) 'Constructing geographies: "race", place and the making of Sydney's Aboriginal Redfern', in P. Jackson and J. Penrose (eds) *Constructions of Race, Place and Nation*. London: UCL Press.

Anthias, F. (1990) 'Race and class revisited – conceptualising race and racisms', *Sociological Review*, xxxviii (1), 19–42.

Anthias, F. (1992a) 'Connecting "race" and ethnic phenomena', *Sociology*, 26(3), 421–38.

Anthias, F. (1992b) *Ethnicity, Class and Migration – Greek Cypriots in Britain*. Aldershot: Gower.

Anthias, F. and Yuval-Davis, N. (1993) *Racialised Boundaries: Race, Nation, Gender, Colour and Class and the Anti-Racist Struggle*. London: Routledge.

Appaduri, A. (1991) 'Global ethnoscapes: Notes and queries for a transnational anthropology', in R. G. Fox (ed.) *Recapturing Anthropology: Working in the Present*. Santa Fe: School of American Research.

Apter, A. (1991) 'Herskovits's heritage: rethinking syncretism in the African diaspora', *Diaspora*, 1(3), 235–60.

Arendt, H. (1973) *The Origins of Totalitarianism*. San Diego: Harcourt Brace.

Asad, T. (1990) 'Ethnography, literature and politics: some readings and uses of Salman Rushdie's *The Satanic Verses*', *Cultural Anthropology*, 5(3), 239–69.

Asad, T. (1993) *Genealogies of Religion: Discipline and Reasons of Power in Christianity and Islam*. Baltimore: Johns Hopkins University Press.

Atkenson, P. H. (1996) *The Irish Diaspora: A Primer*. Belfast: Meany/The Institute of Irish Studies, University of Belfast.

Atkinson, G. (1993) 'Germany: nationalism, nazism and violence', in T. Bjorja and R. Witte (eds) *Racist Violence in Europe*. Basingstoke: Macmillan.

Back, L. (1996) *New Ethnicities and Urban Culture: Racisms and Multiculture in Young Lives*. London: UCL Press.

Balibar, E. (1989) 'Le racisme: encore un universalisme', *Mots*, 18(March), 44–52.

Balibar, E. (1991a) 'Is there a "neo-racism"?', in E. Balibar and I. Wallerstein (eds) *Race, Nation, Class: Ambiguous Identities*. London: Verso.

Balibar, E. (1991b) 'Racism and nationalism', in E. Balibar and I. Wallerstein (eds) *Race, Nation, Class: Ambiguous Identities*. London: Verso.

Balibar, E. (1991c) 'Es gibt keinen Staat in Europa: racism and politics in Europe today', *New Left Review*, 186, 5–19.

Balibar, E. (1991d) 'Racism and crisis', in E. Balibar and I. Wallerstein (eds) *Race, Nation, Class: Ambiguous Identities*. London: Verso.

Balibar, E. and Wallerstein, I. (1991) *Race, Nation, Class: Ambiguous Identities*. London: Verso.

Ball, W. and Solomos, J. (eds) (1990) *Race and Local Politics*. London: Macmillan.

Ballard, C. (1979) 'Conflict, continuity and change: second generation Asians', in V. S. Khan (ed.) *Minority Families in Britain: Support and Stress*. London: Tavistock.

Ballard, J. A. (1992) 'Sexuality and the state in time of epidemic', in R. W. Connell and G. W. Dowsett (eds) *Rethinking Sex: Social Theory and Sexuality Research*. Melbourne: Melbourne University Press.

Ballard, C. and Driver, G. (1977) 'The ethnic approach', *New Society*, 16 June, 543–5.

Banks, J. and Lynch, J. (eds) (1986) *Multicultural Education in Western Societies*. London: Holt, Rinehart and Winston.

Banton, M. (1955) *The Coloured Quarter: Negro Immigrants in an English City*. London: Jonathan Cape.

Banton, M. (1967) *Race Relations*. London: Tavistock.

Banton, M. (1977) *The Idea of Race*. London: Tavistock.

Banton, M. (1987) *Racial Theories*. Cambridge: Cambridge University Press.

Barker, M. (1981) *The New Racism*. London: Junction Books.

Barth, F. (1969) *Ethnic Groups and Boundaries: The Social Organization of Cultural Difference*. London: Allen and Unwin.

Barthes, R. (1977) *Image, Music, Text*. London: Fontana.

Baudrillard, J. (1981) *For a Critique of the Political Economy of the Sign*. St. Lois: Telos.

Baudrillard, J. (1983) *Simulations*. New York: Semiotext(e).

Baudrillard, J. (1988) *America*. Harmondsworth: Penguin.

Bauman, Z. (1992) *Intimations of Postmodernity*. London: Routledge.

Beck, U. (1992) *Risk Society: Towards a New Modernity*. London: Sage.

Benedict, R. (1943) *Race and Racism*. London: Routledge.

Beresford, D. (1987) *Ten Dead Men: The Story of the 1981 Hunger Strike*. London: Grafton Books.

Bhabha, H. (1986) 'Foreword: Remembering Fanon', in F. Fanon (ed.) *Black Skin, White Masks*. London: Pluto Press.

Bhabha, H. (1990a) *Nation and Narration*. London: Routledge.

Bhabha, H. (1990b) 'Introduction: narrating the nation', in H. Bhabha (ed.) *Nation and Narration*. London: Routledge.

Bhabha, H. (1994) *The Location Culture*. London: Routledge.

Bhatt, C. (1994) 'New foundations: contingency, indeterminacy and black translocality', in J. Weeks (ed.) *The Lesser Evil and the Greater Good: The Theory and Politics of Social Diversity*. London: Rivers Oram Press.

Bhavnani, K. K. (1991) *Talking Politics: A Psychological Framing for Views from Youth in Britain*. Cambridge: Cambridge University Press.

Bhavnani, K. K. and Phoenix, A. (1994) 'Shifting identities, shifting racisms: an introduction', *Feminism and Psychology*, 4, 5–18.

Billig, M. (1978) *Fascists: A Social Psychological View of the National Front*. London: Harcourt, Brace, Jovanovich.

Billig, M. (1995) *Banal Nationalism*. London: Sage.

Bock, G. and James, S. (eds) (1993) *Beyond Equality and Difference*. London: Routledge.

Bonnett, A. (1993) *Radicalism, Anti-racism and Representation*. London: Routledge.

Bonnett, A. (1996) '"White studies": the problems and projects of a new research agenda', *Theory, Culture and Society*, 13(2), 145–55.

Bottomore, T. and Brym, R. (eds) (1989) *The Capitalist Class*. Hemel Hempstead: Harvester Wheatsheaf.

Bourne, J. (1983) 'Towards an anti-racist feminism', *Race and Class*, 25(1), 20–32.

Bourne, S. with Sivanandan, A. (1980) 'Cheerleaders and ombudsmen: the sociology of race relations in Britain', *Race and Class*, 21(4), 331–52.

Bradley, H. (1996) *Fractured Identities: Changing Patterns of Inequality*. Cambridge: Polity Press.

Brah, A. (1991) 'Questions of difference and international feminism', in J. Aaron and S. Walby (eds) *Out of the Margins*. London: Falmer Press.

Brah, A. (1992) 'Difference, diversity, differentiation', in J. Donald and A. Rattansi (eds) *'Race', Culture and Difference*. Buckingham: Open University Press.

Brah, A. (1996) *Cartographies of Diaspora: Contesting Identities*. London: Routledge.

Brah, A. and Deem, R. (1986) 'Towards anti-sexist and anti-racist schooling', *Critical Social Policy*, 16, 18–27.

Brah, A., Hickman, M. and Mac an Ghaill, M. (1999a) *Global Futures: Migration, Environment and Globalization*. London: Macmillan.

Brah, A., Hickman, M. and Mac an Ghaill, M. (1999b) *Thinking Identities: Ethnicity, Racism and Culture*. London: Macmillan.

Breen, R., Hannan, D. F., Rottman, D. B. and Whelan, C. T. (eds) (1990) *Understanding Contemporary Ireland: State, Class and Development in the Irish Republic*. Dublin: Gill and Macmillan.

Brubaker, R. (1992) *Citizenship and Nationhood in France and Germany*. Cambridge: Harvard University Press.

Brunt, R. (1989) 'The politics of identity', in S. Hall and M. Jacques (eds) *New Times: The Changing Face of Politics in the 1990s*. London: Lawrence and Wishart.

Bryan, B., Dadzie, S. and Scafe, S. (1985) *The Heart of the Race: Black Women's Lives in Britain*. London: Virago.

Butler, J. (1993) *Bodies that Matter, On the Discursive Limits of 'Sex'*. London: Routledge.

Cambridge, A. and Feuchtwang, S. (eds) (1990a) *Anti-racist Strategies*. Aldershot: Avebury.

Cambridge, A. X. and Feuchtwang, S. (1990b) 'Histories of racism', in A. X. Cambridge and S. Feuchtwang (eds) *Anti-racist Strategies*. Aldershot: Avebury.

Campaign Against Racism and Fascism (1991) 'Comment', *CARF*, 4, 2.

Campani, G. (1993) 'Immigration and racism in Southern Europe: the Italian case', *Ethnic and Racial Studies*, 16(3), 507–35.

Campbell, D. and Connolly, K. (1997) 'Gypsy malady', *The Guardian*, 20 November.

Carby, H. V. (1980) Multicultural Fictions. Occasional stencilled paper. Race Series: SP No. 58. Centre for Contemporary Cultural Studies, University of Birmingham.

Carby, H. V. (1982) 'White women listen! Black feminism and the boundaries of sisterhood', in Centre for Contemporary Cultural Studies (ed.) *The Empire Strikes Back: Race and Racism in 70s Britain*. London: Hutchinson/CCCS, University of Birmingham.

Carmichael, S. and Hamilton, C. V. (1968) *Black Power: The Politics of Liberation of America*. London: Jonathan Cape.

Carter, E., Donald, J. and Squires, J. (eds) (1993) *Space and Place: Theories of Identity and Location*. London: Lawrence and Wishart.

Carvel, J. (1998) 'Muslim schools get the grants', *The Guardian*, 10 January.

Cashmore, E. (1996) 'Review of J. Solomos and L. Back', *Race, Politics and Social Change, Sociological Review*, 44(1), 137–8.

Castells, M. (1983) *The City and Grassroots*. London: Edward Arnold.

Castles, S. and Kosack, G. (1973) *Immigrant Workers and the Class Structure*. London: Oxford University Press/Institute of Race Relations.

Castles, S. and Miller, M. J. (1993) *The Age of Migration: International Population Movements in the Modern World*. London: Macmillan.

Centre for Contemporary Cultural Studies (1982) *The Empire Strikes Back: Race and Racism in 70s Britain*. London: Hutchinson.

Cleeve, B. (1982) '1938: When the British was Best and the £ Rode High – a Vanishing World', *Sunday Telegraph*, 18 November.

Cockburn, C. (1983) *Brothers: Male Dominance and Technological Change*. London: Pluto Press.

Cohen, P. (1986a) *Rethinking the Youth Question*. Working Paper No. 3. Post 16 Education Centre. London: Institute of Education.

Cohen, P. (1986b) *Anti-Racist Cultural Studies*. Curriculum Development Project in Schools and Community Education. London: Institute of Education.

Cohen, P. (1987) *Racism and Popular Culture: A Cultural Studies Approach*. Working Papers No. 9. London: Centre for Multicultural Education, Institute of Education.

Cohen, P. (1988) 'The perversions of inheritance: studies in the making of multi-racist Britian', in P. Cohen and H. Bains (eds) *Multi-racist Britain*. London: Macmillan.

Cohen, P. (1989) *The Cultural Geography of Adolescent Racism*. London: University of London.

Cohen, P. (1990) 'Forward: transitions in transition', in R. G. Hollands (ed.) *The Long Transition: Class, Culture and Youth Training*. London: Macmillan.

Cohen, P. (1992) '"It's racism what dunnit": hidden narratives in theories of racism', in J. Donald and A. Rattansi (eds) *'Race', Culture and Difference*. London: Sage/ The Open University.

Cohen, P. (1993) *Home Rules: Some Reflections on Racism and Nationalism in Everyday Life*. London: University of East London.

Cohen, P. (1997) 'Labouring under whiteness', in R. Frankenberg (ed.) *Displacing Whiteness*. New York: Duke University Press.

Cohen, P. (1998) *Essays on England and Dreaming of Race*. London: CMER.

Cohen, P. and Bains, H. (eds) (1988) *Multi-racist Britain*. London: Macmillan.

Cohen, R. (1994) *Frontiers of Identity: The British and the Others*. London: Longman.

Commission for Racial Equality (1985) *Swann: A Response from the Commission for Racial Equality*. London: Commission for Racial Equality.

Community Relations Commission (1976) *Between Two Cultures: A Study of Relationships between Generations in the Asian Community in Britain*. London: Community Relations Commission.

Connell, R. W. (1990) 'The state, gender and sexual politics', *Theory and Society*, 19(5), 507–44.

Conner, T. (1985) *Irish Youth in London Research Report*. London: Action Group for Irish Youth.

Connolly, C., Hall, C., Hickman, M., Lewis, G., Phoenix, A. and Smyth, A. (1995) 'Editorial: The Irish Issue: the British question', *Feminist Review*, 50, 1–10.

Connolly, W. E. (1991) *Identity/Difference: Democratic Negotiations of Political Paradox*. Ithaca: Cornell University Press.

Coward, R. (1996) 'A stakeholder in exploitation and poverty', *The Guardian*, 22 January.

Crompton, R. (1993) *Class and Stratification: An Introduction to Current Debates*. Cambridge: Polity Press.

Curtis, L. (1984) *Nothing but the Same Old Story*. London: Information on Ireland Press.

Curtis, L. P. (1968) *Anglo-Saxons and Celts*. Connecticut: University of Bridgeport.

Curtis, L. P. (1971) *Apes and Angels: The Irishman in Victorian Caricature*. Washington: Smithsonian Institution Press.

Cutler, T. and Wain, B. (1994) *Managing the Welfare State*. Oxford: Berg.

Davidson, R. B. (1966) *Black British*. London: Oxford University Press.

Deane, S. (1991) *The Field Day Anthology of Irish Writing: Volume One*. Derry: Field Day Publications.

Devine, T. M. (ed.) (1991) *Irish Immigrants and Scottish Society in the Nineteenth and Twentieth Centuries*. Edinburgh: John Donald.

Donald, J. and Rattansi, A. (eds) (1992) *'Race', Culture and Difference*. London: Sage/The Open University.

Driver, G. (1980) *Beyond Underachievement*. London: Commission for Racial Equality.

Duffield, M. (1982) 'New racism . . . new realism: two sides of the same coin', Mimeo. Birmingham: Research Unit on Ethnic Relations, University of Aston in Birmingham.

Duffield, M. (1996) *The Symphony of the Damned: Racial Discourse, Complex Political Emergencies and Humanitarian Aid*. Birmingham: School of Public Policy, University of Birmingham, occasional paper, 2 March.

du Gay, P. (1996) *Consumption, Identity and Work*. London: Sage.

Dummett, A. (1973) *A Portrait of British Racism*. Hammondsworth: Penguin.

Dummett, A. (1991) 'Europe? Which Europe?', *New Community*, 18, 167–75.

Dummett, A. and Nicol, A. (1990) *Subjects, Citizens, Aliens and Others*. London: Weidenfeld and Nicolson.

Dunphy, R. (1997) 'Sexual identities, national identities: the politics of gay law reform in the Republic of Ireland', *Contemporary Politics*, 3(3), 247–65.

Dyer, R. (1993) *The Matter of Images: Essays on Representation*. London: Routledge.

Eade, J. (1989) *The Politics of Community: The Bangladeshi Community in East London*. Aldershot: Avebury.

Edgar, D. (1981) 'Reagan's hidden agenda', *Race and Class*, 22(3), 207–23.

Engels, F. (1969) *The Condition of the Working Class in England*. London: Panther.

Enloe, C. (1989) *Bananas, Beaches and Bases: Making Feminist Sense of International Politics*. London: Pandora.

Epstein, S. (1994) 'A queer encounter: sociology and the study of sexuality', *Sociological Theory*, 12, 188–202.

Fanon, F. (1970) *Black Skins, White Masks*. London: Paladin.

Featherstone, M. (1991) *Consuming Culture and Postmodernism*. London: Sage.

Feminist Review (1995) 'Editorial: The Irish Issue: The British question', 50, 1–4.

Feuchtwang, S. (1990a) 'Preface', in A. X. Cambridge and S. Feuchtwang (eds) *Anti-racist Strategies*. Aldershot: Avebury.

Feuchtwang, S. (1990b) 'Racism: territoriality and ethnocentricity', in A. X. Cambridge and S. Feuchtwang (eds) *Anti-racist Strategies*. Aldershot: Avebury.

Fielding, S. (1993) *Class and Ethnicity: Irish Catholics in England, 1880–1939*. Buckingham: Open University Press.

Fitzgerald, T. K. (1992) 'Media, identity and ethnicity', in P. Scannell, P. Schlesinger and C. Sparkes (eds) *Culture and Power*. London: Sage.

Ford, G. (1992) *Fascist Europe: The Rise of Racism and Xenophobia*. London: Pluto Press.

Foster, R. F. (1993) *Paddy and Mr Punch: Connections in English and Irish History*. London: Allen Lane.

Foucault, M. (1977) *Discipline and Punish*. London: Allen Lane.

Foucault, M. (1980) in C. Gordon (ed.) *Power/Knowledge: Selected Interviews and Other Writings*. Brighton: Harvester Press.

Foucault, M. (1988) 'Technologies of the self', in L. H. Martin, H. Gutman, P. H. Hutton (eds) *Technologies of the Self: A Seminar with Michel Foucault*. London: Tavistock.

Frankenberg, R. (1993) *White Woman, Race Matters: The Social Construction of Whiteness*. Minneapolis: University of Minnesota Press.

Freud, S. (1933) *Standard Edition of the Complete Psychological Works of Sigmund Freud*, Vol. XII. London: Hogarth Press/Institute of Psychoanalysis.

Furlong, A. and Cartmel, C. (1997) *Young People and Social Change: Individualization and Risk in Late Modernity*. Buckingham: Open University Press.

Gabriel, J. (1994) *Racism, Culture Markets*. London: Routledge.

Gabriel, J. and Ben Tovim, G. (1978) 'Marxism and the concept of racism', *Economy and Society*, 7(2), 118–54.

Gamble, A. (1988) *The Free Economy and the Strong State: The Politics of Thatcherism*. London: Macmillan.

Gamson, P. (1995) 'Must identity problems self destruct? A queer dilemma', *Social Problems*, 42, 390–407.

Gates, H. L. Jr. (ed.) (1986) *'Race', Writing and Difference*. Chicago: University of Chicago Press.

Gellner, E. (1983) *Nations and Nationalism*. Oxford: Basil Blackwell.

Gibbons, L. (1996) *Transformations in Irish Culture*. Cork: Cork University Press.

Giddens, A. (1985) *The Nation-state and Violence*. Cambridge: Polity Press.

Giddens, A. (1990) *The Consequences for Modernity*. Cambridge: Polity Press.

Giddens, A. (1991) *Modernity and Self Identity*. Cambridge: Polity Press.

Gilbert, M. (1996) *The Holocaust*. London: Fontana.

Gillborn, D. (1990) *'Race', Ethnicity and Education: Teaching and Learning in Multiethnic Schools*. London: Unwin Hyman.

Gillborn, D. (1995) *Racism and Antiracism in Real Schools: Theory, Policy, Practice*. Buckingham: Open University Press.

Gilley, S. and Swift, R. (1985) *The Irish in the Victorian City*. London: Croom Helm.

Gilman, S. (1985) *Difference and Pathology: Stereotypes of Sexuality, Race and Madness*. Ithaca: Cornell University Press.

Gilroy, P. (1980) 'Managing the "underclass": a further note on the sociology of race relations in Britain', *Race and Class*, XXII(1), 47–8.

Gilroy, P. (1981) 'You can't fool the youths . . . race and class formation in the 1980s', *Race and Class*, 23(2/3), 207–22.

Gilroy, P. (1982) 'Steppin' out of Babylon – race, class and autonomy', in Centre for Contemporary Cultural Studies, *The Empire Strikes Back: Race and Racism in 70s Britain*. London: Hutchinson/CCCS, University of Birmingham.

Gilroy, P. (1987) *There Ain't no Black in the Union Jack*. London: Hutchinson.

Gilroy, P. (1992) 'The end of antiracism', in J. Donald and A. Rattansi (eds) *'Race', Culture and Difference*. London: Sage/The Open University.

Gilroy, P. (1993) *The Black Atlantic: Modernity and Double Consciousness*. London: Verso.

Gilroy, P. (1997) 'Diaspora and the detours of identity', in K. Woodward (ed.) *Identity and Difference*. London: Sage/The Open University.

Glass, R. (1960) *Newcomers: West Indians in London*. London: Allen and Unwin.

Goldberg, D. T. (ed.) (1990) *Anatomy of Racism*. Minneapolis: University of Minnesota Press.

Goldberg, D. T. (1993) *Racist Culture*. Oxford: Blackwell.

Gordon, P. (1990) 'A dirty war: the New Right and local authority anti-racism', in W. Ball and J. Solomos (eds) *Race and Local Politics*. London: Macmillan.

Gordon, P. and Klug, F. (1986) *New Right, New Racism*. London: Searchlight Publications.

Graham, C. and Kirkland, R. (eds) (1998) *Ireland and Cultural Theory: The Mechanics of Authenticity*. London: Macmillan.

Gramsci, A. (1971) *Selection from the Prison Notebooks*. London: Lawrence and Wishart.

Green, M. and Carter, B. (1988) ' "Races" and "race-makers": the politics of racialisation', *Sage Race Relations Abstracts*, 13, 4–30.

Greenslade, L. (1992) 'White skin, white masks: psychological distress among the Irish in Britain', in P. O'Sullivan (ed.) *The Irish in the New Communities, Volume 2*. Leicester: Leicester University Press.

Gribben, P. (1994) 'A community haemorrhage: number of Irish people working in Britain dropped by nearly 100,000', *Irish Post*, 26 June.

Guillaumin, C. (1980) 'The idea of race and its elevation to autonomous scientific and legal status', in UNESCO *Sociological Theories: Race and Colonialism*. Paris: UNESCO.

Guillaumin, C. (1988) 'Race and nature: the System of marks' *Feminist Studies*, 8(2), 25–44.

Guillaumin, C. (1995) *Racism, Sexism, Power and Ideology*. London: Routledge.

Hall, C. (1992) *White, Male and Middle-Class: Explorations in Feminism and History*. Cambridge: Polity.

Hall, S. (1980) 'Race, articulation and societies structured in dominance', in UNESCO *Sociological Theories: Race and Colonialism*. Paris: UNESCO.

Hall, S. (1988) 'The toad in the garden: Thatcherism among the theorists', in C. Nelson and L. Grossberg (eds) *Marxism and the Interpretation of Culture*. London: Macmillan.

Hall, S. (1991a) 'Old and new ethnicities', in A. D. King (ed.) *Culture, Globalization and the World System*. London: Macmillan.

Hall, S. (1991b) 'The local and the global: Globalization and ethnicity', in A. D. King (ed.) *Culture, Globalization and the World System*. London: Macmillan.

Hall, S. (1992a) 'The question of cultural identity', in S. Hall, D. Held and T. McGrew (eds) *Modernity and Its Futures*. London: Polity/The Open University.

Hall, S. (1992b) 'New ethnicities', in J. Donald and A. Rattansi (eds) *'Race', Culture and Difference*. London: Sage/The Open University.

Hall, S., Critcher, C., Jefferson, T., Clarke, J. and Roberts, B. (1978) *Policing the Crisis: Mugging, The State and Law and Order*. London: Macmillan.

Hall, S. and Held, D. (1989) 'Citizens and citizenship', in S. Hall and M. Jacques (eds) *New Times: The Changing Face of Politics in the 1990s*. London: Lawrence and Wishart/*Marxism Today*.

Hamilton, P. (1986) 'Foreword', in J. Weeks (ed.) *Sexuality*. London: Tavistock.

Hamnett, C., McDowell, L. and Sharpe, P. (eds) (1989) *Restructuring Britain; The Changing Social Structure*. London: Sage.

Hardy, J. (1997) 'The sheer horror of my Adams handshake', *The Guardian*, 6 December.

Hardy, J. (1999) 'Two deaths that shame us all', *The Guardian*, Saturday Review, 20 March.

Hargreaves, A. G. (1995) *Immigration, 'Race' and Ethnicity in Contemporary France*. London: Routledge.

Harvey, D. (1989) *The Condition of Postmodernity: An Enquiry into the Origins of Cultural Change*. Oxford: Basil Blackwell.

Harvey, D. (1993) 'Class relations, social justice and the politics of difference', in J. Squires (ed.) *Principled Positions: Postmodernism and the Rediscovery of Value*. London: Lawrence and Wishart.

Harvey, D. (1996) *Justice, Nature and the Geography of Difference*. Oxford: Blackwell.

Hawes, D. and Perez, B. (1995) *The Gypsy and the State: The Ethnic Cleansing of British Society*. Bristol: Bristol University, School for Advanced Urban Studies.

Hay, C. (1996) *Re-Stating the State: Social and Political Change*. Buckingham: Open University Press.

Hazelkorn, E. (1990) *Irish Immigrants Today: A Socio-economic Profile of Contemporary Irish Immigrants in the U.K.* London: Polytechnic of North London Press, Irish Studies Centre Occasional Paper Series No. 1.

Hechter, M. (1975) *Internal Colonialism: The Celtic Fringe in British National Development.* London: Routledge and Kegan Paul.

Heinemann, B. (1972) *The Politics of the Powerless.* London: Oxford University Press/ Institute of Race Relations.

Henriques, J., Hollway, W., Urwin, C., Venn, C. and Walkerdine, V. (1984) *Changing the Subject: Psychology, Social Regulation and Subjectivity.* London: Methuen.

Hewitt, R. (1986) *White Talk, Black Talk: Inter-Racial Friendship and Communication Amongst Adolescents.* Cambridge: Cambridge University Press.

Hickman, M. J. (ed.) (1986) *The History of the Irish in Britain: A Bibliography.* London: Irish in Britain History Centre.

Hickman, M. J. (1993) 'The Irish community in Britain: myth or reality?', in *Irish Dimensions in British Education,* unpublished report on the 10th International Conference.

Hickman, M. J. (1995a) *Religion, Class and Identity: The State, the Catholic Church and the Education of the Irish in Britain.* Aldershot: Avebury.

Hickman, M. J. (1995b) 'The Irish in Britain: Racism, Incorporation and Identity', *Irish Studies Review,* 10, 16–20.

Hickman, M. J. and Walter, B. (1995) 'Deconstructing whiteness: Irish women in Britain', *Feminist Review,* 50, 5–19.

Hickman, M. J. and Walter, B. (1997) *Discrimination and the Irish Community in Britain.* London: Commission for Racial Equality.

Hickman, M. J. and Walter, B. (1999) *The Irish in Contemporary Britain.* London: Longman.

Hillyard, P. (1993) *Suspect Community. People's Experience of the Prevention of Terrorism Acts in Britain.* London: Pluto Press.

Hirst, P. and Thompson, G. (1996) *Globalisation in Question?* London: Polity.

Hobsbawm, E. (1983) 'Introduction: Inventing traditions', in E. Hobsbawm and T. Ranger (eds) *The Invention of Tradition.* Cambridge: Cambridge University Press.

Hobsbawm, E. (1992) *Nations and Nationalism since 1780: Programme, Myth and Reality.* Cambridge: Cambridge University Press.

Holdaway, S. (1996) *The Racialisation of British Policing.* London: Macmillan.

Hollands, R. G. (1990) *The Long Transition: Class, Culture and Youth Training.* London: Macmillan.

Holmes, C. (ed.) (1978a) *Anti-Semitism in British Society, 1876–1939.* London: Edward Arnold.

Holmes, C. (1978b) *Immigrants and Minorities in British Society.* London: Allen and Unwin.

Holmes, C. (1988) *John Bull's Island: Immigration and British Society, 1871–1971.* London: Macmillan.

Hoogvelt, A. (1997) *Globalisation and the Postcolonial World: The New Political Economy of Development.* London: Macmillan.

Hooper, J. (1997) 'Italy "death trap" for immigrants', *The Guardian,* 13 June, 16.

Hout, M., Brooks, C. and Manza, J. (1993) 'The persistence of classes in postindustrial societies', *International Sociology,* 8, 259–68.

Husband, C. (ed.) (1982) *'Race' in Britain: Community and Change.* London: Hutchinson.

Ignatieff, M. (1993) *Blood and Belonging: Journeys into the New Nationalism.* London: Chatto and Windus.

Jackson, J. A. (1963) *The Irish in Britain.* London: Routledge and Kegan Paul.

Jackson, P. and Penrose, J. (eds) (1993a) *Constructions of Race, Place and Nation.* London: UCL Press.

Jackson, P. and Penrose, J. (1993b) 'Introduction: placing "race" and nation', in P. Jackson and J. Penrose (eds) *Constructions of Race, Place and Nation*. London: UCL Press.

James, C. L. R. (1938) *The Black Jacobins*. London: Alison and Busby.

Jameson, F. (1991) *Postmodernism or the Cultural Logic of Late Capitalism*. London: Sage.

Jameson, F. (1993) 'Actually existing Marxism', *Polygraph: an International Journal of Culture and Politics*, 6/7, 171–95.

Jeffers, S., Hoggett, P. and Harrison, L. (1996) 'Race, ethnicity and community in three localities', *New Community*, 22(1), 111–26.

Jenkins, R. and Solomos, J. (1987) *Racism and Equal Opportunity Policies in the 1980s*. Cambridge: Cambridge University Press.

Jessop, B. (1982) *The Capitalist State*. Oxford: Martin Robertson.

John, G. (1981) *In the Service of Black Youth*. London: National Association of Youth Clubs.

Johnson, R. (1992) 'Radical education and the New Right', in A. Rattansi and D. Reeder (eds) *Rethinking Radical Education: Essays in Honour of Brian Simon*. London: Lawrence and Wishart.

Jones, S. (1988) *Black Youth, White Culture: The Reggae Tradition from JA to UK*. London: Macmillan.

Joshua, H. and Wallace, T. with Booth, H. (1983) *To Ride the Storm: The 1980 Bristol 'Riot' and the State*. London: Heinemann.

Joyce, P. (1995) *Class*. Oxford: Oxford University Press.

Katz, J. (1978) *White Awareness*. Norman: University of Oklahoma Press.

Kearney, R. (1985) *The Irish Mind: Exploring Intellectual Traditions*. Dublin: Wolfhound Press.

Kearney, R. (ed.) (1990) *Migrations: The Irish at Home and Abroad*. Dublin: Wolfhound.

Keith, M. (1993) *Race, Riots and Policing: Lore and Disorder in a Multi-racist Society*. London: UCL Press.

Kelly, L. (1992) 'Not in front of the children: responding to right wing agendas on sexuality and education', in M. Arnot and L. Barton (eds) *Voicing Concerns: Sociological Perspectives on Contemporary Education Reforms*. London: Triangle Books.

Kettle, M. (1996) 'Let's party people', *The Guardian*, 31 August.

Kettle, M. (1998) 'Hispanics outstripping blacks as largest American minority', *The Guardian*, 16 July, 18.

Khan, V. S. (1976) 'Pakistanis in Britain: perceptions of a population', *New Community*, 5(3), 222–9.

Khan, V. S. (ed.) (1979) *Minority Families in Britain: Support and Stress*. London: Tavistock.

Kiberd, D. (1996) *Inventing Ireland: The Literature of the Modern Nation*. London: Vintage.

Knowles, C. and Mercer, S. (1992) 'Feminism and antiracism: an exploration of the political possibilities', in J. Donald and A. Rattansi (eds) *'Race', Culture and Difference*. London: Sage/The Open University.

Kowarzik, U. (1997) *Irish Community Services: Meeting Diverse Needs*. London: Action Group for Irish Youth/Federation of Irish Societies.

Kristeva, J. (1982) *Powers of Horror*. New York: Columbia University Press.

Kumar, K. (1978) *Prophecy and Progress*. Harmondsworth: Penguin Books.

Kumar, K. (1995) *From Post-industrial to Post-modern Society: New Theories of the Contemporary World*. London: Blackwell.

Kushner, T. (1989) *The Persistence of Prejudice: Anti-Semitism in British Society during the Second World War*. Manchester: Manchester University Press.

Lacan, J. (1977) *Ecrits: A Selection*. London: Tavistock.

Laclau, E. (1990) *New Reflections on the Revolution of our Time*. London: Verso.

Lash, S. and Urry, J. (1994) *Economies of Signs and Space*. London: Sage.

Lather, P. (1986) 'Research as Praxis', *Harvard Educational Review*, 56, 257–77.

Lawrence, E. (1982) 'In the abundance of water the fool is thirsty: sociology and black pathology', in Centre for Contemporary Cultural Studies *The Empire Strikes Back: Race and Racism in 70s Britain*. London: Hutchinson.

Layton-Henry, Z. (1990) *The Political Rights of Migrant Workers in Western Europe*. London: Sage.

Layton-Henry, Z. (1992) *The Politics of Immigration: Immigration, 'Race' and 'Race-relations' in Post-war Britain*. Oxford: Blackwell.

Lebow, N. (1976) *White Britain and Black Ireland: The Influence of Stereotypes on Colonial Policy*. Philadelphia: Institute for the Study of Human Issues.

Leeming, D. (1994) *James Baldwin: A Biography*. London: Michael Joseph.

Lefebvre, H. (1991) *The Production of Space*. Oxford: Basil Blackwell.

Lennon, M., McAdam, M. and O'Brien, J. (1988) *Across the Water*. London: Virago.

Levine, A., Sober, E. and Wright, E. (1987) 'Marxism and methodological individualism', *New Left Review*, 162, 136–45.

Little, K. (1947) *Negroes on Britain: A Study of Race Relations in English Society*. London: Routledge and Kegan Paul.

Lloyd, C. (1994) 'Universalism and difference: the crisis of anti-racism in the UK and France', in A. Rattansi and S. Westwood (eds) *Racism, Modernity and Identity: On the Western Front*. Cambridge: Polity Press.

Lukes, S. (1984) 'The future of British socialism', in B. Pimlott (ed.) *Fabian Essays in Socialist Thought*. London: Heinemann.

Lyon, D. (1984) *Postmodernity*. Buckingham: Open University Press.

Mac an Ghaill, M. (1988) *Young, Gifted and Black: Student–Teacher Relations in the Schooling of Black Youth*. Milton Keynes: Open University Press.

Mac an Ghaill, M. (1994a) *The Making of Men: Masculinities, Sexualities and Schooling*. Buckingham: Open University Press.

Mac an Ghaill, M. (1994b) '(In)visiblity: sexuality, masculinity and "race" in the school context', in D. Epstein (ed.) *Challenging Lesbian and Gay Inequalities in Education*. Buckingham: Open University Press.

Mac an Ghaill, M. (1996a) 'Irish masculinities and sexualities in England', in L. Adkins and V. Merchant (eds) *Sexualizing the Social: Power and the Organization of Sexuality*. London: Macmillan.

Mac an Ghaill, M. (1996b) '"What about the boys?": schooling, class and crisis masculinity', *Sociological Review*, 44(3), 381–97.

Macdonald, I., Bhavnani, R., Khan, L. and John, G. (1989) *Murder in the Playground: Report of the Macdonald Inquiry into Racism and Racial Violence in Manchester Schools*. London: Longsight Press.

Mac Laughlin, J. (1994) *Ireland: The Emigrant Nursery and the World Economy*. Cork: Cork University Press.

Mac Laughlin, J. (1995) *Travellers and Ireland: Whose Country, Whose History*. Cork: Cork University Press.

Macpherson report (1999) *The Stephen Lawrence Inquiry: Report of an Inquiry by Sir William Macpherson of Cluny*, Cmmnd no. 4262 1. London: Stationery Office.

Mama, A. (1992) 'Black women and the British state: race, class and gender analysis for the 1990s', in P. Braham, A. Rattansi and R. Skellington (eds) *Racism and Anti-racism: Inequalities, Opportunities and Policies*. London: Sage/The Open University.

Mama, A. (1995) *Beyond the Masks: Race, Gender and Subjectivity*. London: Routledge.

Marshall, T. H. (1950) *Citizenship and Social Class*. Cambridge: Cambridge University Press.

Martin, L. H., Gutman, H. and Hutton, P. H. (eds) (1988) *Technologies of the Self: A Seminar with Michel Foucault*. London: Tavistock.

Mason, D. (1992) *Some Problems with the Concepts of Race and Racism*. Leicester: University of Leicester.

Mason, D. (1995) *Race and Ethnicity in Modern Britain*. Oxford: Oxford University Press.

Massey, D. (1994) *Space, Place and Gender*. London: Polity Press.

Mercer, K. (1990) 'Welcome to the jungle: identity and diversity in postmodern politics', in J. Rutherford (ed.) *Identity: Community, Culture and Difference*. London: Lawrence and Wishart.

Mercer, K. (1992a) 'Just looking for trouble: Robert Mapplethorpe and fantasies', in L. Segal and M. AcIntosh (eds) *Sex Exposed: Sexuality and the Pornography Debate*. London: Virago.

Mercer, K. (1992b) 'Skinhead sex thing: Racial difference and homoerotic imagery', *New Formations*, 16, 1–23.

Mercer, K. (1994) *Welcome to the Jungle: New Positions in Black Cultural Studies*. London: Routledge.

Mercer, K. and Julien, I. (1988) 'Race, sexual politics and black masculinity: a dossier', in R. Chapman and J. Rutherford (eds) *Male Order: Unwrapping Masculinities*. London: Lawrence and Wishart.

Mercer, N. and Prescott, W. (1982) 'Perspectives on minority experience', in *Minority Experience*. Open University Educational Studies, Course E254, Block 3, Units 8 and 9. Milton Keynes: Open University Press.

Metcalf, A. (1985) 'Introduction', in A. Metcalf and M. Humphries (eds) *The Sexuality of Men*. London: Pluto Press.

Miles, R. (1980) 'Class, race and ethnicity; a critique of Cox's theory', *Ethnic and Racial Studies*, 3(2), 169–87.

Miles, R. (1982) *Racism and Labour Migration*. London: Routledge and Kegan Paul.

Miles, R. (1989) *Racism*. London: Routledge.

Miles, R. (1993) *Racism after Race Relations*. London: Routledge.

Miles, R. (1994a) 'Explaining racism in contemporary Europe', in A. Rattansi and S. Westwood (eds) *Racism, Modernity and Identity: On the Western Front*. Cambridge: Polity Press.

Miles, R. (1994b) 'A rise of racism in contemporary Europe? Some sceptical reflections on its nature and extent', *New Community*, 20(4), 547–62.

Miles, R. and Phizacklea, A. (1977) 'Class, race, ethnicity and political action', *Political Studies*, 25(4), 491–507.

Miles, R. and Phizacklea, A. (1979) *Racism and Political Action in Britain*. London: Routledge and Kegan Paul.

Miles, R. and Phizacklea, A. (1984) *A White Man's Country: Racism in British Politics*. London: Pluto Press.

Miller, D. (ed.) (1998) *Rethinking Northern Ireland: Culture, Ideology and Colonialism*. Essex: Addison Wesley Longman Higher Education.

Mirza, H. S. (1992) *Young, Female and Black*. London: Routledge.

Mirza, H. S. (ed.) (1997) *Black British Feminism*. London: Routledge.

Mitchell, M. and Russell, D. (1994) 'Race, citizenship and "Fortress Europe"', in P. Brown and R. Crompton (eds) *Economic Restructuring and Social Exclusion*. London: UCL Press.

Modood, T. (1989) 'Religious anger and minority rights', *Political Quarterly*, July, 280–4.

Modood, T. (1992) 'British Asian Muslims and the Rushdie affair', in J. Donald and A. Rattansi (eds) *'Race', Culture and Difference*. London: Sage/The Open University.

Mosse, G. (1985) *Toward the Final Solution: A History of European Racism*. Madison: University of Wisconsin Press.

Murray, R. (1989) 'Fordism and post-Fordism', in S. Hall and M. Jacques (eds) *New Times: The Changing Face of Politics in the 1990s*. London: Lawrence and Wishart/ *Marxism Today*.

Nairn, T. (1977) *The Break-up of Britain*. London: New Left Books.

Nikolinakos, M. (1975) 'Notes towards a general theory of migration in state capitalism', *Race and Class*, 17(1), 5–18.

Nisbet, R. (1959) 'The decline and fall of social class', *Pacific Sociological Review*, 2, 11–17.

Nixon, S. (1997) 'Exhibiting masculinity', in S. Hall (ed.) *Representation: Cultural Representations and Signifying Practices*. London: Sage/The Open University.

Noiriel, G. (1988) *Le creuset Francais. Histoire de l'Immigration XIXe–XXe Siecles*. Paris: Seuil.

Noiriel, G. (1990) *Workers in French Society in the Nineteenth and Twentieth Centuries*. Oxford: Berg.

Offe, C. (1985) *Disorganised Capitalism*. Cambridge: Polity Press.

Omi, M. and Winant, H. (1986) *Racial Formation in the United States*. London: Routledge and Kegan Paul.

O'Toole, F. (1997) *The Ex-Isle of Erin: Images of a Global Ireland*. Dublin: New Island Books.

O'Tuathaigh, M. (1985) 'The Irish in nineteenth century Britain: problems of integration', in R. Swift and S. Gilley (eds) *The Irish in the Victorian City*. London: Croom Helm.

Owen, D. (1992) *Ethnic Minorities in Britain: Settlement Patterns*. University of Warwick, Centre for Research in Ethnic Relations, National Ethnic Minority Data Archive, 1991 Census Statistical paper No. 3.

Pajackowska, C. and Young, L. (1992) 'Racism, representation and psychoanalysis', in J. Donald and A. Rattansi (eds) *'Race', Culture and Difference*. London: Sage/The Open University.

Palmer, F. (ed.) (1986) *Anti-racism – An Assault on Education and Value*. London: Sherwood Press.

Parekh, B. (1991) 'British citizenship and cultural difference', in G. Andrews (ed.) *Citizenship*. London: Lawrence and Wishart.

Parekh, B. (1995) 'The concept of national identity', *New Community*, 21(2), 255–68.

Parker, A., Russo, M., Sommer, D., and Yaeger, P. (1992) *Nationalisms and Sexualities*. London: Routledge.

Parker, D. (1994) *The Cultural Identities of Young Chinese People in Britain*. Aldershot: Avebury.

Parmar, P. (1982) 'Gender, race and class: Asian women in resistance', in Centre for Contemporary Cultural Studies (ed.) *The Empire Strikes Back: Race and Racism in 70s Britain*. London: Hutchinson/CCCS, University of Birmingham.

Parmar, P. (1989) 'Other kinds of dreams', *Feminist Review*, 31, 55–65.

Patterson, S. (1963) *Dark Strangers*. London: Tavistock.

Peach, C. (1968) *West Indian Migration to Britain*. Oxford: Oxford University Press.

Peach, C. (1996) 'A question of colour', *The Times Higher Education Supplement*, 23 August, 17.

Phillips, T. (1998) 'Fantastic voyage', *The Guardian*, 18 May, 6.

Phizacklea, A. (1990) *Unpacking the Fashion Industry*. London: Routledge.

Phizacklea, A. and Miles, R. (1979) 'Working class racist beliefs in the inner city', in R. Miles and A. Phizacklea (eds) *Racism and Political Action in Britain*. London: Routledge and Kegan Paul.

Phizacklea, A. and Miles, R. (1980) *Labour and Racism*. London: Routledge and Kegan Paul.

Phoenix, A. (1987) 'Theories of gender and black families', in G. Weiner and M. Arnot (eds) *Gender under Scrutiny*. Milton Keynes: Open University Press.

Plummer, K. (ed.) (1992) *Modern Homosexualities*. London: Routledge.

Poulantzes, N. (1975) *Classes in Contemporary Capitalism*. London: New Left Books.

Race Today (1976) 'A show of strength', 8(6), 123.

Race Today (1979) 'Southall: what is to be done?', 11(3), 52–4.

Rainbow, P. (ed.) (1984) *The Foucault Reader*. Harmondsworth: Penguin.

Ranson, S. (1988) 'From 1944 to 1988: education, citizenship and democracy', *Local Government Studies*, 14, 1–19.

Rattansi, A. (1992) 'Changing the subject? Racism, culture and education', in J. Donald and A. Rattansi (eds) *'Race', Culture and Difference*. London: Sage/The Open University.

Rattansi, A. (1994) 'Western racisms, ethnicities and identities in a "postmodern" frame', in A. Rattansi and S. Westwood (eds) *Racism, Modernity and Identity: On the Western Front*. London: Polity Press.

Rattansi, A. and Westwood, S. (1994) 'Modern racisms, racialized identities', in A. Rattansi and S. Westwood (eds) *Racism, Modernity and Identity: On the Western Front*. London: Polity Press.

Redman, P. and Mac an Ghaill, M. (1996) 'Schooling sexualities: heterosexual masculinities, schooling, and the unconscious', *Discourse*, 17(2), 243–56.

Reeves, F. (1983) *British Racial Discourse: A Study of British Political Discourse about Race and Race-related Matters*. Cambridge: Cambridge University Press.

Renan, E. (1990) 'What is a nation?' in H. Bhabha (ed.) *Nation and Narration*. London: Routledge.

Rex, J. (1970) *Race Relations in Sociological Theory*. London: Weidenfeld and Nicolson.

Rex, J. (1973) *Race, Colonialism and the City*. London: Routledge and Kegan Paul.

Rex, J. and Mason, D. (eds) (1986) *Theories of Race and Ethnic Relations*. Cambridge: Cambridge University Press.

Rex, J. and Moore, R. (1967) *Race, Community and Conflict*. London: Oxford University Press/Institute of Race Relations.

Rex, J. and Tomlinson, S. (1979) *Colonial Immigrants in a British City*. London: Routledge and Kegan Paul.

Rizvi, F. (1993) 'Critical introduction: researching racism and education', in B. Troyna (ed.) *Racism and Education: Research Perspectives*. Buckingham: Open University Press.

Robertson, R. (1992) *Globalisation: Social Theory and Global Culture*. London: Sage.

Roediger, D. (1992) *The Wages of Whiteness: Race and the Making of the American Working Class*. London: Verso.

Rose, K. (1994) *Diverse Communities: The Evolution of Lesbian and Gay Politics in Ireland*. Cork: Cork University Press.

Rowbotham, S. (1989) *The Past is Before Us: Feminism in Action since the 1960s*. Harmondsworth: Penguin.

Rowbotham, S. (1997) *A Century of Women: The History of Women in Britain and the US*. London: Viking.

Runnymede Trust (1993) *The Runnymede Bulletin*, No. 267, July/August. London: Runnymede Trust.

Rutherford, J. (1990) (ed.) *Identity: Community, Culture and Difference*. London: Lawrence and Wishart.

Safran, W. (1987) 'Ethnic mobilization, modernization and ideology: Jacobism, Marxism, Organicism and Functionism', *Journal of Ethnic Studies*, 15(1), 1–32.

Saggar, S. (1992) *Race and Politics in Britain*. London: Harvester Press.

Said, E. W. (1978) *Orientalism*. London: Routledge and Kegan Paul.

Said, E. W. (1993) *Culture and Imperialism*. London: Vintage.

Samuel, R. (1989) 'Introduction: "The little platoons"', in R. Samuel (ed.) *Patriotism: The Making and Unmaking of British National Identity*. Vol. 11. Minorities and Outsiders. London: Routledge.

Sarup, M. (1996) *Identity, Culture and the Postmodern World*. Edinburgh: Edinburgh University Press.

Savage, S. and Robins, A. (eds) (1990) *Public Policy under Thatcher*. London: Macmillan.

Scarman Report (1981) *The Brixton Disorders 10–12 April 1981, Special Report*. London: HMSO.

Seidler, V. J. (1990) 'Men, feminism and power', in J. Hearn and D. Morgan (eds) *Men, Masculinities and Social Theory*. London: Unwin Hyman.

Seidman, S. (1993) 'Identity and politics in a "postmodern" gay culture: some historical and conceptual notes', in M. Warner (ed.) *Fear of a Queer Planet: Queer Politics and Social Theory*. Minnesota: University of Minnesota.

Silverman, M. (ed.) (1991) *Race, Discourse and Power in France*. Aldershot: Avebury.

Silverman, M. (1992) *Deconstructing the Nation: Immigration, Racism and Citizenship in Modern France*. London: Routledge.

Sivanandan, A. (1976) *Race, Class and the State*. London: Race and Class Publications/ Institute of Race Relations.

Sivanandan, A. (1978) 'From immigration control to induced repatriation', *Race and Class*, 20(1), 75–82.

Sivanandan, A. (1982) *A Different Hunger*. London: Pluto Press.

Sivanandan, A. (1983) 'Challenging racism: strategies for the '80s', *Race and Class*, 25(2), 1–11.

Sivanandan, A. (1985) 'RAT and the degradation of the black struggle', *Race and Class*, 26(4), 1–33.

Sivanandan, A. (1989) 'New circuits of imperialism', *Race and Class*, 30(4), 1–19.

Sivanandan, A. (1990a) *Communities of Resistance. Writings on Black Struggles for Socialism*. London: Verso.

Sivanandan, A. (1990b) 'All that melts into air is solid: the hokum of new times', *Race and Class*, 31(3), 1–30.

Small, S. (1994) *Racialised Boundaries: The Black Experience in the U.S. and England in the 1980s*. London: Routledge.

Smart, B. (1990) 'Modernity, postmodernity and the present', in B. Turner (ed.) *Theories of Modernity and Postmodernity*. London: Sage.

Smith, A. D. (1971) *Theories of Nationalism*. London: Duckworth.

Smith, A. D. (1986) *The Ethnic Origins of Nations*. Oxford: Blackwell.

Smith, A. M. (1994) *New Right Discourse on Race and Sexuality: Britain, 1968–1990*. Cambridge: Cambridge University Press.

Smith, S. J. (1989) *The Politics of 'Race' and Residence*. Cambridge: Polity Press.

Smith, S. J. (1993) 'Immigration and nation-building in Canada and the United Kingdom', in P. Jackson and J. Penrose (eds) *Constructions of Race, Place and Nation*. London: UCL Press.

Smyth, A. (ed.) (1993) *Irish Women's Studies: Reader*. Dublin: Attic Press.

Smyth, J. (1993) 'Nationalism, nightmares and postmodern utopias: Irish society in transition', *History of Education Ideas*, 16(1), 157–63.

Soja, E. (1989) *Postmodern Geographies: The Reassertion of Space in Critical Social Theory*. London: Verso.

Solomos, J. (1988) *Black Youth, Racism and the State*. Cambridge: Cambridge University Press.

Solomos, J. (1993) *Race and Racism in Britain*, 2nd edition. Basingstoke: Macmillan.

Solomos, J. and Back, L. (1995) *Race, Politics and Social Change*. London: Routledge.

Solomos, J. and Back, L. (1996) *Racism and Society*. London: Macmillan.

Spivak, G. C. (1986) 'Three women's texts and a critique of imperialism', in H. L. Gates Jr (ed.) *'Race', Writing and Difference*. London: University of Chicago Press.

Spivak, G. (1988a) 'Can the subaltern speak?', in C. Nelson and L. Grossberg (eds) *Marxism and the Interpretation of Culture*. Urbana: University of Illinois Press.

Spivak, G. (1988b) *In Other Worlds: Essays in Cultural Politics*. New York: Routledge.

Spivak, G. (1990) *The Post-colonial Critic: Interviews, Strategies, Dialogues*. London: Routledge.

Swift, R. and Gilley, S. (1989) *The Irish in Britain: 1815–1939*. London: Pinter Publishers.

Taguieff, P.-A. (1988) *La Force du Prejuge: Essai sur le racisme et ses doubles*. Paris: La Decouverte.

Taguieff, P.-A. (1990) 'The new cultural racism in France', *Telos*, 83, 109–22.

Taguieff, P.-A. (1991) 'Les metamorphoses ideologiques du racisme et le crise de l'anti-racisme', in P.-A. Taguieff (ed.) *Face au Racisme, Vol. 2: Hypotheses Perspectives*. Paris: La Decouverte.

Taylor, D. (1991) 'A big idea for the nineties? The rise of the Citizens' Charters', *Critical Social Policy*, 11, 87–94.

Taylor, I., Evans, K. and Fraser, P. (1996) *A Tale of Two Cities: Global Change, Local Feeling and Everyday Life in the North of England*. London: Routledge.

Thomas, D. E. (1985) 'The making of minorities: the confounding of change', *Multi-Cultural Teaching*, 3(3), 8–14.

Todorov, T. (1986) 'Race, writing and culture', in H. L. Gates Jr (ed.) *'Race', Writing and Difference*. Chicago: University of Chicago Press.

Tomlinson, S. (1981) *Education Subnormality: A Study in Decision-Making*. London: Routledge and Kegan Paul.

Troupe, Q. (1989) *James Baldwin: The Legacy*. New York: Simon and Schuster/ Touchstone.

Troyna, B. (1993) *Racism and Education: Research Perspectives*. Buckingham: Open University Press.

Troyna, B. and Williams, J. (1986) *Racism, Education and the State*. London: Croom Helm.

Turner, B. (1990) 'Outline of a theory of citizenship', *Sociology*, 24, 189–217.

Turner, B. (ed.) (1993) *Citizenship and Social Theory*. London: Sage.

Van Dijk, T. A. (1991) *Racism and the Press*. London: Routledge.

Walby, S. (1994) 'Is citizenship gendered?', *Sociology*, 28(2), 379–95.

Wallerstein, I. (1974) *The Modern World-System*. New York: Academic.

Wallman, S. (1979) 'The scope of ethnicity', in S. Wallman (ed.) *Ethnicity at Work*. London: Macmillan.

Walshe, E. (ed.) (1997) *Sex, Nation and Dissent in Irish Writing*. Cork: Cork University Press.

Walter, B. (1984) 'Tradition and ethnic interaction: second wave Irish settlement in Luton and Bolton', in C. Clarke, D. Ley and C. Peach (eds) *Geography and Ethnic Pluralism*. London: Allen and Unwin.

Walters, M. (1995) *Globalization*. London: Macmillan.

Ware, V. (1992) *Beyond the Pale: White Women, Racism and History*. London: Verso.

Webber, F. (1991) 'From ethnocentrism to Euro-racism', *Race and Class*, 32(3), 11–17.

Weeks, G. (1990) 'The value of difference', in J. Rutherford (ed.) *Identity: Community, Culture and Difference*. London: Lawrence and Wishart.

Weiner, G. (1994) *Feminism in Education: An Introduction*. Buckingham: Open University Press.

Westergaard, J. (1994) *Who Gets What: The Hardening of Class Inequality in the Late Twentieth Century*. Cambridge: Polity Press.

Westwood, S. (1990) 'Racism, black masculinity and the politics of space', in J. Hearn and D. Morgan (eds) *Men, Masculinities and Social Theory*. London: Unwin Hyman.

Westwood, S. (1996) ' "Feckless fathers": masculinities and the British state', in M. Mac an Ghaill (ed.) *Understanding Masculinities: Social Relations and Cultural Arenas*. Buckingham: Open University Press.

Wetherell, M. and Potter, J. (1992) *Mapping the Language of Racism: Discourse and the Legitimation of Exploitation*. London: Harvester Wheatsheaf.

Wieviorka, M. (1991) *L'espace du Racisme*. Paris: Seuil.

Wieviorka, M. (1994) 'Racism in Europe: unity and diversity', in A. Rattansi and S. Westwood (eds) *Racism, Modernity and Identity: On the Western Front*. Cambridge: Polity Press.

Wieviorka, M. (1995) *The Arena of Racism*. London: Sage.

Willems, H. (1995) 'Right-wing extremism, racism or youth violence? Explaining violence against foreigners in Germany', *New Community*, 21(4), 501–23.

Williams, F. (1989) *Social Policy: A Critical Introduction. Issues of Race, Gender and Class*. Cambridge: Polity.

Williams, I., Dunne, M. and Mac an Ghaill, M. (1997) *Economic Needs of the Irish Community in Birmingham*. Birmingham: Birmingham City Council.

Williams, I. and Mac an Ghaill, M. (1998) *Older Irish Men: An Investigation of Health and Social Care Needs*. Birmingham: The Irish Government's Dion fund and focus housing group.

Williams, J. (1985) 'Redefining institutional racism', *Ethnic and Racial Studies*, 8, 323–48.

Willis, P. (1985) *Youth Unemployment and the New Poverty: A Summary of Local Authority Review and Framework for Policy Development on Youth and Youth Unemployment*. Wolverhampton: Wolverhampton Local Authority.

Woodward, K. (1997) 'Introduction', in K. Woodward (ed.) *Identity and Difference*. London: Sage/The Open University.

Worsthorne, P. (1982) 'Why not inequality?', *Sunday Telegraph*, 7 November, 20.

Wrench, J. and Solomos, J. (eds) (1993) *Racism and Migration in Western Europe*. Oxford: Berg.

Wright, E. O. (1997) *Class Counts: Comparative Studies in Class Analysis*. Cambridge: Cambridge University Press.

Young, I. M. (1993) 'Together in difference: transforming the logic of group political difference', in J. Squires (ed.) *Principled Positions: Postmodernism and the Rediscovery of Value*. London: Lawrence and Wishart.

Young, R. (1990) *White Mythologies: Writing History and the West*. London: Routledge.

Young, R. (1995) *Colonial Desire: Hybridity in Theory, Culture and Race*. London: Routledge.

Yuval-Davis, N. (1992) 'Fundamentalism, multiculturalism and women in Britain', in J. Donald and A. Rattansi (eds) *'Race', Culture and Difference*. London: Sage/The Open University.

Yuval-Davis, N. and Anthias, F. (eds) (1989) *Women-Nation-State*. London: Macmillan.

Zaretsky, E. (1996) 'Identity theory, identity politics: psychoanalysis, Marxism, poststructuralism', in C. Calhoun (ed.) *Social Theory and the Politics of Identity*. Oxford: Blackwell.

Index

A SOCIOLOGY OF SEX AND SEXUALITY

Gail Hawkes

A Sociology of Sex and Sexuality offers a historical sociological analysis of ideas about expressions of sexual desire, combining both primary and secondary historical and theoretical material with original research and popular imagery in the contemporary context.

While some reference is made to the sexual ideology of Classical Antiquity and of early Christianity, the major focus of the book is on the development of ideas about sex and sexuality in the context of modernity. It questions the widespread assumption that the anxieties and fears associated with old sexual mores have been overcome in the late twentieth century context, and asks whether the discourses of Queer sexual politics have successfully fractured the binary categories of heterosexuality and homosexuality.

A Sociology of Sex and Sexuality will be of interest to students in the fields of sociology, sexual history, gender studies and cultural studies.

Contents

The specialness of sex – Sex and modernity – Enlightenment pleasures and bourgeois anxieties – The science of sex – Planning sex – Pleasurable sex – Liberalizing heterosexuality – Subverting heterosexuality – Final thoughts and questions – References – Index.

176pp   0 335 19316 1   (Paperback)

RE-STATING SOCIAL AND POLITICAL CHANGE

Colin Hay

Re-Stating Social and Political Change provides a critical introduction to the social, political and cultural changes that have occurred in Britain since the war, and argues that these changes can best be understood in terms of a theory of the state.

Re-Stating Social and Political Change reviews and assesses the major theories of the state that have sought to diagnose and explain the trajectories of western societies. It provides a powerful case for the study of the state, and demonstrates how state theory can shed new light on war, social change, the extension of citizenship, the emergence of a patriarchal welfare state, the crisis of the state and the rise and demise of Thatcherism.

Features:
• focuses on 'real' examples from post-war British society
• makes considerable use of figures, tables and diagrams
• each chapter is structured around a key set of questions and issues
• a genuinely introductory critical account of existing theories.

Colin Hay has written a broad introduction to this pressing topic, which presents a new and distinctive argument about the role of the state in our understanding of social and political change. He also examines the impact of Thatcherism on the state, the possibility of a post-Thatcher settlement and the role of the current Labour Party, and assesses the prognosis for the future.

Re-Stating Social and Political Change will be important reading for students of sociology, social and political theory, politics, social policy and women's studies.

Contents
Part 1: Stating the obvious – What is the state and why do we need it? – Part 2: Stating social and political change – War and social change – The sense and nonsense of consensus – Citizenship – Part 3: Re-stating crisis – Theories of state crisis – From contradiction to crisis – Part 4: Re-stating social and political change – Thatcherism – The state of the present – Bibliography – Index.

224pp   0 335 19386 2   (Paperback)   0 335 19387 0   (Hardback)

YOUNG PEOPLE AND SOCIAL CHANGE

INDIVIDUALIZATION AND RISK IN LATE MODERNITY

Andy Furlong and Fred Cartmel

- How have young people's lives changed over the past two decades?
- Are traditional social divisions such as class and gender still useful in helping to predict life chances and experiences?
- How do young people cope with increased feelings of vulnerability and stress?

Social changes occuring in recent years have had an enormous impact on the lives of young people. In this book, Furlong and Cartmel consider whether the traditional parameters understood as structuring the life chances and experiences of young people are still relevant, and examine the extent to which 'individualization' and 'risk' convey an accurate picture of the changing lives of the young. They argue that life in late modernity revolves around an epistemological fallacy: although social structures, such as class, continue to shape life chances, these structures tend to become increasingly obscure as collectivist traditions weaken and individualist values intensify. As a consequence, the social world becomes regarded as unpredictable and filled with risks that can only be negotiated on an individual level, even though chains of human interdependence remain intact.

This wide-ranging overview is designed to provide an essential text for undergraduate courses on the sociology of youth, education, work, and stratification, and supplementary reading for other courses such as leisure, crime and health as well as vocational courses in youth and community work.

Contents
The risk society – Change and continuity in education – Social change and labour market transitions – Changing patterns of dependency – Leisure and lifestyles – Health risks in late modernity – Crime and insecurity – Politics and participation – The epistemological fallacy of late modernity – References – Index.

160pp   0 335 19464 8   (Paperback)   0 335 19465 6   (Hardback)